The Women's International Democratic Federation, the Global South, and the Cold War

This book examines the role of the Women's International Democratic Federation (WIDF) in transnational women's activism in the context of the Cold War, and in connection to the rights of women from Asia, Africa, and Latin America.

Combining a global history and postcolonial theory approach, this monograph shines light on an underrepresented organization and its important role in the Cold War, 20th-century women's rights and Soviet history. Questioning whether the organization acted for women's causes or whether it was merely a Cold War political instrument, the book analyzes and problematizes the place that the WIDF had in the politics of the Soviet Union, examining the ideology and politics of the WIDF and state socialist propaganda regarding women's equality and rights. Using Soviet archival documents of the organizations, the book offers a new perspective on the complexities of the development of global women's rights movement, which was divided by the Cold War confrontations.

This is an important study suitable for students and researchers in Women's and Gender History, Eastern European History and Gender Studies.

Yulia Gradskova is Associate Professor in History and works at the Department of History, Stockholm University, Sweden. Her research interests include Soviet and postsocialist social and gender history, decolonial perspective on Soviet politics of emancipation of "woman of the East" and gender equality. Gradskova is the author of *Soviet Politics of Emancipation of Ethnic Minority Women: Natsionalka* (Springer, 2018) and co-editor of several books, including *Gendering Postsocialism: Old Legacies and New Hierarchies* (Routledge 2018, with, I. Asztalos Morell); *Gender Equality on a Grand Tour. Politics and Institutions – the Nordic Council, Sweden, Lithuania and Russia* (Brill, 2017 – with E. Blomberg, Y. Waldemarson and A. Zvinkliene).

Global Gender

The *Global Gender* series provides original research from across the humanities and social sciences, casting light on a range of topics from international authors examining the diverse and shifting issues of gender and sexuality on the world stage. Utilising a range of approaches and interventions, these texts are a lively and accessible resource for both scholars and upper level students from a wide array of fields including Gender and Women's Studies, Sociology, Politics, Communication, Cultural Studies and Literature.

Early Motherhood in Digital Societies
Ideals, anxieties and ties of the perinatal
Ranjana Das

Nordic Gender Equality Policy in a Europeanisation Perspective
Edited by Knut Dørum

Gender-Based Violence in Latin American and Iberian Cinemas
Edited by Rebeca Maseda García, María José Gámez Fuentes, and Barbara Zecchi

Queering the Migrant in Contemporary European Cinema
Edited by James S. Williams

Bisexuality in Europe
Sexual Citizenship, Romantic Relationships, and Bi+ Identities
Edited by Emiel Maliepaard and Renate Baumgartner

Men in the American Women's Rights Movement 1830–1890
Cumbersome Allies
Hélène Quanquin

The Women's International Democratic Federation, the Global South and the Cold War
Defending the Rights of Women of the 'Whole World'?
Yulia Gradskova

Gender and Australian Celebrity Culture
Edited by Anthea Taylor and Joanna McIntyre

https://www.routledge.com/Global-Gender/book-series/RGG

The Women's International Democratic Federation, the Global South, and the Cold War

Defending the Rights of Women of the 'Whole World'?

Yulia Gradskova

LONDON AND NEW YORK

First published 2021
by Routledge
2 Park Square, Milton Park, Abingdon, Oxon OX14 4RN

and by Routledge
52 Vanderbilt Avenue, New York, NY 10017

Routledge is an imprint of the Taylor & Francis Group, an informa business

© 2021 Yulia Gradskova

The right of Yulia Gradskova to be identified as author of this work has been asserted by her in accordance with sections 77 and 78 of the Copyright, Designs and Patents Act 1988.

All rights reserved. No part of this book may be reprinted or reproduced or utilised in any form or by any electronic, mechanical, or other means, now known or hereafter invented, including photocopying and recording, or in any information storage or retrieval system, without permission in writing from the publishers.

Trademark notice: Product or corporate names may be trademarks or registered trademarks, and are used only for identification and explanation without intent to infringe.

British Library Cataloguing-in-Publication Data
A catalogue record for this book is available from the British Library

Library of Congress Cataloging-in-Publication Data
Names: Gradskova, IUliia, author.
Title: The Women's International Democratic Federation, the Global South and the Cold War : defending the rights of women of the 'whole world'? / Yulia Gradskova.
Description: Abingdon, Oxon; New York, NY : Routledge, 2021. | Includes bibliographical references and index.
Identifiers: LCCN 2020033187 (print) | LCCN 2020033188 (ebook) | ISBN 9780367504786 (paperback) | ISBN 9780367504762 (hardback) | ISBN 9781003050032 (ebook)
Subjects: LCSH: Women's International Democratic Federation. | Women's rights--Developing countries--History--20th century. | Cold War.
Classification: LCC HQ1236.5.D44 G73 2021 (print) | LCC HQ1236.5.D44 (ebook) | DDC 305.4209172/4--dc23
LC record available at https://lccn.loc.gov/2020033187
LC ebook record available at https://lccn.loc.gov/2020033188

ISBN: 978-0-367-50476-2 (hbk)
ISBN: 978-1-003-05003-2 (ebk)

Typeset in Saban
by SPi Global, India

Contents

Abbreviations vii
Acknowledgements ix

1 A forgotten women's organization? The WIDF, in between women's history and Cold War studies 1

   A combination of macro- and micro-historical approaches, and materials on the WIDF in the Soviet Archives 7
   Previous research on women's rights during the Cold War, the WIDF, and "Third World" women's activism 11
   This book's main themes and structure 20

2 The WIDF, the Soviet state, and Cold War battles 23

   The Soviet state, the Antifascist Committee of Soviet Women, and the WIDF 24
   The WIDF's internal life in the correspondence of the Soviet members of the CSW between Berlin and Moscow, from the second half of the 1950s to the early 1980s 41

3 Protecting peace, mothers, and children: WIDF's ideology and activities in its first decades 63

   Peace as the main condition for women's and children's rights 63
   Women need rights in order to fulfil their duties as mothers 70

4 Anti-colonialism, anti-racism and social rights 77

   The WIDF's understanding of the problems of women in Asia, Africa, and Latin America 77
   The WIDF meets the anti-colonial struggle and decolonization 84

5   **The state socialist model of women's emancipation as an example to follow for the "Whole World"**   98

State socialist equality and "women of colour" from the Soviet borderlands 99
Encountering state socialism and its women – impressions, personal connections, and memories 109

6   **Women from Asia, Africa, and Latin America make themselves visible in the WIDF**   118

Discussion on the WIDF's structures, leadership, and agenda 118
Decolonization and women's activism in the Global South make an impact on the WIDF 127

7   **Activists from the Global South and the WIDF: A biographical perspective**   136

Argentinian communist women as WIDF leaders 137
Representing Nigerian women in the WIDF 141
Organizing women in Northern Africa and the Middle East 147

8   **The WIDF on the eve of the IWY and during the UN decade for women**   158

The WIDF and the UN agenda on equality and non-discrimination 158
From anti-colonialism to development? speaking the language of transnational women's rights in the Global South 170
Successes and disappointments of the WIDF work in Africa, Asia, and Latin America 175

9   **The WIDF and the end of the three worlds: Concluding remarks**   193

Appendix   198
List of Literature   200
Index   211

Abbreviations

AAPSO	Afro-Asian People Solidarity Organization
ACSW	Antifascist Committee of Soviet Women
AFŽ	Women's Anti-Fascist Front of Yugoslavia
ANC	African National Congress
ARAB	Arbetarörelsens Arkiv och Bibliotek (Archive and Library of Working Movement, Sweden)
CC	Central Committee
CEDAW	Convention on Elimination of All Discrimination Against Women
CIA	Central Investigation Agency
Comintern	Communist International
CPSU	Communist Party of the Soviet Union
CSW	Committee of Soviet Women
DEDAW	Declaration on the Elimination of Discrimination Against Women
DRV	Democratic Republic of Vietnam
ECOSOC	United Nations Economic and Social Council
FMC	Federación de Mujeres Cubanas (Federation of Cuban Women)
GARF	Gosudarstvennyi Arkhiv Rossiskoi Federatsii (State Archive of the Russian Federation)
GDR	German Democratic Republic
IAW	International Alliance of Women
ICW	International Council of Women
ILO	International Labor Organization
IWY	International Women's Year
IISH	International Institute of Social History
JWU	Jordanian Women's Union
KGB	Komitet Gosudarstvennoi Bezopasnosti (Committee of State Security)
LAI	League Against Imperialism
NGO	Non-Governmental Organization
NIEO	New International Economic Order
PAWO	Pan-African Women's Organization

RFE	Radio Free Europe
RGASPI	Rossiskii Gosudarstvennyi Arkhiv Sotsialno-Politicheskoi Istorii (Russian State Archive of Social and Political History)
SKV	Svenska kvinnors vänsterförbund (The Left Union of Swedish Women)
SNDL	Finnish Women Democratic League
SWU	Sudanese Women's Union
UDI	Unione Donne Italiane (Union of Italian Women)
UFF	Union des Femmes Françaises (Union of French Women)
UMA	Union de Mujeres Argentinas (Union of Argentinian Women)
UN	United Nations
UNCHR	United Nations Commission on Human Rights
UNESCO	United Nations Educational, Scientific and Cultural Organization
VKP(b)	Vesesoiuznaia Kommunisticheskaia Partiia (bolshevikov) (All-Russian Communist Party (Bolsheviks))
VOKS	Vsesoyuznoe Obshchestvo Kulturnoi Sviazi s zagranitsei (All-Union Society for Cultural Relations with Foreign Countries)
WILPF	Women's International League for Peace and Freedom
Zhenotdel	Zhenskii Otdel (Department of Work among Women)

Acknowledgements

How is it possible to do research about a transnational women's organization? And, in particular, about one whose history got to be "forgotten" after the end of the Cold War? Of course, in the case of all the research projects realized by the individual researcher, there are behind them colleagues and institutional structures, but also those who helped on the different stages of the book's progress, not least with scanning and correction. In the case of the transnational research, however, the number of people who, in one way or another, contributed to the realization of the project increases disproportionally and it is difficult to name all of them in this short message. Even to establish the correct spelling of the names of the WIDF participants from different countries often required multiple email messages and phone conversations with my friends and colleagues in Sweden, and in many different parts of the world! Indeed, the research on the transnational organization required establishing and maintaining transnational contacts and having transnational conversations that were crucial for the development of this project.

This project started from a research grant that I received from the Swedish Research Council (Vetenskapsrådet, pr. 1599201) in 2017, for which I am very grateful. I also want to express my gratitude to the History Department of Stockholm University which provided me with a workplace and the stimulating environment of the "Modern History Seminar" during the years in which I realized my project. I am also extremely grateful to Professor Elisabeth Elgán (Stockholm University) and Professor Irina Sandomirskaja (Södertörn University, CBEES), who inspired me to start thinking about the WIDF as a possible project for research.

I am particularly thankful to my longtime colleague, Monica Quirico, PhD in History, (Institute of Contemporary History, Södertörn University) who read the earlier version of the manuscript of this book and, using her experience with research on the European left thought and politics, provided me with invaluable comments.

The writing of this book would have been impossible without travel and exchange. And here, in particular, one week of my ERASMUS teaching exchange visit to the Women's Study Center of the University of Jordan (Amman) became an invaluable possibility for learning about Middle Eastern women's movement in the past and present. In particular, my conversations with Dr. Amani Al-Serhan and Dr. Abeer Dababneh became an important point of reflection around my material. I am also very grateful for the possibility of taking part in the exchange programme with the History Department of the University of Sheffield and the possibility of discussing my research on the WIDF with Dr. Miriam Dobson and Dr. Hannah Parker.

In the process of working on this book, I also presented my ideas and preliminary findings at multiple conferences and research seminars both in Sweden and abroad. Particularly important were my participation in Gender History Conference (Jornadas de Historia de Genero) in the University of Mar del Plata, Argentina, and the BASEES conference in Cambridge 2019.

I am very thankful to Professor Francisca de Haan of the Central European University, historian of the WIDF, for allowing me the possibility of discussing my research with her in June 2019 and for getting her opinion about my project.

The correspondence and a personal meeting in Mar del Plata (Argentina) with Professor Adriana Valobra offered me a rich experience of learning more about the perspective of Argentinian researchers on the WIDF's history in Latin America and on the history of the WIDF's Argentinian member, the Union of Argentinian Women (UMA).

I want to express my gratitude to all the participants of the workshop organized by Professor Elisabeth Elgán at Stockholm University (September 2019) and of another one organized by Associate Professor Celia Donert at the University of Cambridge (December 2019). And I am also grateful to many researchers – both in Sweden and across the world – who helped me with their advice, ideas and critique: (in alphabetic order) Maryam Adjam, Anders Ahlbäck, Eva Blomberg, Håkan Blomquist, Helene Carlbäck, Manuel Chicharro, Christian Gerdov, Irina Gordeeva, Norbert Götz, Heidi Kurvinen, Andrej Kotljarchuk, Iva Lusic, Julia Malitska, Carl Marklund, Katarina Mattson, Maija Runcis, Tuichi Rashidov, Yuliya Yurcuk, Vladislava Vladimirova, Ann Werner, and Ylva Waldemarson.

I also want to thank the participants of the seminars in Södertörn University (Institute of Contemporary History, Center for Baltic and East European Studies and Gender Studies), the Gender History seminar in Stockholm University, the seminar at the Institute of Russian and Eurasian Studies at Uppsala University and gender research days at the Mid-Sweden University, Sundsvall, 2020. Stimulating discussions at these seminars helped me to get more confidence in my research methods and approach as well as a variety of new ideas and ways of looking at transnational activism, the Cold War and the Soviet politics being brought to my attention.

I also want to express my gratitude to those working in the Moscow archives, in particularly in GARF where I collected the main part of my material. I am very grateful to those working at the library of the IISH in Amsterdam for possibility of receiving copies in spite of the pandemic. I am also grateful to the librarians of the Slavica Library in Helsinki. My special gratitude is to Maria Pinaeva and Nika Kokhanovskaia, who helped me with copying archive materials in GARF.

And last but not least, during all these years of working on my project I received support, inspiration (and just as importantly – useful IT and language advice) from my sons – Damian and Yakov.

1 A forgotten women's organization? The WIDF, in between women's history and Cold War studies

This book scrutinizes the activities of a transnational women's organization, the Women's International Democratic Federation (WIDF), which campaigned for women's rights in countries beyond Europe and North America during the Cold War. The WIDF was founded in 1945, and declared the protection of peace and the rights of women and children to be its main goals. It played an important role in the declaration of 1975 as the International Women's Year (de Haan 2018), and during the succeeding United Nations Decade for Women (1975–1985). Its work was also crucial in terms of the adoption of the Convention on the Elimination of All Forms of Discrimination Against Women (CEDAW) in 1979. Yet the WIDF was frequently referred to as a "communist organization" and a "Soviet front". After the collapse of the Soviet Union (1991), and the end of the Cold War, the WIDF lost most of its international visibility and members and, it seems, it has also disappeared from history. Even though this organization was one of the biggest and most important transnational women's organizations during this period, this book is the first account of the WIDF's activities during the whole period of the Cold War.

Why was this organization ignored? Why was such a large organization, whose period of activity corresponded with the lifetimes of many people still living, forgotten? In order to understand this strange "memory loss" and the general lack of interest from feminist historians in the WIDF, it is necessary to learn more not only about this organization per se, but also about the historical context in which it was established, and the context surrounding its demise. This context includes the Cold War and its ending (1989), and also the Universal Declaration of Human Rights (1948), and the step-by-step recognition of the equality of rights between women and men in international law. (The UN's CEDAW convention of 1979 was the most important achievement in this regard.) The context also includes the fundamental transformation of world geopolitics – from a planet divided between imperial masters and the colonized majority, towards the contemporary political map of more than 200 independent states – and also from a world divided into three (First, Second and Third Worlds) to one divided between the Global North and the Global South. What were the relations between the global women's rights movement, the Cold War confrontation, and the anti-colonial struggle? How did the WIDF navigate through Cold War "hot" conflicts and cultural battles?

In order to understand why this organization was "forgotten", it is also important to explore how the history of the state socialist vision of gender equality, and the women's movement in the Soviet Bloc, was, and continues to be, written. For example, how are global issues, ranging from public childcare to anti-racism, presented? Or, how did the mass involvement of women in the productive economic sectors of the Eastern Bloc countries change global attitudes towards women's right to work? In her 2011 article, Jennifer Suchland suggested that "experiences and voices from the former second world" find almost no place in post-Cold War transnational feminist discourses or, at least in US academia (2011, 838).

However, as a person born in the Soviet Union, I consider the reasons for the "forgetting" of the WIDF, as well as the nature of the organization itself, to be more complex. Indeed, if the WIDF was "forgotten" by the majority of feminist and women's history researchers merely on account of the dominance of the post-Cold War American/Western perspective, according to which the former "Second World" is "no region" (Suchland 2011, 843), why is it equally forgotten in Russia and the other formerly state socialist countries? Understanding the "lack of memory" with regard to this organization, known internationally as a "Soviet front", demands attention be paid to the striking contrast of the state socialist construction of rights, and the practice of the "rights" (such as declarations on the equality of citizens versus the realities of the GULAG). It also demands discussing the contrast of the state socialist interpretation of a "woman" – recognized as an equal member of the society – but, together with the majority of the society, mostly lacking the possibility of influencing the most important decisions concerning her body, wellbeing, and life itself.

Finally, the historical role of this organization, and its "disappearance" from history, cannot be studied without bringing in questions concerning the status and role of women from Asia, Africa, and Latin America in the organization. The WIDF used to issue declarations in the name of "women of the whole world", claiming to speak on behalf of women from different countries and continents. Speaking for women "of the whole world", particularly in that historical period, meant speaking about women experiencing transformation from colonial subjects into citizens of independent countries. It also entails speaking about the intersections of women's rights activism with national liberation and anti-racist movements, as well as leftist ideas on redistribution of national wealth, social equality, and the New International Economic Order (NIEO). Did the WIDF really overcome the Eurocentric conception of rights and women's activism and become a political instrument for women from Latin America, Africa, and Asia?

The **main aim** of this book is to explore the WIDF's work for, and in the name of, women from Asia, Africa, and Latin America in the context of the Cold War, and the participation of women from these parts of the world in the work of the WIDF on different levels. In order to explore this, several questions will be of particular importance.

The first concerns the WIDF's self-positioning with respect to the Cold War confrontation between "East" and "West", a confrontation that was significant in the development of both the transnational discussion of women's rights, and the political process in Asia, Africa, and Latin America (see Westad 2005; Olcott 2017). Benefitting from the use of materials from Soviet archives, I try to find answers to questions about the Soviet state's role in the federation: How much, and in which way, can we speak about the WIDF as a "Soviet front"? How much did the Soviet Bloc influence the political agenda aimed at women from the Global South? I explore what Soviet and Communist influence meant for the everyday work of the federation, if and how it changed during different periods of the Cold War, and what importance it had for the countries of Asia, Africa, and Latin America.

The second question concerns the role that women, and organizations, from Latin America, Africa, and Asia played in setting the WIDF's political agenda, and in managing the organization. I am particularly interested in how the agenda, internal power relationships, and decision-making processes of the federation, as it concerned the Global South, changed over time.

Thirdly, I explore the federation's internal life, and conflicts between women who had different (and sometimes, multiple) worldviews: female Communists from different parts of the world, female activists from the Global South, and European women of different political orientations. What were their thoughts on women's rights? How did they perceive decolonization, political independence, and the social rights of women from Asia, Africa, and Latin America? While I assume that women who were members of the Communist parties of their respective countries played special role in the WIDF, I consider it important to explore not only the similarities, but also the differences in their opinions and priorities. I am particularly interested in individual female leaders from the Global South in the WIDF. What can we learn about their motivation, successes, and failures during their time at the WIDF, and how did their participation impact the federation?

The book focuses mainly on the period between 1955 and 1985. 1955 was the year of the Bandung conference, which first showed the importance of the "Third World" countries as a new political force, and questioned the then-dominant system of international law (Eslava et al. 2017); 1985 was the year Perestroika began, leading to the development of new geopolitical visions in the Soviet Union, and to growth of the mass anti-government uprisings in other countries of the "Eastern Bloc", beginning with Poland in the early 1980s. However, the WIDF was founded in 1945 and, even if the first years of its activities were touched upon in previous research, the WIDF's politics with respect to women from the Global South before 1955 were analysed mainly using examples of certain countries and regions (Drew 2014; McGregor 2013, 2016, Armstrong 2016; Valobra 2017). Most of this scholarship did not look at the WIDF's policies towards the colonial world from the perspective of the broader context of the WIDF's ideology and work. Therefore, some parts of the book will also explore the WIDF's activities in the Global South before 1955. My study explores the WIDF's ideas and practical activities for, and relationships with, women's organizations from these countries. By doing so, it contributes to research on decolonization, and on the role of transnational and national women's organizations in the Global South in terms of political and social change.

Theoretical perspective: The book combines the transnational approach to the study of organizations and Cold War history with a postcolonial approach to women's rights and feminism.

The transnational approach draws the focus away from nation-states, or relationships among them, and pays special attention to the role of organizations, movements, and ideas that are "not contained by national borders" (Snyder 2013, 102; see more on transnational approach in Iriye 2013, 28–30; Scholte 2005; Sluga & Clavin 2017). Following Maud Bracke and James Mark, I see transnationalization as complex processes "in which locally acting agents adapt, re-interpret and re-contextualize" and in some cases "betray" the ideas found elsewhere (2015, 413). Consequently, I study how the WIDF's ideas on the defence of peace, and on the rights of mothers and children, travelled through and subverted national borders and the "Iron Curtain". I also explore how national organizations and the local context (in this case, women's organizations from the Global South doing work to transform women's status in the context of anti-colonialism, anti-racism, and development) may have influenced the WIDF as an organization, and its transnational women's activism. I also explore the impact that women's rights leaders and organizations from the Global South had on the WIDF after their visits to the state socialist countries, both on their work locally, and on cooperation between the respective organizations.

The transnational perspective of the cultural Cold War approaches the history of the period after the Second World War as not just a political and economic confrontation between the USSR and the USA. However, it also pays special attention to the permeability of the Iron Curtain, as well as to confrontations and interactions between norms, beliefs, values, and identities (Saunders 2000; Scott-Smith & Krabbendam 2003, 3–4; Autio-Sarasmo & Miklossy 2011; Devinatz 2013; Scott-Smith et al. 2014; Bechmann Pedersen & Noack 2020). Hence, I explore how Cold War divisions and politics impacted the interactions and confrontations on gender norms, rights, and equality.

Following Arne Westad (2005), I am interested in the Cold War's global effects. More specifically, I focus here on the effects of the WIDF's pro-Moscow and pro-Communist leadership on the federation's discourses with respect to the Global South, and its politics of alliances there. I am also interested in the effects the Cold War confrontation had on the positions women's organizations and leaders from Africa, Asia, and Latin America took towards the WIDF.

Furthermore, my interest in the cultural Cold War allows me to explore what "Moscow" actually denoted, how "Moscow" acted with respect to the WIDF and the rights of women in the Global South, and what were the limits of its influence. Thus, I do not see the actions of "Moscow" as somehow obvious per se, but rather explore how and through which channels and forms these actions were practiced, and what kinds of internal conflicts and discussions they provoked within the federation.

On the other hand, by giving attention to the role of "Moscow" in the WIDF's activities for, and in the name of, women from the Global South, I can pose a broader question about the nature of relationships between the transnational women's movement during the Cold War, and the Cold War pressures, developments, and turning points. In particular, I explore the possibilities and limitations of independent women's rights activism, with a focus on the newly independent countries of Africa and Asia, as well as on women's organizations in Latin America.

The *postcolonial approach to women's movements and feminism* criticizes the domination of Western interpretations of the "Third World" woman, gender inequality, sexism, and the aims and tactics of women's political mobilizations (Mohanty 2003, 40–41; bell hooks 1989). Postcolonial feminism questions the subject of feminism itself. For example, according to bell hooks, the assumption "that resisting patriarchal domination is a more legitimate feminist action than resisting racism and other forms of domination" is an assumption made by "the White feminist movement in the West" and it is criticized by the "Black women and women of color" (hooks 1989, 19–20).

In spite of my focus on the "Global South", the title of this book may appear to be an attempt to homogenize "women" outside of Europe – what Mohanty warned against – my use of this problematic (see below) concept is connected with my questioning of the WIDF's self-presentation. The WIDF declared itself to be an organization that represented the interests of women from Asia, Africa, and Latin America better than the pro-Western transnational organizations. Thus, taking the "Global South" as a starting point allows me to find similarities and differences in the politics of a transnational organization created by the "West's" Cold War opponents with the women' organizations that originated in the "West" – the subject of Mohanty's criticism.

Employing Mohanty's critique of the way "feminism" is used as a term to define activism in the "West" (while "Third Word" feminisms are mainly ignored) helps me to address the history of the WIDF, an alternative to "Western" transnational organizations that was usually associated with the "Second" and the "Third" Worlds, as a variation of the "conflictual histories" of feminisms outside of the "First World" (Mohanty 2003, 46). Indeed, while WIDF members usually did not call themselves "feminists" (they understood the term as denoting the women's movement of its Cold War adversary), using Mohanty's and bell hooks' approach[1] allows me to see the WIDF, an organization advocating women's rights, as a part of the women's movement, and as a variant of feminist organization.[2]

Furthermore, following Mohanty's claim regarding the importance of deconstructing the image of the uniform and dominated "Third World" woman (2003), I pay attention to the diversity of problems and demands of the different organizations and groups from the Global South that were cooperating with the WIDF. I differentiate between those emphasizing anti-racism, and their countries' independence, those focusing on the social rights of working mothers, those who joined the WIDF during a military struggle for social change and independence, and those who advocated for some changes in women's education and everyday life, but preserved a respect for local traditions. Even if the Soviet archives do not seem to be a place to look for alternative voices and interpretations of the WIDF's ideology and activism, some of the documents kept there clearly indicate dissent, and reveal the voices of women who did not share a "communist", "Soviet" or "Euro-centric" way of thinking.

On the other hand, close reading of the presumably "universal" (written for women of "the whole world") WIDF's documents and declarations through a post-colonial lens allows me to explore their internal contradictions and silences. Here, I follow Ann Laura Stoler's approach on how a researcher can perform a post-colonial investigation in the colonial archive (Stoler 2009). She proposed, for example, to differentiate between "what was 'unwritten' because it could go without saying and 'everyone knew it,' what was unwritten because it could not yet be articulated, and what was unwritten because it could not be said" (Stoler 2009, 3). This allows me to find and expose the silences and internal contradictions during changing times, while the WIDF was still promoting a "uniform" (using Mohanty's definition) image of those women from Africa, Asia, and Latin America in the name of whom the organization claimed to speak for. Hence I can use the Soviet archive for a post-colonial investigation.

I also follow Madina Tlostanova's discussion of colonial/imperial differences with respect to the position of the former "Second World" and its women. I pay attention not only to the hierarchical relationships between the "Second" and "Third" Worlds, in terms of discourses on the benefits of Soviet modernization for "Third World women", but also to the colonial differences inside of the "Second World" women themselves (2009). In particular, I pay attention to the importance of the Soviet borderlands, such as Central Asia, as well as to the special position of Soviet "women of colour", and their role in the WIDF during the period of decolonization in Africa and Asia.

Finally, the postcolonial perspective allows me to pose a question on possible changes in the power relationships inside the federation that were provoked by the growing diversity of the WIDF's membership during the 1960s–1970s.

The geopolitical concepts used throughout this book require special discussion. During the period under research, the countries of Asia, Africa and Latin America were often referred to as the "Third World", indicating their difference from the two main geopolitical blocs: the "First World" (the capitalist West) and the "Second World" (the state socialist countries or the "Eastern" or "Communist" Bloc). However, these concepts were never accepted by the Soviet Union and its allies, who preferred to define independent countries outside Europe and North America as "developing", dividing them into those that chose the "socialist way of development" and the rest. The Bandung conference (Indonesia, 1955) brought together representatives of many of the post-colonial countries of Asia and Africa, and elaborated principles according to which the Non-Aligned Movement – a union of countries not part of the two Cold War blocs – would be created in 1961 (Eslava et al. 2017). However, even though the geopolitical term "Non-Aligned country" was widely used, the applicability of this concept for discussing non-European women is limited: the Non-Aligned Movement did not encompass all of the countries of Latin America, Asia, and Africa, but did include several "Communist countries" such as Yugoslavia and Cuba.[3] Thus, it is possible to say that while all these concepts and definitions could be found in my primary sources, and in previous scholarship, none of them can be seen as satisfying the needs of this study. Nevertheless, I use these concepts when they are found in primary or secondary materials.

The current widely used concept of the "Global South" has also been questioned by several researchers (Wolvers & Salvedra 2015). The term is used by the World Bank, and is often based on a developmental approach – economic growth measured through GDP per capita. However, its geographical definitions are not stable (Wolvers & Salvedra 2015). Thus, this term does not correspond fully to the aims of my historical study, as it often includes the countries of the former "Third World", and newly independent countries formerly part of the "Second" or "Communist" world (e.g., Uzbekistan or Albania), while, at the same time, it excludes several countries having a long history of colonialism and anti-colonial struggle (e.g. Singapore or South Korea). Thus, I am aware of the limitations of this term, and use it mainly as a substitute for "Third World" – to indicate the geographical area outside the former "First" and "Second Worlds". However, I also use a longer, but less contested geographical definition of this region: the countries of Asia, Africa, and Latin America.

A combination of macro- and micro-historical approaches, and materials on the WIDF in the Soviet Archives

The history of a transnational organization poses many challenges, especially for the individual researcher. These organizations have complex structures, issue their documents in several languages, while their members reside in different countries, and do not necessarily organize their work or have the same priorities on the national level (see, e.g., research by Rupp on transnational organizations such as the International Alliance of Women (IAW) and International Council of Women (ICW), 1997). On the other hand, the work of a transnational organization depends greatly on the politics surrounding the selection of leaders, the adoption of new members, methods of organizing communications inside the organization, and the adoption of changes in the organization's statutes and priorities. All of this requires important attention to be given to both macro- and micro-level analyses of a transnational organization's work.

In this book, attention to the most visible events in the organization's history (i.e. congresses or important changes in the top leadership) was combined with micro-level analysis. The means special attention was given to correspondence between individual members of the transnational leadership, as well as to individual biographies of some of the key female activists and leaders. This micro-analysis allowed me to learn more about the internal management and decision-making process of this organization, as well as, in some cases, about the individual motivations for accepting certain positions inside the leadership, or starting/ending cooperation with the organization.

There are many surviving materials from the WIDF that were printed during the Cold War, including the WIDF's own periodical, *Women of the Whole World* (published from 1951), that was published in several languages. Documents concerning the federation can also be found in the archives of those countries that had women's organizations that were members of the WIDF. However, the WIDF's central archive, from 1951 to 1991, was located at the WIDF's headquarters in East Berlin, it seems to have become lost to researchers, permanently or temporarily, some time after 1991 (see de Haan 2012).

Thus, the Soviet collection of WIDF materials, preserved in the archive of its Soviet member organization, the Antifascist Committee of Soviet Women (ACSW, which changed its name to the Committee of Soviet Women in 1956) in the State Archive of the Russian Federation (GARF, fond 7928) seems to be crucial for historical research on the WIDF.[4] Due to the special importance of the WIDF for the Soviet authorities, which I will discuss in more detail later, the Soviet archives preserved Russian translations of most of the protocols, minutes, and decisions of WIDF meetings from 1945 to 1991. This collection of documents, as well as internal correspondence between the Soviet representatives in the organization, constitute the main source material for this book.

Since the opening of Russian archives after the fall of the Soviet Union, opportunities and problems connected to the use of the Soviet archives continues to be discussed (see, e.g.; Fitzpatrick 1996; Livshin et al. 2002; Kozlova 2005). Scholars have drawn attention to a range of problems concerning documents from the Soviet period; from falsification of statistical data (Fitzpatrick 2015, 387) to self-censorship and use of the Soviet ideological language in personal documents, such as letters, diaries, or memoirs (Kozlova and Sandomirskaja 1996). At the same time, according to Sheila Fitzpatrick, in spite of all the difficulties related to writing "history from below" on the basis of the Soviet, mainly state-generated and state-controlled, archives, these difficulties are comparable with writing such history in other countries. Furthermore, the use of state-preserved documents paradoxically challenges the presumed "monolithic identity" of the Soviet state itself (Fitzpatrick 2015, 394).

The use of Soviet archival and printed materials for studying a transnational organization obviously differs from the task of understanding Soviet history "from below". Even so, I deem it important to consider the discussion above regarding the possible problems and challenges of using Soviet archival material and publications by the (Soviet-friendly) WIDF in order to understand how the federation worked in practice, and how its activities were perceived "from below" by its member organizations and lower-level representatives from various countries. Thus, I was particularly concerned with possible falsifications of reality presented in the WIDF's official publications (*Women of the Whole World*) and documents. A critical deconstruction of depictions of the Soviet and state socialist achievements with respect to women's rights played a particular role here. Furthermore, when using documents from the archive of the ACSW/CSW, I consider it important to pay special attention to the intentions of the authors of these documents, to the context where these documents were created, as well to the possible reasons for their preservation in the archive. In particular, I find it useful to pay attention to the personal position and possible motivations, as well as the (self-)censorship's restrictions the individual women – Soviet and international – who were the authors of classified and non-classified letters I used – lived under.

Following Chiara Bonfiglioli, I differentiate between how I used the publications and documents aimed at external readers (Bonfiglioli calls them "representative"), on the one hand, and materials that circulated internally, such as protocols, minutes, and letters, on the other (Bonfiglioli 2012, 47–48). The WIDF's appeals, official speeches of its leaders, bulletins, and other publications (including most of the materials published in *Women of the Whole World*) were aimed at spreading the WIDF's ideas and attracting new members and sympathizers. Thus, these documents often gave a very selective picture of reality. I approached these documents mainly when exploring changes in the federation's discourses with respect to one or another aspect of its activities, for example, peace or anti-colonial struggle. When doing so, I mainly pay attention to the use of language, and the context of the main message of the particular document. I also used the WIDF's official publications to discern the general orientation of its activities – for example, for information on bureau meetings, members of the WIDF governing bodies in a particular year, as well as on the WIDF's leaders' participation in international events.

The internal documents available in the GARF include protocols and minutes of the WIDF congresses, council and bureau meetings, as well as reports and personal letters. The protocols and minutes were often produced via stenography and thus offer rather exact content of the discussions that were going on at the meetings; the protocols often included full-length speeches of the representatives of the organizations from the Global South. While self-censorship should obviously be taken into account when analysing the content of the individual speeches, still, as opposed to the official documents of the WIDF aimed at a broader public, the protocols and minutes could be more reliable sources of information about the work, achievements, and concerns of women from the different member organizations. The protocols also contain some information about internal conflicts inside the federation.

Finally, the most revealing documents found at the ACSW/CSW archive in the GARF, in Moscow, are the classified correspondence between the Soviet representatives at the WIDF headquarters (in Paris and later, East Berlin) and the leadership of the ACSW/CSW in Moscow. The correspondence of the Soviet WIDF delegates provide information regarding discussions and rumours within the WIDF leadership that were not recorded. The choice of events to be reported obviously followed instructions that the Soviet representative at the WIDF Secretariat received before departing from Moscow, but personal choice and individual assessment of the situation did largely define how a report was formed. This material is a unique source for a less official and inside view of the situation at the WIDF headquarters, and for the non-protocolled opinions of its leadership. At the same time, the main aim of these letters, and its main addressee, obviously influence the choice of topics, and the style and language of these letters. While the accounts of discussions and events mentioned in the letters cannot be approached as "historical facts" per se, they could inform us about changes in the general environment inside the WIDF's leadership, as well as in the views of its leaders, and in the priorities of the Soviet leadership. The last item can be also learned from other classified documents preserved in the Moscow archives – reports on WIDF activities sent to different bodies of the Communist Party of the Soviet Union (CPSU), preserved in the GARF, and in the Russian State Archive of Social and Political History (RGASPI).[5]

Language always constitutes a difficulty when researching transnational organizations and activism. Most of the documents preserved in the Moscow archives are in Russian, which contributes to my difficulties when dealing with the history of women from the Global South, using them as a main source. The translation of the original documents into Russian could not only somehow change the initial meanings of the speeches and letters of the WIDF leaders and activists from other countries, but the Cyrillic versions of the names used in most of the documents often constitute an extra difficulty when trying to identify these women and find additional information on them. These difficulties particularly relate to the earlier period of the WIDF's history, because the archives from the 1970s to 1980s include documents in English (and also other languages such as French or Spanish) more often.

As mentioned above, the WIDF periodical publications – most of all, its journal, *Women of the Whole World* – were issued in several languages – French,

English, Russian, German, Spanish and, from the 1970s on, Arabic. Due to availability and accessibility problems, I mainly used the Russian – *Zhnenshchiny mira* – and the English – *Women of the Whole World* – versions of the WIDF's main publication.[6]

Alongside the material from the archives in Moscow, I also used archival materials from several different collections, including those of the Institute of International Social History in Amsterdam (IISH, the WIDF collection), the Archive and Library of the Working Movement (ARAB) in Stockholm, and individual documents from the CIA's online collection. The documents from the first two – mainly in English – include the WIDF's circular letters and bulletins, while the CIA declassified documents contain information on the "Communist fronts".

Finally, while writing this book I consulted a few published memoir accounts written by important representatives of the WIDF in the Global South. They were helpful as additional sources of information on different approaches towards evaluating the WIDF's role in women's rights activism in the Global South, as well as on the impact participating in the WIDF had on an individual's life.

Previous research on women's rights during the Cold War, the WIDF, and "Third World" women's activism

Francisca de Haan, who was the first to bring attention to the "forgotten" history of the WIDF, explained the lack of scholarship on this organization, in one of her early articles from 2010, as resulting from "continuing Cold War paradigms in women's history" (2010). In particular, she showed that, as a leftist organization, the WIDF did not fit into the well-established progressive narrative paradigm on the liberal transnational struggle for women's rights, nor into the theories about the developing of feminism through waves.

While the WIDF's in-house publications dedicated to its anniversaries (e.g., *WIDF 40 years* 1985; Gryzunova 1975) mainly praised its achievements in defending the rights of women and protecting peace, historians on the other side of the Iron Curtain explored this organization from the perspective of its realizing and supporting Soviet foreign policies. Thus, Roger Kanet, for example, published a list of such organizations, "the Soviet fronts", that should be seen not as transnational bodies, but as instruments of Soviet foreign policy (Kanet 1988). The WIDF was named as one of several organizations of this kind, which included the World Federation of Trade-Unions, the International Democratic Youth Organization, and the Organization of Women with University Education.

In the following pages, I will present the most important developments in post-Cold War scholarship concerning the relationships between the Soviet bloc and the Third World, as well as on women's transnational organizations and the WIDF's cooperation with "Third World" women.

A forgotten women's organization?

The Cold War, the "Soviet fronts" and the "Third World"

After the end of the Cold War, and the partial opening of the archives, Cold War studies became a popular object of research, and publications on different aspects of the Cold War now include hundreds of volumes. As opposed to "hot" military operations and security issues, cultural Cold War research deals with issues of ideology, values, and politics of cultural exchange and cooperation. In particular, scholars explored the roles of transnational legislation (Reilly 2009; Eckel & Moyn 2014), information agencies (see Feinberg on RFE 2016), and bodies of global governance (Mazower 2008) in establishing and regulating norms of individual rights and freedoms, the fate of dependent territories, and citizenship laws. For example, Peo Hansen and Stefan Johnson showed that the process of European integration during the early Cold War period saw the possibility of integrating Western European countries into a new union of European states, together with their dependent territories in Africa (Hanson & Johnson 2014). As for bodies of global governance, Mark Mazower demonstrated that during the first part of the Cold War, the United Nations was seen by the US government as an important instrument for supporting and propagating its geopolitical interests (Mazower 2008).

Ideas of human rights have a particularly important place in research on the cultural Cold War. According to a pioneering book by Samuel Moyn, human rights ideologies during the first decades of the Cold War usually did not include women's rights or anti-colonial struggles (Moyn 2010), while the 1970s was the era of the human rights "breakthrough". In that decade, human rights became the subject of heated discussions involving, among others, feminist activists and political dissidents from the state socialist countries and, at the same time, human rights first began to be applied to problems ranging from racial discrimination to the NIEO (Eckel & Moyn 2014). However, other publications have further problematized the history of human rights and women's human rights. In particular, Niamh Railly indicated that, initially, feminists played an important role in the UN, and the Commission on the Status of Women was created to be an institution that would guarantee women's rights. However, after the establishing of the UN Commission on Human Rights, the Commission on the Status of Women found itself isolated and underfunded (Reilly 2009, 28). At the same time, human rights protection activism created often-complex alliances that crossed the Cold War dividing line, including one described by Sara Snyder between American Civil Rights movement activists in the 1960s (an object of solidarity by the Soviet bloc), and those supporting the rights of Soviet Jews to immigrate to Israel (Snyder 2018, 28). Thus, human rights seem to have been a particularly contested area of cultural confrontations during the Cold War, and it deserves further research, especially with regard to women's rights and trans-blocs activism.

During the Cold War, the WIDF was typically described as one of the "Soviet (or Communist) fronts", the organizations and people acting in the interests of the Soviet state or "Eastern Bloc", as I said above. However, while documents from the Communist International (Comintern), the organization that coordinated Communist activities abroad[7] became partially available, the "Communist fronts" started to be studied as a part of the inter-war history. Nevertheless, these studies showed that the organizations were more complex than Cold War history had previously presented them. For example, Fredrik Petersson (2013), who studied one of these organizations, the League Against Imperialism (LAI, created in 1927), questioned the internal unity and uniformity of this Communist-sympathizing organization (2013, 5–6). Peterson insisted on the use of the term "sympathizing organization" instead of "Communist front". Such an organization, according to him, "depended on the willing participation and benevolence of non-communist actors, which preferably already had a prominent position within their own political context" (Petersson 2013, 8). Thus, "willing participation and benevolence" seem to be important components here. In recent years, attention to the "willingness" of participants in these organizations has been reflected in the use of another concept – "public" or "cultural" diplomacy, i.e. government-sponsored efforts for communicating directly with a foreign public, or cultural institutions (see e.g., David-Fox 2012; Devinatz 2013). Michael David-Fox applied it in his study of the Soviet Society for Cultural Relations with Foreign Countries (VOKS)'s activities during the 1920s–1930s. In spite of these concepts being somewhat useful when approaching the beginning of the WIDF's history, they seem to be inadequate for grasping the growing internal complexity of such "cultural diplomacy" or "sympathizing" organizations. In particular, in the case of the WIDF, these concepts leave no space for exploring different interests, as well as the power and agency of communist (and non-communist) women from different countries inside the federation's leadership.

Further, scholarship on the cultural Cold War suggested that the Iron Curtain was not a wall dividing the world into two parts, but rather a permeable membrane that allowed for cooperation and encounters to occur (Bechmann Pedersen & Noack 2020 3). However, every aspect of cooperation and encounters – youth politics, population politics, music, science, tourism, or sport – became an arena for Cold War rivalries (Desfosses 1980, 85–93; Bechmann Pedersen & Noack 2020; Koivunen 2011). Indeed, many actors on different levels were trying to reach their goals by using temporary alliances on both sides of the Iron Curtain, or attempted to compromise or even cooperate with the two camps (on solidarity with Chile, see Christiaens et al. 2014; see also Autio-Sarasmo 2011 on scientific-technical cooperation). At the same time, the research also showed that most of the civic and humanitarian initiatives, projects, and organizations that were initiated and promoted as global were, to some extent, subsumed by the superpowers' geopolitical strategies or, at least, had to take geopolitical confrontation into consideration (Berger & Weber 2014). This was the case for Western and "Eastern" developmental aid programmes for the countries of Asia and Africa (Hong 2015), the education of "Third World" students (Matusevich

2012; Katsakioris 2019, 2020) and adolescents (Müller 2014), anti-war movements (Wernicke 2003), and human rights (Eckel & Moyn 2014; Snyder 2018). The competition between the USA and the Soviet bloc for influence over women's organizations in the "Third World" countries can be seen as one aspect of this broader competition.

However, research on the Cold War in the "Third World" demonstrated that the competition for influence over nations, leaders, and women in the Global South encompassed several directions, and a multiplicity of actors. Soviet political ambitions in the countries of the Global South met obstacles, not only due to the confrontation with its Cold War political adversary, but also as a result of internal conflicts and competitions inside the bloc. Researchers studying the Sino-Soviet conflict (mid-1960s–1970s) showed that it was one of the most serious crises of "Communist solidarity", and suggested that this confrontation within the "Second World" was comparable to the confrontation between the two camps divided by the Iron Curtain (Westad 1999; Friedman 2015). Friedman showed, in particular, that already at the time of the Bandung conference, Chinese political leaders started to think that the Soviet Union "has failed to adequately evaluate the revolutionary significance of movements in the developing world" (Friedman 2015, 28). It is possible that the competition with China during that later period was an important driver of Soviet support for anti-colonial movements in Asia and Africa. Additionally, according to Mazower, from the 1960s onwards, the Soviets were also competing with Cubans in Africa (Mazower 2008, 231). On the other hand, new research about the Eastern bloc shows that some of the Communist elites of these countries saw cooperation with the "Third World" not as following the Soviet lead, but rather as an opportunity to escape its domination. Cooperation with the "Third World" was also seen as a means of getting economic benefits and international recognition (on Hungary, e.g., see Mark & Apor, 2015).

At the same time, scholarship on Soviet policies in the Global South have noted its contradictory results and different grades of success. Sergei Mazov, for example, in his book on Soviet politics in West Africa, showed that the Soviet Union expected some of the new African leaders to embrace socialism, in the context of decolonization, and intended to provide African countries with radio programmes and printed information about the construction of the socialism in the USSR (Mazov 2008). However, when this tactic proved to be unsuccessful – by the mid-1960s, many countries saw cooperation with the West to be more important, or did not find Soviet production and technical help to be of sufficient quality – the Soviet leaders took a more pragmatic approach to choosing their allies (Mazov 2008).

As for the Global South, the researchers named many reasons for why many countries there became interested in cooperating with the state socialist countries. For researchers from the Cold War period, such as MacFarlane, the reasons were mainly economic: some of the local national leaders preferred to follow Soviet expectations, for example, such as establishing a national front government with Communists participating in power-sharing, in order to extract more economic benefits from the USSR (MacFarlane 1985, 176). However, post-Cold War researchers showed that the situation was more complex, and there were a number of reasons contributing to that cooperation. Westad has demonstrated (2005) the importance of Communist universalism to "Third World" anti-colonial movements, and stressed that the appeal of the Communist message of progress and justice should not be overlooked. In this regard, it is interesting to note that, according to Peterson, LAI, the inter-war Soviet "sympathizing organization", evoked some nostalgic feelings among the participants at the 1955 Bandung conference (Petersson 2013, 3). Recent publications on cooperation between the Eastern bloc and countries in Africa, Asia, and Latin America, in the spheres of university education, architecture, and legislation, explored this problem further; and pointed out various overlapping mutual interests between the representatives of the "Third" and "Second" Worlds (Lee 2010a; Eslava et al. 2017). Finally, several researchers have written about the attractive image the Soviet and Eastern bloc modernization's experiences had for many nationalist leaders in the newly independent countries (Byrne 2016; Kalinovsky 2018; Mark et al. 2020). For example, Byrne, author of a book on independence and revolution in Algeria from 1960 to 1962, suggested that, although the Algerian leaders did not have any special sympathies for the Communists or the Soviet Union, the experience of Soviet modernization looked quite attractive to them (Byrne 2016, 158). A recently published book by James Mark, Artemy Kalinovsky, and Steffi Marung (2020) also explores the attractiveness many ideas, principles, and technical and organizational solutions coming from the Eastern bloc had for the nations of the Non-Aligned Movement, leading to the setting up of distinct cooperation and solidarity structures in the countries of Asia and Africa.

Recent publications exploring trans-Atlantic, African-Asian, and trans-Asian cooperation and solidarity questioned the bipolarity of the Cold War power relationships. They focused on the role of the Non-Aligned Movement, and transnational networks of Black and Asian Americans with activists and revolutionaries in Asia and Africa (Lee 2010a; Wu 2013; Byrne 2016, see also Roman 2011 on Black Americans' use of Soviet anti-racism in the 1930s). For example, Judy Wu, in her book on solidarities with Vietnam, showed that many radical Western intellectuals preaching anti-colonialism, anti-imperialism, and anti-racism were involved with the campaign against the war in Vietnam, and to support Vietnamese women, but they were not necessarily supporters of the Soviet bloc (Wu 2013).

History of transnational women's organizations and the WIDF

The history of international women's movements and feminisms is a relatively new direction of research. For a long time, national movements or developments in particular geographical regions were more common subjects of research (see Leon 1994; Molyneux 2001). However, in the late 1990s, Leila Rupp explored the early history of three transnational women's organizations: ICW, IAW, and Women's International League for Peace and Freedom (WILPF) (Rupp 1997). Rupp's research not only showed that international coordination played an important role in women's rights activism, but also indicated that these organizations could be seen as important transnational political actors, contributing to discussions on the most important global political issues, including militarism and democracy.

On the other hand, research on the engagement of women from the countries of the Global South in these transnational organizations showed that they had problems addressing the specific issues that were important for their members from newly independent countries, and countries involved in the anti-colonial struggle. For example, Laura Bier, who studied the Egyptian feminist movement, wrote that most of the transnational women's organizations originated in the West, and they rejected ethnic and national differences between women in favour of a notion of solidarity on the basis of biological sex, and a shared experience of oppression and disenfranchisement (Bier 2010, 148).

In recent years, more scholarship has appeared concerning the activities of the UN Commission on the Status of Women (founded in 1947), the International Women's Year (IWY), 1975, and the UN Decade for Women, 1975–1985 (Antrobus 2004, 37–67; Gaer 2009; Popa 2009; Ghodsee 2010; Sluga 2016; Olcott 2017; de Haan 2018). This scholarship showed that during the period after the Second World War, transnational events and organizations were influenced by Cold War tensions and rivalries, and the UN women's conferences (Mexico City 1975; Copenhagen 1980; Nairobi 1985) became sites of open confrontation between women's organizations from the "Third World" and organizations from the USA and Western Europe (Ghodsee 2010; Olcott 2017; Ghodsee 2018). The meeting of non-governmental organizations in Mexico City, which took place parallel with the meeting of official governmental delegations, was described as particularly confrontational, with tensions between women from Europe and North America on the one hand, and women from Africa, Latin America, and Asia on the other (Olcott 2017, 238–240). At the heart of the conflict were what the priorities of global coordination for women's activism should be, and attitudes towards important political events and ideologies. Hence the participants of the Mexico conference had differing views on socialism, peace, Zionism, and the 1973 Chilean military coup (Ghodsee 2010; Bonfiglioli 2016; Olcott 2017). Ghodsee especially focused on the confrontation between American feminists and the Soviet bloc delegations. According to her, American women "believed that their leadership of the movement was challenged by the strident anti-capitalist rhetoric of the Soviet Union and its allies" (2010, 5).

The WIDF did not receive much attention from these researchers of transnational women's history; Olcott (2017) and Sluga (2016) only discuss it very briefly. As I already stated, it was de Haan who began to study the WIDF's activities, and came to the conclusion that the WIDF was "a progressive, 'left-feminist' international umbrella organization, with an emphasis on peace, women's rights, anti-colonialism and anti-racism" (de Haan 2012, 1). De Haan explored the activities of the organization with a focus on its earlier years, its 1963 Moscow congress and a few others. She also created a timeline of its development and main changes from 1945 to 1989 (de Haan 2012, 2013, 2018). De Haan stressed that the women who belonged to this organization had their own political agency, and it cannot be seen as only a "Soviet front" (de Haan, 2012, see also de Haan, Bonfiglioli, Popa in discussion on Communism and Feminism 2016). These findings were supported by those of Melanie Ilic, who studied the WIDF's history with a focus on the development of the organization between the congresses of 1963 and 1969. Ilic saw the WIDF's activities in the defence of women's rights as important (Ilic 2011). Both de Haan and Ilic stated that the history of the WIDF requires further study because there is yet no comprehensive history of this organization. De Haan, in particular, stressed the importance of further research on the WIDF due to its key role in the development of a global understanding of women's rights (de Haan 2010, 2013).

In contrast to de Haan and Ilic, other historians recognized the importance and visibility of the WIDF in the global debate on women's rights, but suggested that its role was more complex and rather contradictory. Bonfiglioli analysed the development of relationships between Italian and Yugoslav women's organizations, both members of the WIDF, and showed the important role this organization had in defending women's rights in post-war southern Europe. At the same time, Bonfiglioli stressed the negative role the WIDF played during the Soviet/Yugoslav split in 1949, and in the cooperation between Yugoslav and Italian women (Bonfiglioli 2012). She also noted that there were important "differences between the leadership and the rank-and-file members" of the WIDF (Bonfiglioli 2012, 147). Celia Donert used materials from the GDR archive and demonstrated the dependence of the WIDF on the Communist leadership of the Eastern bloc. She stressed that "women's rights were swiftly embedded in Soviet and East European cultural diplomacy 'in defence of peace'" (Donert 2013, 190). Donert analyzed the WIDF's 1975 Berlin Congress, and showed that it was quite popular, especially among women's organizations from the "Third World", but it occurred in a context of growing concern about the persecution of political dissidents and human rights violation in the state socialist countries (Donert 2014).

A heated discussion around state feminism, and the agency of women under Communism as such, and in state-supported women's organizations like the CSW or the Chinese Communist women's organization (see Zheng 2017), was provoked by a 2014 article by Nanette Funk. In this article, the state feminist organizations were called "transmission belts" of the communist parties of the state socialist countries, while researchers insisting that women still had some space for demands and influence inside these organizations were called "feminist revisionists" (Funk 2014, 345). While this discussion – see the answer to Funk by several researchers in the journal *Aspasia* (de Haan et al. 2016) – did not concern transnational organizations such as the WIDF per se, it is important to discuss the agency of communist women during the Cold War era more broadly. The discussion on the definition of a "feminist organization" seems to be less important if we look at it from a post-colonial perspective (see Mohanty 2003). However, the issues of agency – the intentions and possibilities that women from state socialist countries, and in communist parties from different countries of the world – to influence the decision-making and ideology of the organizations seem to be of a particular importance. The use of the documents from the Moscow archives, and the focus of this book on women from the Global South, can be fruitful for further development of this discussion.

Thus, it is possible to say that, although some aspects and periods of the WIDF's history have already been studied, and some of the contradictions in its activities have been noted, many economic and political aspects of the organization's work continue to be underexplored. Biographies of its leaders and activists, as well as a systematic analysis of its periodical publications and relationships with UN governing bodies, and other transnational organizations, are waiting to be written.

Women from Africa, Latin America, and Asia and the WIDF

While publications on women's movements in different regions of the Global South simply ignored the WIDF and Communist women's organizations for a long time (a very informative and well-written book edited by Leon (1994) on Latin America is one example of this), in recent years, the role of the WIDF for women in Africa, Asia, and Latin America was explored by researchers from several different perspectives. Indeed, focusing on Vietnam and Algeria, Katherine McGregor has argued that the "WIDF's support for anti-colonialism was remarkably progressive". In particular, she has specified three strategies the organization adopted to support anti-colonialism. First, forging networks with colonized women by publicizing accounts of how women were affected by colonialism. Second, providing a platform for colonized women to articulate their ideas at the WIDF's congresses and in its official publications. And, finally, pressuring European powers "to uphold the new human rights standards" (2016, 926).

Several researchers also explored the WIDF's member organizations from various countries in Asia, Africa, and Latin America. In particular, several contributors to the book *Communist Women*, edited by Adriana Valobra and Mercedes Yusta (2016) in Spanish, discuss WIDF women's organizations in Chile, Argentina, Brazil, Costa Rica, Uruguay, and Cuba, mainly during the 1940s–1950s. The explicit focus on "communist women", expressed in the title of the book, allowed the contributors to contextualize the activities of the women's organizations, and to show important differences in their work methods locally, and in their relationships with the WIDF and Moscow. Similarly, McGregor (2013) provides a complex picture of the work of the WIDF member organization from Indonesia,

Gerwani, which combined a struggle for independence with campaigns for women's rights and social reforms in the 1950s–early 1960s.

Several researchers – Armstrong (2016), Pieper Mooney (2013b), de Haan (2013, 2016), Sandwell (2018), and some others – have discussed the importance of transnational cooperation and, in particular, the WIDF's networks for organizations and individual women activists from the countries of Asia, Africa and, Latin America. They stressed, in particular, that while the WIDF was organizing many regional events (several conferences in Latin America, de Haan 2017), many prominent female leaders from different regions were interested in cooperating with the WIDF as a means of gaining new knowledge and ideas, as well as it being a means of strengthening solidarity in their struggle against colonialism, fascism, and Apartheid. One relevant example is, according to Sandwell, the participation of women from the African National Congress (ANC, South Africa) in "rich transnational networks" of which the WIDF was an important part, contributed to their vision of themselves as being part of a wider context of anti-colonial struggle (2018, 101).

Finally, the book by Ghodsee (2018), to which I have already referred, focuses specifically on one case of cooperation between women from the "Second World" (a Bulgarian women's organization") and women from Zambia during the last phase of the Cold War. Ghodsee analysed the work of the special courses for female cadres from Africa that were organized in Sofia in the late 1970s. She showed the enthusiasm Bulgarian women expressed while helping their African sisters and, on the basis of the interviews with some of the former Zambian activists, Ghodsee concluded that this cooperation was important, and that the courses were useful. Ghodsee also showed the negative impact that the collapse of the "Second World" had for established cooperation, and for the livelihood of individual women activists in Bulgaria and Zambia (Ghodsee 2018).

In spite of these important contributions, research on the participation of women from the countries of Latin America, Asia, and Africa in the WIDF is only beginning. Whole regions (like Northern Africa and the Middle East), and many individual countries, that had active member organizations of the WIDF haven't been studied at all. The same can be said for the prominent women leaders of these national organizations, WIDF secretaries, and the representatives of its governing bodies. Additionally, most of the existing research on the participation of non-European women deals with specific periods in the WIDF's history (usually its beginning and the IWY), while a more general overview of the WIDF's policies with respect to women from the Global South, and the changing patterns of their activism and participation during the WIDF's Cold War history, is still waiting for researchers to produce.

Finally, the prevailing focus on the positive aspects of the WIDF's work for, and with, women from the countries of the Global South leaves unanswered questions regarding conflicts, problems, and misunderstandings, in particular, after considering previous research on the Cold War, with regard

20 A forgotten women's organization?

to "Communist fronts" and "sympathizing organizations". The effects of the gender equality model that was at the heart of the WIDF's ideology, as well as changes of Soviet policies towards the "Third World", and the conflicts inside of the Eastern bloc, are only some of these questions.

This book's main themes and structure

Existing scholarship on the WIDF's activities in different geographical regions, as well as the enormous amount of material available in the Russian archives, suggests that one book obviously cannot hope to critically analyse the WIDF's role in the transnational women's movement. Neither can it encompass the history of its relationships with women's organizations in all of the countries of Latin America, Africa, and Asia. Thus, due to my main interest being in the WIDF's work for the women of the Global South, and in their cooperation with the WIDF, and due to the specificity of the sources available, I have limited my study to an analysis of the most general tendencies, successes, and problems of this work. Nevertheless, this general review offers a series of more focused and detailed studies of examples of particular events (seminars, congresses), countries, and individual women from Asia, Africa, and Latin America who were directly involved in the federation's activities.

The first two chapters, after this introduction, aim to explain how the WIDF worked, what its main ideology was, and how it changed over time. These chapters also explore different aspects of the Soviet role in the federation; from the place of the CSW in the WIDF's decision-making to the influence of Soviet foreign policy priorities (such as détente or cooperation with particular leaders in the Global South) on the federation's activities.

The next chapter, –'The WIDF, the Soviet State, and Cold War Battles', analyses and problematizes the place that the WIDF had in the politics of the Soviet Union, including the ways that Soviet policies were realized in practice, and how successful they were. The chapter also problematizes the notion of the "Communist organization" through exploring complex and shifting power hierarchies between Communist female leaders of the WIDF from different countries, and their relationships with non-Communist members of the WIDF leadership. Chapter 3 – 'Protecting Peace, Mothers, and Children – WIDF's Ideology and Activities in its First Decades' – explores the WIDF's ideology and politics, with a special focus on the main changes that occurred over the first 25 years of its existence. I am especially interested in how the main components of the WIDF's ideology – the protection of peace and the protection and rights of mothers and children – were connected and put into practice, and what changes occurred later. I also explore the changing attitudes of the WIDF towards other organizations that had women's rights as part of their agenda.

The next five chapters are dedicated to the WIDF's work with issues, organizations, and individual female activists from Africa, Asia, and Latin America, and to female activists from these regions, and their influence on the federation. Chapter 4, 'Anti-Colonialism, Anti-Racism and Social Rights – the WIDF Defends Women in the Global South', analyses how the problems of women from the countries of Asia, Africa, and Latin America were addressed by the WIDF's official documents, and how they were discussed in unofficial correspondence and Soviet reports. The chapter shows that the WIDF, from its first days, was interested in the situation of women in colonial and dependent territories, and the WIDF's official publications expressed support for anti-colonialism and the social and political rights of women in Africa, Asia, and Latin America. At the same time, the study of archival documents suggests that even if the WIDF always demonstrated support for the rights of women in the Global South, their circumstances and intersectional concerns were often underestimated by the WIDF's leaders. Chapter 5 – 'The State Socialist Model of Women's Emancipation as an Example to Follow for the 'Whole World'" – is dedicated to the WIDF's advertising regarding the state socialist solution to the "woman question" as the best way of achieving women's emancipation and gender equality. The chapter shows that women's rights in the state socialist countries were exemplified in the WIDF's publications, as well as demonstrated to the participants of different events organized by the WIDF in the Eastern bloc, and those organized in the Global South itself, for women from non-European countries. In particular, I show that the images of, and female representatives from, the Soviet Central Asian republics – former colonies of the Russian Empire – were used by the WIDF to convince women from the Global South of the benefits of the state socialist system for women. Chapter 6 – 'Women from Asia, Africa and Latin America Make Themselves Visible in the WIDF' – is dedicated to the participation of the "Third World" women's organizations, and their female leaders, in the WIDF structures. The archival materials suggest that the incorporation of women from Africa, Asia, and Latin America into the WIDF's decision-making bodies was rather slow. Issues relating to the differing priorities for women's movements in the North and the South, as well as those connected to the struggle for independence and the use of "anti-imperialism", provoked major disputes in the WIDF's governing bodies. Chapter 7 – 'Activists from the Global South and the WIDF – A Biographical Perspective' – has an in-depth exploration of some of the individual women who worked with the WIDF. Unlike the other chapters of the book, this one takes a biographical approach, and attempts to indicate and problematize the complexity of the identities, as well as grounds and forms of participation in the WIDF, of women from the Global South. Finally, Chapter 8 – 'The WIDF on the Eve of IWY and During the UN Decade for Women' – is dedicated to the WIDF's work during the late Cold War period, and as a part of the UN Decade for Women. The chapter explores the continuities and changes in the WIDF's activities aimed towards women from the countries of Africa, Asia, and Latin America during the mid-1970s–1980s. This chapter also shows that from the 1970s onwards, the organizations from the Global South not only became numerically bigger and more visible in the WIDF, but also influenced its development towards the achievement of a certain degree of regionalization.

Notes

1 See also de Haan discussing Communism and Feminism in *Aspasia* 2016, 105.
2 The self-definitions of women from the Global South can also be important here. For example, Loomba wrote that many Indian communist women could be seen as feminist even if they did not "identify as such" (Loomba 2018, 6). Jeanne Martin Cissé, a general secretary of the Pan-African Women's Organization from 1962 to 1972, described the WIDF, in her memoirs, as an organization that united "women's and feminist organizations from the whole world" (Cissé 2009, 75).
3 The position of Cuba, the main Soviet ally in Latin America from the 1960s onwards, should be seen as particularly relevant with respect to several aspects of its politics, especially its support of revolutionary movements in Latin America, and its cultural politics (see, e.g., Gordon-Nesbitt 2015).
4 All translations from Russian and Spanish are mine.
5 The declassified RGASPI collections offer only a small portion of the documents concerning the WIDF, and only those from its earlier period (late 1940s–early 1950s).
6 These two versions were mainly identical, with the exception of some individual articles.
7 Comintern was organized in 1919 at a congress in Moscow, it included Communist parties from about 40 countries. It supported several other international organizations, including Red Aid and the Communist Women's International. The Comintern was dissolved in 1943.

2 The WIDF, the Soviet state, and Cold War battles

As already stated in the introduction, Cold War scholars have identified a number of transnational humanitarian and civil society organizations that acted internationally on behalf of the Soviet Union and, in general, were seen as "Communist" agents abroad or "sympathising organizations" (Petersson 2013). Even if these organizations presented themselves as independent, the common opinion was that all the instructions and money for their activities came "from Moscow". Moscow, in this case, never meant the concrete geographical place; rather, it designated the centre of communist activities (see Kanet 1988, 90). Thus, this chapter explores what was behind the Cold War period's definition of the federation as "a Soviet front" or "sympathizing organization". The next questions seem to be of particular interest here. What were the Soviet aims for the WIDF, and how were they realized in practice? How much power, in regard to the federation's activities, finances, and cadre politics, did the Soviet Union have? Did this power change over time? Who were the agents of the realization of "Moscow's interests"? What can be said about internal discipline within the organization, and the relationships between "Moscow" and female communists, from different countries and regions, in the WIDF's leadership? How well did the Soviet representatives in the organization and the women from different countries cooperate? How did other participants in the federation react to Moscow's control, or attempts to control it? What made women from different countries join and stay in the organization, and become a part of its leadership?

While this chapter cannot give the full answer to all of these questions, it aims to study the WIDF materials available in the Soviet archives to help detect, map, and explain the role of "Moscow" in this organization. It also pays attention to how external Cold War pressures over the WIDF influenced the role of "Moscow". Hence, the materials explored in this chapter could be seen as an introduction to the forthcoming analysis of how the WIDF acted in the case of women's rights in the countries of the Global South, presented in the chapters that follow.

I begin by exploring the relationships between the Soviet state, the Antifascist Committee of the Soviet Women (ACSW), and the WIDF, during the first 10 years of WIDF's history, and in the context of the beginning of the

Cold War. The second part of this chapter analyses changing power dynamics inside the WIDF during the latter part of that period. I mainly use the correspondence between those working for the ACSW/CSW in Moscow, and those who were sent by them to work at the WIDF Secretariat in Paris and Berlin (GARF). For the first period of the history of the Soviet women's organization's work within the WIDF, I also use the documents of the Commission on Foreign Politics of the Central Committee of the Communist Party of the Soviet Union (hereafter CC of the CPSU) that were preserved in RGASPI.

The Soviet state, the Antifascist Committee of Soviet Women, and the WIDF

As stated before, to the best of my knowledge, there are no documents available to researchers that would clearly expose a possible Soviet "hidden" agenda with respect to the WIDF, or explicitly show the amount of money transferred from "Moscow" to the WIDF unofficially year by year. However, in this subchapter, I address a question concerning the plans and aspirations that the Soviet state had with respect to the WIDF with the help of documents from the Soviet member of the federation – the ACSW. I commence with a short overview of Soviet politics regarding women's organizations inside and outside the country after 1917, and then focus mainly on the correspondence between the ACSW and its representative in the WIDF's Secretariat.

As is known, after taking power in October of 1917, the Bolsheviks declared the equality of rights of men and women, and also produced a series of laws that contributed to gender equality in regard to marriage, parenthood, work, and education (Engel 2004). At the same time, the Bolsheviks considered feminism to be a bourgeois political ideology, it was seen as dangerous to socialism. This led to a closing down of liberal women's organizations and their publications in Russia after 1917 (Engel 2004; Yukina 2007). Additionally, the *Zhenotdel*, the special department for work among women in the Soviet Communist Party, was closed down in 1930, when the "women's question" was declared to be "solved" in the USSR (Wood 1997). Furthermore, while the Comintern had some active female participants, the separate organization of communist women, the Communist Women's International, was also shut down in 1930 (Waters 1989). At the same time, the Soviet Union supported attempts to create a broader, international, women's anti-fascist organization, as a part of its struggle against fascism during the late 1930s. At that time, fascism was seen by a part of the leftist women's organizations as the "main enemy to the empowerment of women" (Yusta 2016, 168; see also Pieper Mooney 2013b; on anti-fascism in Soviet history see also Faraldo 2016). In 1934, the "World Congress of Women against War and Fascism" was organized in Paris by Gabrielle Duchêne (1870–1954), the head of the French section of the WILPF (de Haan 2012, 7; Yusta 2017, 50–56). Mercedes Yusta stresses that many of the organizers of, and participants in this congress were sympathizers of the Soviet Union, while some others came to antifascism through feminism (Yusta 2016, 170). The USSR also expressed its support to the Congress.

As for the big international liberal women's organizations – the IAW, or the ICW – they were usually seen by the Soviet leaders as bourgeois feminist organizations, and the Soviet women were not represented there. Thus, the participation of Soviet women in the WIDF, a big transnational organization created after the Second World War, outside of Soviet territory, was quite a new experience for the Soviets. It was particularly true when considering that it was mostly male members of the Soviet *nomenklatura*[1] (the Communist party bureaucracy) who were trained to work in the field of international relations. The CPSU and the Soviet state had very few female cadres in the highest levels of the hierarchy. Indeed, Aleksandra Kollontai was the only female Soviet ambassador during the 1940s, while the CPSU Central Committee had no female members at this time, and not until Valentina Furtseva was elected a member in 1952. One more prominent woman, a member of the Comintern leadership during the 1930s, and a former member of the CPSU Central Committee (during the Bolshevik revolution), Elena Stasova, retired soon after the end of the Second World War. Finally, the Cominform, the organization created in 1947 for coordinating Communist activities in Europe, where the Soviet and Yugoslav communists played the central role (Swain 1992), did not have participation from prominent Soviet women.

Thus, it is possible to state that, even if the Soviet leaders considered the transnational women's movement to be an important arena for post-war politics, they had to expect some difficulties at the practical level. Indeed, the degree of Soviet participation in the WIDF, and the participation of the Soviet representative in the WIDF's leadership, required that the international work would be performed exclusively by female cadres. They had to be well informed, knowledgeable, and eloquent, in order to be convincing while discussing the Soviet arguments for women's rights and global peace. Thus, in order to explore how the Soviet Union could influence the WIDF it is important to understand how the Soviet Union acted within the WIDF on a practical level, and what role Soviet women played in this organization.

The Antifascist Committee of Soviet Women and the Soviet "foreign front"

The ACSW was founded in 1941 as an organization aimed at channelling female support for the Soviet struggle against fascism (Ilic 2011). The official role of the ACSW in the WIDF during the federation's earlier years has been the subject of considerable study (de Haan 2010, Ilic 2011). The first head of the ACSW – from 1941 to 1968 – was Nina Popova, who, at the time of its establishment, was the secretary of the party committee of one of the districts of Moscow (Grigorieva 2010). Representatives of the ACSW took part in the founding congress of the French Women's Union (Union des Femmes Françaises – UFF) in December 1944. After that, the ACSW sent a large delegation (about 40 women) to Paris for the constituting meeting of the WIDF in 1945 (Ilic 2011, 158).

Being one of the members of the WIDF, the ACSW/CSW always occupied the position of one of the vice-presidents there. Thus, as I already said, the correspondence files of the WIDF in the ACSW archive in Moscow include some documents, or copies and translations, that were sent to the federation's headquarters from women's organizations of different countries. While the protocols of WIDF meetings were open and official documents, the reports of the Soviet representative in the Secretariat, and parts of other materials (outside of the protocols), were mainly sent to Moscow as classified letters. It is these letters that seem to be particularly interesting from the viewpoint of analysing Soviet strategies and tactics in the federation.

I will begin with a non-classified letter from 1956, sent by one of the representatives of the ACSW, Blinova, to an Italian activist from Turin, Renata Antonicelli (GARF 2 1773, p. 52; from 18 February 1956). The letter is preceded by a Russian translation of a letter by Antonicelli to Blinova, and by a short dossier concerning this Italian woman activist (GARF 2 1773, p. 49). According to this information, Antonicelli did not belong to any political party, but, in 1952, she visited the Soviet Union, thanks to the invitation of VOKS, an organization responsible for establishing contacts with intellectuals abroad, and organizing their visits to the Soviet Union.[2] After returning from her trip to the USSR, according to the Soviet information, Antonicelli became an active member of the society of friendship between Italy and the USSR. In her answer to Antonicelli, Blinova communicated that she worked at the ACSW at the time, and explained further that "This is an organization similar to VOKS, but it establishes contacts not with cultural, but with women's organizations from different countries" (GARF 2 1773, p. 52). Even considering the context – both women most probably first met via an event organized by VOKS – it is quite remarkable that Blinova emphasizes that ACSW's main activity is maintaining contacts with women's organizations abroad, rather than defending women's rights, or working for the women's cause per se. Thus, this presentation of the ACSW by one of its members allows us to suggest that, in communication with foreign women, Blinova, the member of the ACSW, presented her organization as: (1) merely a cultural organization; (2) an organization oriented primarily for communication and exchange with women from abroad (not for defending the rights of the Soviet women).

The contacts with women abroad, and the similarity of the earlier ACSW to VOKS named by Blinova in her letter, seem to be a good method of explaining what the ACSW was doing in practice. Such an explanation can also be proposed after considering several other documents and biographical data from the ACSW. Indeed, it was not only Blinova who moved between the VOKS and the ACSW in her professional life. The ACSW's president (and the vice-president of the WIDF), Nina Popova, also had close connections to both organizations. In 1956, Popova became a candidate member of the Central Committee of the CPSU (Ilic 2011, 159), and later she was chosen by the CPSU to be the head of the VOKS[3] (Tonchu 2004, 351–355). Thus, it is possible to say that Popova could use her experience of contacts with women from different countries acquired during her work in ACSW and WIDF for her work in the organization that, in 1956, was characterized by Blinova as "similar" to ACSW.

The structure of the ACSW's archival collection in Moscow also suggests that the external activities were more important to the leaders of the ACSW than the internal problems and concerns of Soviet women. In fact, while some meetings organized by the ACSW against fascist aggression during the Second World War were aimed at Soviet women, the ACSW's archived files between 1945 and 1955 are mainly dedicated to the activities of the ACSW and the WIDF abroad. They include correspondence with women of various (mainly European or North American) countries, or the travel of the ACSW's members to different countries in order to meet with women's organizations there. Thus, the archive does not offer much information on ACSW's discussions or actions regarding Soviet women during the difficult post-war years, when millions of women suffered from hunger, lack of housing, hard working conditions, and repression (see Zubkova 1998). For the most part, together with activities connected to WIDF, "friendship" – establishing contacts with women's organizations sympathizing with the Soviet Union abroad – seems to have been the main occupation of the majority of those working for ACSW, and not only of Blinova and Popova.

The documents from the CPSU's CC's Commission for Foreign Politics that were declassified at the Russian State Archive of Social and Political History (RGASPI), some years ago, show that the ACSW was acting under the supervision of this party Commission. The ACSW had to report to the Commission in regard to certain events, and certain financial issues connected to its activities abroad, in the context of its participation in WIDF. For example, the documents dedicated to the preparations for the conference for the defence of children in Vienna in 1952, supported by the WIDF, illustrate well how the relationships between the ACSW, on the one hand, and the Commission and the Ministry of Foreign Affairs, on the other, were functioning. These documents also show the place of the ACSW in the Soviet state and party hierarchy. The decision on the participation of the Soviet delegation (representing the ACSW at this WIDF event) was approved by the Commission. Information about this decision was sent by V. Tereshkin, the head of one of the departments of this Commission, to the Secretariat of Georgii Malenkov, member of the CC. The copy of this decision was preserved in the Commission's files (RGASPI 17 137 818, p. 37):

To the Secretariat of c. Malenkov G.I

To N 136415 from 22 February 1952

21 March 1952 the CC of the VKP(b)[4] took the decision about participation of the Soviet delegation in the international conference

for defence of children. The request of the Antifascist Committee of the Soviet Women that is described in the information about the preparation for the conference is approved in operative order.

The Head of the Department of the Commission for Foreign Politics of the CC VKP(b), V. Tereshkin. 27.03.1952

This document not only suggests that the participation of Soviet women representing the ACSW in WIDF's activities abroad could only occur on condition that the special department of the Central Committee of the CPSU sanctioned its participation, but also implies that the CPSU's Central Committee was well informed about the main activities of the ACSW abroad. In the context of the late Stalinist period, it meant also that most of the ACSW's international actions were planned in coordination with the CC of the CPSU.

In some cases, the Commission on Foreign Politics of the CPSU was receiving the reports of the ACSW or copies of the letters and reports that the Soviet representative in the Secretariat sent to the leaders of the ACSW. For example, the whole file from 1947 is documenting the materials that were sent to the CC (GARF 1 7). Part of these consist of the documents from the meeting of the WIDF Executive committee in Prague in March of the same year; the information was sent as a classified file to Comrades Stalin, Zhdanov, Molotov, Kuznetsov and Pankshin (GARF 1 7, p. 52). The archive materials do not offer any confirmation, however, that these materials really were read by Stalin himself. Neither are similar files from later years are available. However, it is possible to find other documents that indicate that the ACSW in one or another form was reporting to the CC of the CPSU and to other Soviet governing bodies about important events in connection to the WIDF activity.

For example, in connection to the conference in Vienna in 1952 that I discussed above, the files of the Commission preserved a letter sent from the Soviet representative in Berlin to the ACSW's president, Nina Popova, and to Petrova, the vice-president of the organization (RGASPI 17 137 818, pp. 39–48). The letter contained information about delegates to the conference from different countries, and a request for help with the visas for prospective participants. In the situation of the post-war Europe separated by old and new borders of zones of occupation, many delegates, according to this report, had a lot of difficulties with coming to Vienna. Thus, the ACSW leaders had to ask the Soviet Ministry of Foreign Affairs to make an exception for the delegates travelling to this conference. The ACSW asked to allow the visa for entering the territory of Soviet-occupied Austria to be granted faster than the 24 days it was usually taking (RGASPI 17 137 818, p. 41).

This document not only supports the conclusion regarding the hierarchical structure of the relationships between the Commission for the Foreign Politics of the CPSU and ACSW, but also suggests the existence of broader cooperation between different party and state institutions in the Soviet Union and the ACSW. Indeed, through applying to the CPSU's Commission, the ACSW expected to get help with visas from the Soviet Ministry of Foreign Affairs. At the same time, it is apparent that the ACSW had a closer relationship with the Communist Party of the Soviet Union than with the Ministry of Foreign Affairs.

The decisions regarding the financing of both Soviet delegations travelling abroad, as well as foreign delegations, and some individual female leaders vising the Soviet Union, also were mainly taken by the CPSU Commission on Foreign Politics during the federation's early years. For example, the letter from the ASWC informed Com. Grigoryan from this Commission on 19 January 1952, that the Union of Danish Women, a member organization of the WIDF, invited the Soviet delegation to visit Denmark (RGASPI, 17 137 819, p. 6). A list of four names was attached to this letter – one of the prospective members of the delegation was responsible for the work among women in the Central Committee of CPSU in Ukraine, another one was a distinguished shoemaker who had received the Stalin Prize, while the other two were ACSW functionaries. Along with asking for the approval of the chosen candidates, the letter also requested finances for the delegation's travel within Denmark (RGASPI, 17 137 819, p. 6).

The GARF collection concerning the ACSW's first years of activities in connection to WIDF preserved many documents that can help us understand the important principles used to determine the selection of the Soviet representatives who participated in the international events. For example, the archive of the ACSW preserved the list of participants of a rather large Soviet delegation (44 women) who travelled to Paris in 1945 to take part in the WIDF's constituting congress. This list included both the ACSW members headed by Nina Popova, as well as women-workers, engineers, and peasants from different parts of the Soviet Union (GARF 1 4, p. 26). The congress participants named in the list were characterized by stating their place of living, profession, or education. For example: "Kapustina, Anna Terentievna – architect. [..] was given a special diploma for projects of construction of the school building at the World Exhibition in Paris in 1937"; "Gurina, Zinaida Alekseevna – engineer-metallurgist of the aviation plant". Along with women who were professionally successful, some others were described also as mothers of heroes – those who perished in the war defending the motherland: "Ivatsek Nadezhda Fominichna – director of sanatorium of the Central Organization of Trade Unions, mother of the hero of the Soviet Union" (GARF 1 4, p. 26).

However, the ACSW also kept in its records several lists of the international participants at the constituting congress of the WIDF. While in some cases the lists contained only the names of women representing one or another country, in other cases, the participants were described in greater detail, with often about a paragraph of text. It first describes the participants from the USA, whose individual data seem to have been collected by one of the members of the American delegation, M. Draper (GARF 1 4, pp. 1–2).

The data show that, alongside members of the American Communist party, such as Elisabeth Gurley Flynn, the delegation included several prominent Black American activists. For example, "Missis Vivian Meson, National Council of Negro Women" or "Miss Henrietta Bookmaster, known American writer whose books are mainly about Negroes" (GARF 1 4, pp. 1–2). Some other participants were described through their social activism and/or sympathies to the Soviet Union in the data: "Miss Cornelia Brace Pinchot, leader of civil and political life in Pennsylvania. […] worked in organizations dealing with help to loyal Spaniards, Help to Russia,[5] 'France forever'" (GARF 1 4, p. 9). In the case of the participants from Yugoslavia, the information was not so detailed, albeit in a style to that provided for the Soviet participants: "Eugenia Selic, Montenegro, mother-hero", "Milena Rodic, Bosnia, partisan-fighter, peasant" (GARF 1 4, p. 11). Thus, the leadership of the ACSW and, obviously, the representatives of the CC of CPSU's Commission, from the very beginning of the WIDF, were very attentive to the social position and political views of the women from different countries who were participating in the WIDF's activities.

As for the financial aspects of the ACSW's activities of establishing and maintaining contacts with women abroad – through or without the WIDF – the documents preserved in GARF suggest that the Committee and its representatives abroad, including at the WIDF's Secretariat headquarters, were receiving their salary and were provided compensation for expenses from the Soviet state. They could be considered employees of the ACSW, rather than simply members of the organization. It is apparent, for example, from the ACSW's budget for the work of its representative in Paris in 1946 (GARF 4 5, p. 6), as well as from the letter discussing salary payments for the Soviet representative at the WIDF in Paris, and Soviet membership fees for participation in WIDF in 1950 (GARF 4 45, p. 11). The first document shows that the salary of the Soviet representative in Paris was determined on the basis of the ordinary Soviet salary form. In this case, an extra sum was paid, for example, if the employee had knowledge of foreign languages, and as compensation for the costs of improving her qualifications – in the case of this employee, for attending French language courses. The Soviet employee dispatched to work at the WIDF's headquarters also received some money to cover her representational expenses (GARF 4 45, p. 6). The letter from 1950 demonstrates that the salary of the Soviet representative, and money for paying the Soviet membership fees for the WIDF, came directly from the Soviet state – through its Foreign Money Department (*valutnoe upravlenie* – GARF 4 45, p. 11).

Being Soviet employees, the ACSW's representatives at the WIDF Secretariat were responsible to the CPSU through the ACSW's leaders – also CPSU employees at a higher level. At the same time, the Soviet representatives working abroad, at the WIDF's Secretariat, seemed to not be considered a part of the Soviet diplomatic corps and, thus, had a lower status compared to the employees of Soviet diplomatic missions. This is visible, for example, in the letter from the Soviet representative at the WIDF's Secretariat in Berlin, Galina Goroshkova, sent to ACSW, to Lidiia Petrova, on 1 December, 1952. Among other things, Goroshkova discusses her problems with using the library facilities at the Soviet Embassy in Berlin:

> Please, write to the Ministry of Foreign Affairs about permission for using the reading room [she means reading room for classified documents] of the special department of the USSR diplomatic mission. All documents I need for my work are preserved there, but I can read them only in the corridor. Even if comrades there are treating us very well they cannot allow us [to use the reading room] without the special permission of the Ministry of Foreign Affairs.
> (GARF 4 66, pp. 155–156)

The relatively low status of the Soviet representatives at the WIDF's Secretariat in the hierarchy of Soviet employees working abroad is also visible in letters from another ACSW representative, Zoya Ivanova, written in 1956 (GARF 4 106, p. 67), during the tense atmosphere after Khrushchev's speech on Stalin's "cult of personality". As the document shows (I will return to other aspects of this letter later in this chapter), the first weeks after this speech were particularly difficult for the Soviet women working at the WIDF Secretariat. In a situation where women from different countries working at the WIDF Secretariat were interested in the opinions of the Soviet representative regarding events in the USSR, Ivanova felt a lack of information and advice. According to the letter from Ivanova, the Soviet Embassy employees, and representatives of the party committee for Soviet employees working abroad in Berlin, "refused to help" her with advice on how she should behave with respect to discussions after Khrushchev's speech. (GARF 4 106, p. 67)

Some of the documents suggest that the Soviet representative at the Secretariat had to play an important role in the realization of Soviet foreign policy goals. However, they also show that, in many cases, the Soviet expectations were far from practical realization. For example, the letter sent by Zinaida Gagarina from the ACSW to Tatiana Kosheleva, in Paris on 8 August 1946, discusses several mistakes that Kosheleva made in her work:

> Tatiana Kirillovna! It was very strange to read that the Secretariat allowed the Antifascist Front of Yugoslav women to accept the invitation of the International Women's Assembly (Eleanor Roosevelt). It is against the decisions taken by the WIDF Executive Committee. It is also very unclear why the delegation of Republican Spain, Greek women from EAM, Yugoslavian and some other women decided to travel to Luxembourg? What aim do they have when they decided to travel to

this congress? The Executive Committee has decided to send only one representative of our federation and only as observer.

(GARF 4 5, p. 21)

It is obvious here that the responsible person from the ACSW in Moscow, Gagarina, is frustrated with several countries, members of the WIDF, who accepted an invitation to take part in a conference that Moscow sees as being organized by the Cold War enemies of the Soviet Union. At the same time, it can be assumed that neither Gagarina herself, nor any other female employee at AWSC in Moscow, had enough power to prevent the Greek, Spanish, and Yugoslavian delegations from travelling to that conference in Luxembourg. It also appears that Moscow learned about their decision post-factum, not in the least due to the communication means available at the time. In other words, the letter allows us to suppose that in spite of Moscow's constant control over what was going on in the Secretariat, and in spite of all its efforts to guarantee that the Secretariat and WIDF's members would make decisions that best corresponded to Soviet foreign policy interests, neither the ACSW nor the Soviet leaders had a mandate to give direct orders to foreign women's organizations.

Some documents preserved in the archives indicate the importance of the observing of the rules prescribed by Moscow on the side of those who were sent by the ACSW to work abroad. For example, the letter from the ACSW to Zoya Ivanova shows that the rules regarding classified information had to be observed strictly:

Dear Zoya Petrovna!

On December 28 we received the correspondence from you containing letters addressed to N.V. Popova, transcription of the conversation with Levon, letter by Lilly Wächter and newspaper clips. All these materials have a secret character but they were sent by the ordinary post. We ask you to pay more attention to how you make your post packages in the future, the packages should correspond to the content.

(GARF 4 106, p. 6)

Thus, as is obvious to see, most of the correspondence, not only reports but even newspaper clippings, were considered classified information. This regime of classification was designed by the Soviet state and Communist party structures, and applied to many foreign and internal policy documents of the time.[6] The special attention to observing the classification protocols in the documents on WIDF confirms that the Soviet employees of the ACSW, in addition to working for the goals proclaimed by the WIDF – protection of the rights of women and peace – also had obligations that could not be made public. Such obligations included the collection of information on important activists of the women's movement from different countries, information that could help influence the development of the WIDF in a direction suitable for the Soviet state and its communist party leaders.

The documents studied in this section indicate that the Soviet Union intended to control the work of the WIDF; at the same time, however, they demonstrate that the possibilities of such a control were rather limited, not in the least due to the lack of cadres having knowledge and experience in the sphere of women's issues in an international perspective. Also, the activities of ACSW's representatives in the WIDF, and women's activity abroad as such, does not seem to have been placed very high on the list of Soviet foreign political priorities. It is possible to suppose that it was the leaders of the CPSU who formulated the general policy with regard to desirable developments in WIDF's activities, defined the priorities of the ACSW work abroad, and demanded reports on the actual developments. However, it was the ACSW who had to elaborate tactics, and influence the development of events in the direction desired by Moscow through its representative at the WIDF's Secretariat. It also seems that the female leaders of the ASWC – first of all, Nina Popova, herself on her way to becoming a candidate member of the CPSU Central Committee – were considered competent enough to manage the observation of Soviet interests in the WIDF.

In the sections that follow, I explore the relationships between the CPSU, the Soviet state, and the Soviet women's organization, a member of the WIDF, further, by using examples of some cases and situations from WIDF's history.

ACSW and foreign communist female leaders and activists in the WIDF

The special status of the ACSW's representatives in the WIDF as employees of the Soviet state, and of the Communist party of the Soviet Union, should be also considered in the more general context of the participation of many representatives of Communist organizations, and female communist leaders, in the WIDF, and their presence at the Secretariat. Previous research has already shown that such famous female communist leaders as Dolores Ibarruri from Spain, Marie-Claude Vaillant-Couturier from France, and several Italian and Yugoslav communist women constituted an important part of the WIDF's leadership during the organization's early years (see de Haan 2012; Pojmann 2013; Yusta 2016; Bonfiglioli 2012). First among them was Vaillant-Couturier, a journalist and former prisoner of the Ravensbrück concentration camp, who was also known as someone who testified about Nazi crimes at the Nuremberg tribunal. She served as WIDF's general secretary from 1945 to 1955. Ibarruri, known as the hero of the Spain's civil war under the name of *Passionaria*, was one of the WIDF's vice-presidents during the 1950s. Several researchers already indicated that these two leaders had a particularly strong pro-Soviet and hard-line communist viewpoint: Vaillant-Couturier was characterized by Celia Donert as a "Stalinist" (Donert 2016, 319), Grigorieva noticed her very friendly relationships with the Soviet representatives and, in particular, with Popova, with whom she spoke Russian (Grigorieva 2010, 144). Finally, the Spanish organization of women (UME), where Ibarruri played a central role during the postwar period, was classified by Mercedes Yusta as "too dependent" on the interests of the Spanish Communist party (Yusta 2017, 69). The documents that were available to me mainly confirm these assumptions of previous scholarship.

The materials preserved in the Moscow archives suggest that, along with Ibarruri and Vaillant-Couturier, other communist women who had central roles in the WIDF also had very close relationships with some of the Soviet women from the ACSW, mainly with Nina Popova. For example, Jeannette Vermeersch, WIDF member and well-known French communist and women's rights activist, was the partner of the leader of the French communist party, Maurice Thorez. During the Second World War, she spent several years in the Soviet Union accompanying her husband, who found refuge in the USSR. Thus, this letter from Jeannette from 1946 to the head of the ACSW, Nina Popova, shows a lot of care and affection:

> I hope very much that you are in good health! Last time I saw your face it seemed to be so tired. You should check with the doctor and have some rest, dear Ninochka, our way is still so long and so difficult… My pregnancy does not cause me many problems and I think I will work to the end. I kiss you from all my heart as a sister and my hugs for your daughter.
>
> (GARF 1 4, p. 47)

On the other hand, the friendly relationships seem to coincide with the strict observance of ideological purity and party discipline. As previous scholarship already showed, it is possible to see the coincidence between the changes of the political line of the Soviet Communist Party, and the changes in the politics of the WIDF. Research by Bonfiglioli showed that, in the case of the Yugoslavian women's organization, the AFŽ, decisions made by the CPSU, and by Stalin personally, directly influenced the decisions of the WIDF (Bonfiglioli 2012). The AFŽ was expelled from the WIDF after the split between Stalin and the Yugoslavian leaders in 1948–1949.[7] Even though some years later the Yugoslavian organization was re-accepted into the WIDF, it never regained the position it had in the federation before 1948.

At the same time, I found a number of documents suggesting that some individual foreign female communist leaders and organizations expressed and defended their quite independent position with regard to the WIDF's strategies and working methods at different periods in its history. I refer specifically to the Italian Communists. The specific role of the Italian women's organization (Unione Donne Italiane – UDI) in the WIDF was explored in the dissertation by Bonfiglioli (2012), and in the monograph by Wendy Pojmann (2013). Both researchers showed that UDI was a broad coalition of leftist women, including socialist and independent women, and was one of the biggest and most active women's organizations in Europe at that period of time. The existing research also suggested that a special combination of factors inside the WIDF, as well as inside the Italian women's organization, and the internal political situation in Italy, influenced the decision of the UDI to cease from active participation in the WIDF in 1963. However, for almost 20 years before that, several Italian women, members of UDI and of the Italian Communist Party, played a very important role in the WIDF, and their names are very frequently mentioned in the documents I studied. They include: Angiola Minella (1920–1988), Carmen Zanti (1926–1979), Rosa Montagnana (1895–1979), and Maria Magdalena Rossi (1906–1995).

The biographies of these prominent women have certain similarities. Angiola Minella, the WIDF's general secretary in 1956–1957, and Carmen Zanti, the WIDF's general secretary in 1957–1964, as well as Rosa Montagnana, and Maria Magdalena Rossi took part in the Italian resistance movement, and enjoyed a high degree of popularity in post-war Italy. Two of these women – Rossi and Minella – were also members of the Italian Constituent Assembly, and of the Italian Parliament, in the 1940s and 1950s. Carment Zanti became a member of Parliament after 1963 (Bonfiglioli 2012, 211–213, 236). In the 1950s, Rossi was also the head of the UDI (Bonfiglioli 2012, 73–75).

The documents from the Soviet archive further show that Italian communists enjoyed a relatively independent position inside the federation as early as the mid-1950s, and they often showed their disagreements with Soviet strategies and tactics.

For example, Rossi and Minella are named in a letter by the Soviet representative in Berlin, Ivanova, that she sent to Moscow on 2 April 1957. While discussing the work of the Soviet representative on the publication committee for the WIDF's main publication, *Women of the Whole World*, the Italians seemed to not be satisfied with its overly ideological character:

> Angiola and Maddalena Rossi are not happy with the situation[...]. Angiola said to Maddalena and Odette Roux [a French representative] that Nina [Drynina, the Soviet representative on the publication committee] wants to make the journal like 'Pravda'. It means that she does not listen to our Italian friends.

Ivanova continued stating that:

> [According to Rossi] Everything is meaningless because the Soviet [members] do not understand their position. But the time will pass and everybody will understand that they [Rossi and other Italian women in WIDF] are right, similar to how the mistake with Yugoslavia is understood now.
> (GARF 4 115, pp. 76–82)

According to this letter, Rossi also complained that the WIDF was too much of 'a party mechanism' (*makhovik partii*), and implied that it needed to become a mass organization (GARF 4 115, pp. 76–82).

According to a letter from another Soviet representative in Berlin, Zinaida Lebedeva, from 19 January 1961, the WIDF general secretary, Carmen Zanti, after coming back from her trip to Italy, said that, according to her opinion, the representatives of France and Italy should not be the leaders of the federation. By this, she implied that the European communist women have too much power in the federation, and this power should be redistributed to improve the position of the representatives of the newly independent countries of Asia and Africa in the WIDF (GARF 4 149, p. 1).[8] Later correspondence shows that on 24 July of that same year, Carmen Zanti visited Moscow and discussed the situation of the UDI and the WIDF with several representatives of the Committee of Soviet Women (GARF 4 149, pp. 139–144). Among other things, Zanti suggested that:

> The problems of peace require creating possibilities of exchanging opinions between women of different continents. The development of contacts is important: we have to get on our side those forces that currently do not participate in the peace movement. It would be good to organize exchanges of delegations from different countries dedicated to these issues. For example, [to organize some activities] dedicated to the issue of Berlin.[9] And of course, the WIDF could have its special role here. To organize the meeting of women from Western Germany and the GDR would be even more important. Delegations from some other countries could be invited there as well and the problem would be discussed.
>
> (GARF 4 149, p. 144)

From this letter, it is possible to suppose that the members of the CSW came to the conclusion that Zanti's views were somehow dangerous, and sent a copy of the meeting transcript to the Commission on Foreign Politics of the CC. Further correspondence shows that after consultations with S.V. Tereshkin, the functionary at the department of foreign politics of the CC of CPSU, who is also named in several other CSW documents (see above), the Soviet representative at the Secretariat in Berlin, Lebedeva, seemed to try to cancel the next meeting of the Secretariat. In her letter to Moscow, Lebedeva stated that after communicating with Popova and Tereshkin, she understood completely why the Soviet Union should not support the idea of inviting more participants to the planned Secretariat meeting (*rashshirennyi secretariat* in the document) as suggested by Zanti. According to this letter, the next meeting of the Secretariat was postponed and relocated to Budapest (GARF 4 149, pp. 147–148).

Thus, with only the information from these examples, it is perceivable that some European communist women elected into the WIDF's leadership were ready to express their own views on the WIDF's goals, strategies, and developments; their views sometimes differed significantly from those of the CPSU. Thus, getting and maintaining alliances, even with Communist women from other countries, was an important task of the Soviet representatives, and this task was becoming only more difficult with the passing of time. As I will show in Chapter 6, the disagreement of the Italian leaders, in particularly Carmen Zanti, with the WIDF's strategies for work with women from Africa and Asia could be seen as one more reason for the ending of the active participation of the Italian female communist leaders in the work of the WIDF.

Still, the documents also show that the female representatives of the foreign communist parties, and non-party members working for the WIDF, had certain privileges in the Soviet Union; these privileges allow them to be compared to the Soviet *nomenklatura*, the hierarchical Soviet elite. In particular, they had the opportunity to spend holidays, and receive free medical treatment in the Soviet Union. [10] In spite of many changes in the WIDF during the 40 years of its history, these privileges seem to have been preserved up to the years of Perestroika (see more in the last section of this chapter).

However, such privileges seem to have been particularly significant in the construction of a hierarchy between women during the first years of the activities of the federation. Indeed, during the first post-war years, the majority of women in the Soviet Union suffered from hunger, shortages of everyday goods, clothes, and adequate housing, not to speak about repression (see Zubkova 1998, about situation for mothers see also Gradskova 2007). Thus, the hospitality offered by the Soviet state to the WIDF's leaders visiting the USSR was in a particularly sharp contrast with the level of life and rights of ordinary Soviet women. In the archive files, one can find the application to spend a holiday in the Soviet Union made by Rossi in 1949. In her application, Rossi asked about the possibility of spending 20 days of her summer holiday in the Soviet Union, together with her husband. Her request received a fast and positive decision. The ACSW informed Molotov, a member of the CC of the CPSU, about Rossi's application, and supplied a short datasheet on her and her husband (RGASPI 17 137 40, p. 86; 20 June 1949). The ACSW letter also noted that the Soviet ambassador in Italy had no objection to their visit to the USSR, and to the provision of financial support by the Soviet Union. The letter has a handwritten note by Molotov – "please do it immediately" – addressed to his secretary, Grigoryan. The sum stated in the letter – 3,500 rubles in foreign currency, and 12,000 Soviet rubles – indicates the relatively high level of comfort offered to the guests. The fast decision, and the large sum allocated for Rossi and her husband's visit to the USSR, suggests that Rossi's activity in the WIDF was particularly important to the CPSU and the Soviet leaders.

Nevertheless, as is shown by the case of the Italian communist leaders in the WIDF, and of Rossi herself, such privileged treatment from the Soviet authorities did not per se guarantee the full loyalty of the foreign communists to the Soviet position. As for many non-communist female leaders and activists from different countries that joined the WIDF during different periods of its history, their loyalty to the Soviet vision of the development of the federation always was under suspicion in Moscow.

These complicated relationships inside the WIDF leadership, and the WIDF's Secretariat, are revealed mainly in the classified correspondence between the Soviet representative at the WIDF Secretariat and the ACSW/CSW. This correspondence will be discussed further later in this chapter, while the next section aims to provide more information about the Soviet representatives working abroad.

Soviet members of the ACSW working abroad: between state duties and personal concerns

The relationships between the Soviet female employees involved in the work of the WIDF were organized through a hierarchical structure, where those in the Moscow CSW always had a higher position compared to the representatives in Paris or Berlin. As I showed, being employees and receiving a salary from the state, the Soviet representatives in the Secretariat had to follow protocol, for example, with respect to what kind of information had to be classified, and how it should be done. Thus, most of the letters I read do not exhibit any personal flourishes: opinions, feelings, experiences or memories are practically absent from the correspondence. It is particularly visible in terms of attitude to motherhood. While, in its political publications, the WIDF paid special attention to women's roles as mothers, and connected maternity to happiness, issues relating to the personal lives of Soviet women as mothers appear to be largely absent from the correspondence. The formalized official congratulations from the ACSW on the occasion of childbirth by one of the Soviet representatives in the Secretariat, Tatiana Kosheleva, gives a clear illustration of just how unimportant the issue of maternity had in communications between Moscow and its representative in the Secretariat.

The letter sent by Zinaida Gagarina from the ACSW to Tatiana Kosheleva in Paris, on 8 August 1946, starts with formal congratulations to Tatiana on the occasion of the birth of her son, and ends with brief wishes of good health for mother and child (GARF 4 5, p. 21). In contrast to the emotional letter from the French communist Vermeersch to Popova where she wrote about her pregnancy that I quoted above, this letter, however, is remarkable because of the absence of emotional expression or friendliness connected with the similarity of the gendered reproductive bodies. With the exception of these brief references to Kosheleva's maternity at the beginning and the end of the letter, it has an exclusively business tone, and clearly shows the hierarchical relationships between the sender and the addressee (the quote from this letter was discussed in the beginning of this chapter). Indeed, in this letter, Kosheleva received many reproaches on how she fulfilled her duties. The letter allows us to see how little attention the members of the ACSW paid to embodied female experiences.

The special role that the Secretariat played in the realization of Soviet policies within the federation makes it important to explore the process of recruitment of the prospective Soviet representatives at the Secretariat, and their individual biographies. Unfortunately, very little information is available, and even the biographies of the central persons in the ACSW, like Nina Popova or Nadezhda Parfenova, are not easy to find (exceptions are the Soviet-style biographies in dictionary published by Elena Tonchu in 2004).[11] Thus, I will present my attempts to recreate at least some aspects of their careers and personal lives.

Particularly illuminating in this respect is a document – a circular letter from the WIDF sent to all the members of the federation, in English – from 19 January 1951, (Paris) preserved in the Swedish archive (ARAB), in the files of the Swedish member organization of the WIDF, the Swedish Women's Left Union (SKV). The letter expresses "great pain" in connection with the sudden death of the Soviet representative in the Secretariat, Zinaida Gurina.[12] The WIDF general secretary, Vaillant-Couturier, in her two-page circular letter dedicated to the memory of Gurina, follows the established patterns of Soviet biographies. According to this letter, "Zina Gurina was a living example of the Soviet woman liberated by the socialist system". The letter stated that Gurina was a member of the Supreme Soviet of the Soviet Union, which she combined with her work in the Secretariat of the WIDF. Gurina is characterized as one of the heroic Soviet women "who were working for their homeland during WWII", and as one of those whose "hearts bled" because their husbands perished in the war. The letter also mentions that Gurina was a mother, and implied that her interest in protecting peace was inspired by her motherly position: "She did not want other women or her beloved daughter to endure what she had gone through, she wanted all women to live happily in a world of peace" (fond of SKV, p. 2, ARAB, 3340).

In the case of other women, who worked at the Secretariat in Berlin during the 1950s (and even early 1960s) as secretaries, or as Soviet representatives for the WIDF official publication, *Women of the Whole World*, the Soviet archival collection contains only very partial information, coming mainly from correspondence. For example, the letter from Zoia Ivanova to Popova from 1956, complaining that the Soviet representative on the editorial committee of the magazine, Drynina, did not fulfil her duties, mentions Drynina's previous occupation (GARF 4 115, pp. 75–76). According to Ivanova, Drynina was rude to her foreign colleagues, did not listen to their comments about her work, and she also often missed meetings. In spite of Drynina's bad work habits, the author of the letter confesses that she does not know how to discipline her Soviet colleague. One of the reasons for this is Drynina's age, and her previous work experience:

> I will try speak to her one more time, ask what is the problem and if it is something else that prevents her from working well and what might be interesting to her. But, Nina Vasilievna, she is an adult person, she is 35, she worked in the regional party committee and I feel it difficult to speak to her in such a way.
>
> (GARF 4 115, p. 76)

Some other letters suggest that most of the women were mothers; however, sometimes their children already were grown up. Indeed, one of the rare examples of letters exposing quite friendly relationships between the Soviet representative in Berlin and her correspondent in the ACSW discusses issues of employee's communication with her grown-up daughter. Lidiia Petrova, one of the ACSW's leaders in Moscow, wrote to Galina Goroshkova to Berlin in 1952 (most probably answering Goroshkova's questions) about her daughter, a student of the Moscow university:

> Galina Nikolaevna!
>
> I spoke to Innochka. Why do you think that she is sad? No, she is very optimistic, she goes to the university and does her homework after the classes. Of course, it is difficult to find her home – there are not enough textbooks, she and her friends are doing homework together. Sometimes she has to do her homework at the house of some of her friends. But do not worry, everything is going well at home.
>
> (GARF 4 66, p. 157)

Finally, it must be noted that, even if the Soviet representatives at the Secretariat were the employees receiving their salary from the CPSU and thus a subject of the strong work discipline, there were women who dare to have and express their own opinion. Indeed, in some cases the employees were acting according to their understanding of what is the best for the "Soviet interests" in the WIDF. For example, Goroshkova, the secretary I referred to above, worked in Berlin during the period of the war in Korea, when the WIDF published a special reports on American military crimes there (something which I will discuss in more detail in Chapter 4). This report also was the reason for the WIDF to get the label of the "Communist front". During this difficult period for the members of the WIDF's Secretariat, Goroshkova often had to take the risk of deciding by herself. For example, Goroshkova insisted on her own interpretations of WIDF's publication for women:

> It is very difficult to fully implement your demands concerning the pamphlet about women's rights. I already have written to you that this pamphlet should address broader masses of women. It is not a textbook or theoretical publication. That is why we should not hope that we would be able to place everything into the framework of this popular publication.
>
> (RGASPI, 17 137 818, 28.10.1952, p. 193)

At the same time she wanted to present herself as an obedient employee and in the same letter she asked to "educate her" and complained for the lack of information:

> To the Antifascist Committee of the Soviet Women. Classified
> To Com. Popova N.V., Com. Parfenova N.M

Dear Comrades!

Because here I am disconnected from the sources of information that are available to you, sometimes it is difficult for me to find answers to the questions that have big political importance. For example, that one about the publication of letter by Roosevelt in the Soviet press.[13] That is why in such cases I ask you to write me more in detail why is it important to do this and not that. It will help me to solve some other problems, to improve my political vision and educate me.

(RGASPI, 17 137 818, 28.10.1952, p. 192)

In her answer to Goroshkova's letter Popova, the head of the ACSW, stressed the importance of discipline and recommended to Goroshkova to consult Moscow in the cases of doubts and do not take decisions individually:

For us here it is obvious that you should follow our decisions. It is your main task to do so that the Secretariat should not try "finding solution", but to act according to the agreements we had previously [...]. It is always better to ask first our advice and only after that to express your opinion ... you can also ask to postpone the decision under some pretext – for example, because you should better understand the problem and to think.

(RGASPI 17 137 818, pp. 118–119, from 4 November 1952)

Thus, on the basis of the documents studied in this subchapter, it is possible to say that the ACSW, and, later, the CSW, was an organization that worked in accordance with the decisions of the CPSU, and cannot be considered an autonomous women's organization. At the same time, the activities of the ACSW in the WIDF combined democratic (proposing candidates and programmes, building coalitions) and non-democratic (collecting personal information, enforcing party discipline) methods of work. The Soviet representatives in the WIDF's Secretariat played an important role in these activities. As a result of several factors, including the quite independent position of some of the foreign female communist leaders in the WIDF, compared with the absence of widely recognized Soviet female leaders, the low position of the ACSW in the Soviet state and party hierarchy, as well as the Soviet secretaries' lack of experience in international work on women's rights, the practical control of Moscow over the WIDF's activities should not be exaggerated.

The WIDF's internal life in the correspondence of the Soviet members of the CSW between Berlin and Moscow, from the second half of the 1950s to the early 1980s

This subchapter is dedicated to the correspondence between Moscow and the Soviet representatives at the WIDF's headquarters. While in the previous subchapter, I analysed official and non-official power structures inside the federation and its governing bodies, here I want to explore more in depth how the relationships between Moscow and the WIDF worked in the context of the changing pressures of the Cold War confrontation, as well as global political developments. In particular, I analyse what kind of information on the Secretariat's internal operations and work was demanded by Moscow from its representatives, and what kind of problems/conflicts or discontents inside the Secretariat were observed and reported by them to their employers. While it is easy to suppose that the Soviet representative at the Secretariat could not be aware of and observe/report all the conflicts or discontents, these documents are still important to analyse, as they are almost the only "unofficial" observations available now about the Moscow–WIDF relationships, and the internal life of the Secretariat. The correspondence can also inform us further about implicit assumptions with respect to the federation's work style, and the most frequent tasks and problems of the Secretariat's members.

After moving to East Berlin in 1951, the WIDF and its Secretariat changed not only a geographical location, but also a geopolitical one. As opposed to France, East Berlin clearly signified the "pro-communist" character of the organization and, at the same time, promised a friendlier and more relaxed environment for its work. Especially with regard to important technical aspects of the work of the Secretariat – for instance, the problems with visas for Secretariat employees or visitors – East Berlin was a more suitable location. At the same time, the organization continued to experience pressures in connection with further development of the Cold War confrontation.

In order to show better how the power relationships inside the organization were changing in connection to the changing balance of power between the participants of the Cold War confrontation, I have chosen several issues that can help to explore the character of the internal and external challenges that the WIDF experienced. I also paid attention to the part of the correspondence that could help further shed light on the forms and methods Moscow employed to attempt to influence the WIDF's policies, and the degree of the success of some of these attempts. In what follows, I look more closely at the internal crises at the WIDF's Secretariat connected to the Khrushchev speech at the 20th congress of the CPSU as interpreted by the Soviet representative at the Secretariat. In the second part of this subchapter, I explore how the Soviet representatives at the Secretariat reported on other members of the Secretariat, and the internal relationships there at different points in the history of organization. Finally, I also explore the role of Moscow in the cadre politics of the federation. In analysing the Soviet letters and reports, I pay attention to how the authors of the reports were positioning themselves with respect to the federation, Soviet interests, women's rights, and communist ideology. When possible, I also analyse how the reaction of the women from other countries to Soviet policies is described.

The WIDF's Secretariat in Berlin and Khrushchev's Critique of Stalin's "Personality Cult" (1956)

The WIDF's documents and official publications frequently showed the Soviet Union, and other countries of state socialism, as countries where women's rights are protected in practice, and not only declared (see Chapter 5). In the WIDF's official documents, the countries of the Soviet bloc were described as "democratic countries", implying both the importance of democracy, and the incompatibility of true democracy with capitalism. This positive attitude towards state socialism included respect for the Soviet leader, Josef Stalin. The death of Stalin in March 1953 occurred during the World Congress of Women in Copenhagen, organized by the WIDF and the WIDF's official publication quoted the words of Eugénie Cotton, the WIDF's president, on this occasion:

> It is impossible to grasp the truth of the news that Stalin is dead; for the man who has given millions of men and women the sense of their value as human beings will live forever in the hearts of mankind.
>
> Stalin fulfilled the dearest hope of women in proclaiming that human capital is the greatest wealth of a nation, and in giving to children the full care of his government, for nothing is more precious to mothers than the children they bring into the world.
>
> Stalin, the man of justice, raised the women from their former humiliating position, by making them the equals of men in all fields.
> (see Special Bulletin, 20 March 1953, collections of IISH)

The special section dedicated to Stalin's life was also published by the journal *Zheshchiny mira* (ZM 1953, 2). It contained some quotations from Stalin's speeches, and pictures of him with children around.

The process of de-Stalinization, however, did not obtain much publicity in the WIDF's official publications as far as I could find. However, classified correspondence between the Soviet representatives allows us to think that the events of the 20th Congress of the CPSU, and Khrushchev's speech on the "cult of personality", contributed to an important crisis inside the organization.

Zoia Ivanova, the Soviet representative at the Secretariat in Berlin, sent several quite emotional classified letters describing the atmosphere at the Secretariat during the first weeks after the 20th Congress:

> I want to inform you that our situation at the Secretariat became more difficult: after getting different messages by radio and press our friends started to ask us about the cult of personality and, in particular, about the role of Stalin in the history of our party, our state and the international workers movement.
> (GARF 4 106, p. 64, from 24 March 1956)

According to Ivanova, several Secretariat members were affected by the news. Indeed, Elisa Urriz, communist and Spanish representative at the Secretariat, started to discuss the Stalin Prize: "how would it be now – if Stalin is a despot and tyrant, the way the Western press is saying, would anybody be interested in receiving such a prize" (GARF 4 106 p. 65). The Polish representative in the Secretariat, Zlava Sobierajska, who was described by Ivanova as having negative feelings towards the USSR even earlier (*otnosilas k nam plokho*), started to say that "she always knew that Stalin was a dictator" while the Soviet people are "eager to believe everything they are told" (*sovetskie kak peshki, chto im skazhut, oni vsemu veriat*) (GARF 4 106, p. 65).

Ivanova made the following suggestion:

> It is not convenient for us to be silent now – it might lead to alienation of our friends and can damage our work here. It seems that we have to offer more concise information about the role of Stalin in the history of our society. We cannot allow that our friends would get all the information from the evil Western press and would get the wrong interpretations that are benefitting our enemies.
>
> (GARF 4 106, p. 66)

While discussing the situation, Ivanova uses "us" and "we", indicating her feeling of belonging to a community whose interests were dear to her. However, this "we" can hardly refer to "we-women" or "we-WIDF activists", but rather to "we-Soviets". This "we" opposing them – the Cold War enemy, but also representatives of other transnational women's organizations – is an important part of the Cold War rhetoric that seems to have been widely used within the federation. However, in her letter, Ivanova also suggests that her own views on Stalin were changing:

> As for the personality of com. Stalin and others, I answered this question in such a way that it would not provoke false interpretations. Also, I myself did not know at that moment what I learned later from Khrushchev's speech.
>
> (GARF 4 106, p. 64)

When feeling left without enough information and advice, Ivanova and other Soviet representatives in the Secretariat went to the Soviet Embassy and the Soviet organization of the Communist Party for Soviet employees in Berlin, but did not get help:

> … We asked for advice from the local party committee and the Soviet embassy but they categorically refused to help us with more information. It is a pity that in the case of such important and central issues

for the international front, we, the workers of this front (even if not so important ones)[...] get the information at the last moment.
(GARF 4 106, p. 67, from 24 March 1956)

Thus, Ivanova felt an obvious dissonance between the interpretation of her international role she learned in Moscow, and her real situation in the context of the political and ideological crises. It is also interesting how she described her functions: "we, the workers of this front (even if not important ones)" (*rabotniki etogo fronta, khotia i malenkie*). It seems that, in her case, Ivanova considered herself to be working for the Soviet political ideals, but general confusion and the lack of help in the context of the beginning of the politics of de-Stalinization made her feel herself to be "not so important".

The archival documents from the same file show that Ivanova was not alone in her perception of the 20th Congress of the CPSU as having a serious and long-lasting effect on the work of the federation. One of her reports was accompanied by the translation into Russian of two letters that were sent by the West German leader of the women's organization, and one of the WIDF's vice-presidents, Lilly Wächter. One of these letters was sent to Maria Ovsiannikova, at the time the main editor of the journal *Soviet Woman*, and the second one – to Angiola Minella, the general secretary of the WIDF. In the accompanying classified note to Popova, Ivanova informed the head of the CSW that Wächter "declared that she will work as a functionary of the social-democratic party due to her disagreement with the work methods of our women's organization" (GARF 4 106, pp. 72–75 from 29 June 56).

Wächter's letter has many interesting comments about the Soviet system, and the work of the WIDF. That is why I think that it is important to discuss it here in more detail. Lilly Wächter was of Jewish decent, and many members of her family had perished in the Nazi concentration camps. She joined the WIDF delegation reporting on the American War Crimes in Korea (as well as Ovssiannikova – *We accuse*, 1951), and after returning back to Germany, she was arrested and tried by the US court of the Allied High Commission, on suspicion of spreading of communist propaganda. Celia Donert described Wächter's trial in detail in her article (2016, 325–331). Donert also showed that this trial was used by the Soviet and GDR authorities to raising the prestige of East Germany, through mobilizing female solidarity behind Wächter; during the trial, Wächter was presented as an ordinary West German housewife who shared the ideals of the peace movement (Donert 2016, 331).

In the beginning of her several-pages-long letter to Maria Ovsiannikova[14] (GARF 4 106, pp. 77–85, in Russian translation), Wächter stated that she lost almost all of her family under the Nazis, and expressed her sympathies for the Soviet Union and the CPSU that she had had for a long time (GARF 4 106, p. 77, p. 79). In particular, Wächter claimed that she was a sympathizer of the Soviet Union because "it was fighting against racial discrimination and because it stopped the pogroms that were frequent in the previous period" (GARF 4 106, p. 79).[15] However, Wächter also stated that from 1933 on, she was carefully observing the work of the CPSU (in the letter it is "your party" – the party Ovsiannikova belongs to), and found that the 20th Congress revelations confirmed the suspicions she had felt for a long time. Wächter disclosed, for example, that she did not join the Communist Party due to her fears. She conveyed that the latest revelations on the 20th CPSU Congress confirmed that the "methods of justice and full faith that is required from the party members [by its leaders]" were the main cause of her fears and doubts. She continued by stating that the absolute faith in the party required from the Communist Party's members is similar to that one "that can be found inside the Catholic Church". Indeed, the Communist party, like the Church, "does not allow doubts or mistakes and promises paradise" (GARF 4 106, p. 77). In explaining some of her fears and doubts, Wächter showed a very high awareness of political developments inside and outside the Soviet Union:

> this country again became a source of fear for me due to the killing hand of the God brought on the pedestal – Stalin! Thousands were killed, innocent people were sentenced on the basis of wrong accusations; they died just because they honestly expressed their opinion.
> (GARF 4 106, p. 79)

While stating that the decisions of the 20th Congress were not so surprising for her, Wächter then tells of her meeting an unnamed old female Soviet communist during some time she spent in Moscow receiving medical treatment in the Kremlin hospital (GARF 4 106, p. 79). There, Wächter shared a ward with this old communist, who informed her about what was going on in the Soviet Union under Stalin. Wächter's letter contains several facts that she learned in Moscow, facts that seem to be important in her decision to leave the WIDF. For example, Wächter felt outraged when she heard Otto Grotewhol, the GDR head of government, say that the Soviet Union had "never started a war":

> but how was it with little Finland?[...] (and how was it with Estonia, Latvia and Lithuania?)[...] And how was it after the agreement between Hitler and Stalin? All antifascist literature disappeared at once and the history course in the universities was suspended.
> (GARF 4 106, pp. 78–79)

In another part of the letter, Wächter criticizes the introduction of paid secondary education in the Soviet Union during the early 1940s,[16] and the growth of the Soviet *nomenklatura*:

> In 1940, the fellowships in secondary schools and universities were stopped. And, in contradiction to the Constitution, payment for

secondary education was introduced in schools. Thus, children of the workers and peasants had to leave universities[...] The high-level bureaucrats appeared and the privileges that the privileged people had become "hereditary".

(GARF 4 106, p. 79)

Thus, this letter shows that some of the WIDF leaders were not only well informed about events and policies that were censored in Soviet publications and official international declarations, but that they probably cooperated with the Soviet representatives and the WIDF for tactical reasons, and the temporal lack of other options for activism.

In contrast to the first letter, addressed to a high-ranking Soviet female communist, Wächter's letter to Minella, an Italian communist, and WIDF's general secretary, mainly discussed internal problems of the federation (GARF 4 106, pp. 87–92). According to this letter, the WIDF's Secretariat functioned as too closed a structure, and too much in line with communist ideas:

If the local organizations get only bureaucratic guidelines from above, even if these guidelines are perfectly formulated, they will remain on paper. Thus, if the Secretariat or bureaus of the national organizations cannot enrich their activism with a "new life" – i.e. new people and new ideas that inspire them – the local groups would also be passive. Indeed, now the member of the local groups often say: "first you have to show us how to do it".

(GARF 4 106, p. 88)

In order to avoid negative effects from a similar organizational structure inside her organization in Germany, the Union of German Women, Wächter considered it important to have more open organizational arrangements, and to not have a Secretariat (GARF 4 106, pp. 87–88). At the end of her letter, Wächter complained about the lack of development of the WIDF with respect to getting more support for the rights of children after the congresses in Copenhagen (1953) and Lausanne (1955), and connected it to "narrowness (*uzost*) of organization that we have created ourselves" (GARF 4 106, pp. 89–90).[17]

Lilly Wächter does not seem to be the only person who decided to stop her active participation in the WIDF or to be part of the leadership of the national organizations, its members in the context of the discussions about Stalin's crimes after the 20th Congress of the CPSU. In her information to Moscow a few weeks later, Ivanova informed Nina Popova about "complicated relationships" between the Communist Party members and independent female activists. Several important members of the federation decided to stop taking official positions in their respective national organizations:

I want to bring your attention to the abnormal relationship between the communist women and women from other parties and social backgrounds. It led to a situation where Lilly Wächter, the leader of the Democratic Union of German Women, Frida Engel, the head of the All-German Council of Women (West Germany), the Head of the Democratic Union of Danish women, Ruth Hermann and members of the leadership of this organization – Ida Bazman, Kristina Borum, Anna Peterson, Viveka Gaardman – and the head of the National Assembly of Women of England, Monica Felton, [...] left [their position].

(GARF 4 106, p. 102)

Thus, on the basis of the correspondence from 1956, it is possible to conclude that the leaders of the Soviet women's organization in Moscow were receiving a lot of information about the discontent felt by many women, representatives of both Western countries and the Soviet bloc. However, it does not appear that the ideas and concerns of these women were taken into consideration, or that changes in the Soviet line within the WIDF, or the federation's structures and politics, were ever proposed. The correspondence also shows that during big ideological shifts in Soviet politics, such as the 20th CPSU Congress, the Soviet representatives in the WIDF experienced huge difficulties in maintaining their status and respect within the organization. Thus, in spite of all the attempts to manage it from the Soviet centre, improvement of the Soviet image was possible only to a certain degree, and required a lot of effort and creativity from the Soviet representative in Berlin. This all suggests that the Soviet representatives should have been more careful when pursuing "Soviet interests" and that they should have attempted to win sympathies rather than demanding them.

Soviet representatives reporting on the WIDF leadership and Secretariat members

The documents collected in the correspondence files of the archive also contain a lot of information about individual members of the WIDF's leadership, and their attitudes towards their Soviet colleagues, and towards the Soviet Union itself. While, in most of the cases, these documents are reports from semi-official meetings and conversations, in some cases, the reports of the Soviet representatives were accompanied by translations and copies of letters of other (non-Soviet) members of the Secretariat, translations from press reports, and even medical reports.

For example, the correspondence from 1957 contains a report about a medical examination of Angiola Minella, at that time the WIDF's general secretary. The report communicated that medical doctors in the Soviet hospital in Berlin examined Minella upon her request; she complained of insomnia and other psychological disorders (GARF 4 115, pp. 84–85). This report was sent to Moscow in connection with previous letters and reports informing about Minella's health problems, and the distortions in the Federation's work that they caused:

> Angiola came from Italy not feeling good. We [most probably other members of the Secretariat, not only Soviet] suggested that she go on holiday. Her sickness influences our work very negatively. Thus, she plans to traveling on holiday to Czechoslovakia.
> (GARF 4 106, p. 74)

In most reports, the information transferred by the Soviet representatives concerned members of the WIDF leadership, or leaders of women's organizations cooperating with the WIDF, from the viewpoint of existing or possible danger they could cause to the WIDF and/or to Soviet interests. Individual opinions and utterances regarding the WIDF's aims and tactics that were partially different from Moscow's vision were considered important information worth reporting to Moscow. For example, two reports of the Soviet representatives in Berlin from the 1950s suggest that one of the prominent WIDF leaders of that period, Andrea Andreen, the representative of the Swedish member organization, the Swedish Women's Left Union (SKV), expressed some ideas that were not compatible with the Soviet vision of the WIDF.

Andreen had a medical degree, and during the 1930s, she participated in peace and women's rights activism in Sweden. In 1945, Andreen took part in the WIDF constituting Congress as an activist who did not belong to any political party (Andreen 1974). Internationally, Andreen became particularly known after her participation in the Commission investigating the use of bacteriological weapons by US troops in North Korea in 1951(Andreen 1974). Similar to Wächter in Germany (Donert 2016), Andreen was accused of sympathizing with communism by the Swedish press (Andreen 1974; Larberg & Andreen Sachs 2015). During the 1950s, Andreen worked as one of the vice-presidents of the Federation. She received the Lenin Prize in 1953, and in 1955, she was elected as a head of the Committee of Mothers that was created at the World Congress of Mothers organized by the WIDF in Lausanne. While Andreen's status as an independent women's rights and peace activist (similar to that of Eugénie Cotton) seemed to be very important for the WIDF, the letters of the Soviet representative in Berlin show that Andreen did not enjoy the trust of all the members of the WIDF leadership. Some of the doubts and suspicions against her can be found in the letters sent to Moscow by the Soviet representative, Ivanova, in 1956.

In the first one, in her letter to Popova, Ivanova wrote that Angiola Minella, the WIDF general secretary, met Andrea Andreen in Stockholm at the beginning of 1956. According to Ivanova, Minella noted that Andreen:

> Considers it important that while organizing cooperation with other women's organizations we [the WIDF] should take the position that

is different from one insisting that everything in the USSR is good and everything in the USA is bad. We have to criticize both. She also suggested to make an appeal to the governments of the USA, UK and the USSR demanding a ban of atomic weapons.

(GARF 4 106, pp. 36–38)

The second report is a summary of a conversation with Andrea Andreen at the Secretariat that took place on 7 January 1956. Along with Zoya Ivanova, the participants at the meeting included the representative of French women, Simone Bertrand, and two Spanish representatives, Dolores Ibarruri and Eliza Urriz. According to Ivanova, after the end of the meeting, she was approached by Ibarruri, who asked her to communicate to the Soviet representatives in the WIDF her private opinion about Andreen:

Dolores Ibarriri is afraid that Andrea Andreen is a difficult person and she might tend to separate the Committee [of Mothers] from the WIDF and to start developing it in accordance with feminist ideas. Ibarruri said that it is a pity that she herself is not able to take part in the next meeting of the WIDF's bureau: she could speak to Andreen and to convey her all that the Soviet friends cannot say to her.

(GARF 4 106, pp. 25–27)[18]

Thus, these two reports indicate that, as a non-communist leader of the WIDF, Andreen was seen by many communist members of the organization as a member that was particularly prone to taking a "wrong" position in the Cold War confrontation, and damaging the organization.

The WIDF leaders also experienced mistrust towards another kind of female activists – the representatives of leftist organizations supporting socialist and communist ideas different from the Soviet interpretations of Marxism and communism. For example, the handwritten letter (probably indicating that the message was sent urgently) sent by Lebedeva to Moscow from Berlin on 29 September 1961 warned the representatives of the CSW about the "problematic" political orientation of the person who was invited at the last moment to substitute for one of the initially scheduled keynote speakers at the WIDF event:

Sudha Roy, the vice-president of the National Federation of Indian Women, should come [...]. She is the member of the WIDF's council from Bengal. But, according to information from Vimla Farooqui,[19] Sudkha Roy is one of the leaders of the Trotskyist party, so called party of Bolsheviks.

(GARF 4 149, p. 164)

While the archive does not contain information regarding the further development of events in connection with this guest, it is possible to suppose that the Soviet representative in Berlin used some lobbying techniques in order to replace the "Trotskyist" woman with some other activist at the planned WIDF event.

In a few cases, the WIDF files preserved some well-elaborated, Soviet-style, personal information sheets (*kharacteristika*) on the members of the Secretariat that were created via collaboration between the Soviet representative in Berlin and the heads of the CSW. For example, I found some information files, signed by Ionova and Parfenova, from 1961. These files, most probably, were aimed at informing the CPSU's Commission on Foreign Policy. This document allows us to explore more closely the Soviet perception of power relationships inside the Secretariat, as well as their perception of the members of the Secretariat with respect to their work qualities and possible ideological deviations.

The document shows that, at the beginning of the 1960s, all of the WIDF secretaries were members of their respective communist parties. In contrast to several other Secretariat collaborators who were simply named in the reports,[20] all of the secretaries received an evaluation by the Soviet representatives of the CSW.

The report on the Secretariat's staff began with its head, the WIDF's general secretary from 1957, Carmen Zanti. She was described as the "daughter of a professional revolutionary who was murdered by fascists [during the Second World War]" (GARF 4 149, p. 122). The report also stated that Zanti took part in the resistance movement, was the leader of the organization of Italian women in the province of Reggio-Emilia, and, between 1950 and 1953, she worked at the WIDF Secretariat as a secretary, and representative of the Union of Italian Women (UDI). After this short biography, the document moved to describing Zanti's political views and personal qualities:

> During her first years of work at the Secretariat, Carmen Zanti showed herself as a diligent worker who was very attentive to the opinions of the representatives of the Committee of Soviet Women. During the last years, and in connection to the changed international situation, and the difficulties in the work of the WIDF Secretariat, Carmen is less concentrated. Her sickness also has had an effect on her work during this time. One can see that Carmen is unsure of the correctness of the WIDF's political line as elaborated by the leadership of the federation [rukovodyashchimi organami]. Possibly, it is also connected to the fact that she gets some ideas about what the federation should do from her national organization, and they contradict the current decisions of the leadership of the federation.
>
> (GARF 4 149, p. 123)

Thus, this description mainly supports the materials discussed earlier in this chapter: the policies of the federation were affected not only by Soviet geopolitical visions, but also by the positions taken by the national communist parties and national women's organizations. The description of Zanti's working habits and relationship to communist ideology was followed by a description of her negative qualities and examples of dissent:

> Carmen's main problem in her role of general secretary is her lack of persistence and skills for organizing work to fulfil the decisions that were made. It has been particularly visible recently, and in connection to the activism of women from Asia and Africa. It seems that she (Carmen) is somehow lost, and does not know how to organize work in order to increase the influence of the federation on these women. This was the reason why she raised the question of leaving her position as General Secretary, explaining it by stating the importance for women from Asia and Africa, and not those from France and Italy, to be the leaders of the federation in the current moment. But her decision was not supported by the leaders of the Italian Communist party.
> (GARF 4 149, p. 123)

Thus, the report clearly shows that from the perspective of the CSW, Zanti had many problems, and did not correspond fully to the Soviet expectations of how the general secretary of the federation should act. In particular, she was seen by the CSW as an overly independent actor.

As opposed to Zanti, some other WIDF secretaries were criticized by the report due to their passivity, as well as lack of skills and interest in their work. The Spanish Communist Eliza Urriz, who worked at the Secretariat beginning in 1947, was described as being disconnected from Spain and women's activism there.[21] While Urriz was seen as a "honest and loyal (*predannyi*) communist and friend", the authors reported difficulties with respect to her understanding the problems of women in the capitalist, colonial, and dependent countries, adding that Urriz also did not fully understand the role of women in the socialist countries. It is interesting to note, however, how the Soviet authors of the report noted that, in spite of the WIDF's complains with respect to Urriz's work at the Secretariat, the leadership of the Spanish Communist Party did not agree to replace her.

The analysis of the report on Urriz suggests that, similar to the case of Zanti, the dissatisfaction of the leaders of the Soviet women's organization with a particular member of the WIDF's leadership did not lead to her immediate replacement, and required lobbying, pressuring, and coalition building.

Two other secretaries, Vimla Farooqui from India (who worked at the Secretariat from 1957) and Adela Betinelli, from Argentina (worked in the Secretariat from 1960), both members of the Communist parties of their countries, are described as rather useful members of the Secretariat, with regard to their work in their respective regions. However, the document stated that Farooqui and Betinelli were quite passive with respect to other problems in the work of the federation, and other regions. Yet the document shows that, in the case of Betinelli, the Union of the Argentinian Women (UMA), prolonged her period of work at the Secretariat in spite of the WIDF's complaints about her work performance (GARF 4 149, p. 126).

On the other hand, the report offers information regarding a deep division that existed in the early 1960s between the majority of the WIDF's female communist and leftist leaders, and Chinese female activists.[22] Indeed, the Chinese representatives were frequently recalled to China, and then replaced by new ones. According to this report, communications with the Chinese women's organization was practically broken, and they did not participate in the work of the Secretariat (GARF 4 149, p. 124).

On the basis of these documents, it is possible to understand how the WIDF leadership was working. While most of the important positions in the leadership, in general, and almost all in the Secretariat, were given to women who were members of the communist parties of their respective countries, it was the independent women, who did not belong to a communist party, who were particularly important. In spite of this, however, these women, along with all of the foreign women in the WIDF's leadership, were closely watched by the Soviet representatives, who feared their possible defection in the context of the Cold War confrontation.

The Committee of Soviet Women and the cadre politics in the WIDF

The previous sections of this chapter already showed that Moscow's influence over the work of the WIDF was conveyed, to a large extent, through the work of its Secretariat – the special administrative body that managed the activities of the Federation between meetings of its representative organs. However, due to the greater openness of the Secretariat, and a growing number of members from countries outside Europe, during the mid-1960s, the Secretariat's special role seems to have become diminished (see more in Chapter 6). At the same time, the roles fulfilled by the WIDF's top leaders, its president and general secretary, seems to have become more important to the Soviet intentions of controlling the organization. The nomination and support of candidates for these posts who would agree to follow the "Soviet line" was central for the CSW's work.

I did not find in my materials any letters, reports, or references shading new light on Moscow's relationships with the WIDF's first president, Eugénie Cotton. Due to Cotton's independent status (she was not a member of the French Communist Party), it seems that the Soviet and communist influence in the federation emanated from the general secretary and the staff of the Secretariat, who were responsible for preparing all documents, and for planning the WIDF's work.

The post of the general secretary, as has been shown, was occupied by communist women. However, while this combination worked well with the first general secretary, Marie-Claude Vaillant-Couturier, in the case of the next two, Italian communists Angiola Minella and, in particular, Carmen

Zanti, the established channels of Soviet influence in the federation showed their weakness.

Thus, following Cotton's death in 1968, the repertoire of means through which Moscow was trying to influence the WIDF's policies was partially changed. On the one hand, the increased number of archive files dedicated to the CSW's bilateral relationships with women's organizations in different countries suggests that they became an important priority. It allowed the CSW to find new allies on the level of the national organizations. On the other hand, the CSW started to pay even more attention to the cadre politics at the higher levels of the federation. I will analyse it further on via the example of correspondence concerning the nomination and work of the WIDF's later presidents – Hertta Kuusinen (1969–1974) and Freda Brown (1974–91) – and some of the general secretaries of the corresponding period.

As opposed to the earlier period of the WIDF's activities, when it was led by an independent woman, after 1969, the WIDF was led by communist women. On the other hand, the communists, including the communist women in Europe, were much less united as a result of the split over attitudes towards Stalin and Stalinism, as well as growing differentiation in views over the development of the welfare state in the capitalist "West", and Soviet policies in Eastern Europe and the Third World, inside and between different communist parties. The Soviet invasion of Czechoslovakia in 1968 provoked multiple protests against the Soviets, even inside the communist parties, including the Finnish one.[23] Attitudes towards the issues of women's rights inside communist parties and their women's organizations were also influenced by the grassroots women's activism calling for a radical transformation of society, and ending the discrimination of women, in the late 1960s–early 1970s, usually defined as the "second wave" of feminism. It was at this moment that Hertta Kuusinen was first nominated and then, at the WIDF congress in Helsinki in 1969, elected as the WIDF's president.

The Finnish communist Hertta Kuusinen was a long-time ally of the Soviet Union – she moved there in 1922 to live with her father, a well-known Finnish communist, Otto Kuusinen. According to Pirkko Kotila, during the 1930s, Hertta Kuusinen worked as a Comintern representative in Finland and Germany, and, in 1933, she became a full member of both the Soviet and Finnish communist parties (2006). Thus, her relationship to the Soviet Union reminded one of Dolores Ibarruri, the Spanish communist who spent many years in the USSR. However, Kuusinen was arrested in Finland, first in 1934, and again during WWII. In 1945, Kuusinen was elected as a MP in Finland from the pro-Soviet Democratic League of the People of Finland (SKDL); she was then re-elected, and served as MP until 1971. Although Kuusinen was well-known in Finland because of her interest in social reforms, including the introduction of child and maternity benefits (Kotila 2006, 47–53), she seems to not have been known as a women's rights activist before she was nominated to be the WIDF's president in 1968.

In discussing the cadre politics inside the WIDF, it is important also to note that in 1968, significant changes happened inside the Soviet member organization, the CSW. Nina Popova retired, and was replaced by Valentina Tereshkova, the first female cosmonaut, who had spent three days in space in 1963. According to de Haan, Tereshkova's participation in the WIDF's 1963 Congress in Moscow, as an honorary guest, made this congress particularly remarkable (de Haan 2018, 233-234). In 1969 Tereshkova also became a member of the Central Committee of the CPSU, and one of the vice-presidents of the WIDF. The CSW was expanded, and had direct relationships with women's organizations from more than 100 countries, while Tereshkova was seen as an important symbol demonstrating the achievements of state socialism with regard to women's rights and career opportunities. At the same time, the archival documents from Moscow indicate that power inside the CSW, and in connection to the WIDF after 1968, started to be distributed differently.

During the 1970s and 1980s, Valentina Tereshkova became a world-wide representative of Soviet women. Tereshkova was a member of the presidium of important international conferences and UN-supported events,[24] and she travelled to different countries on the WIDF's missions, or representing the CSW and the Soviet Union. However, internal correspondence between the Soviet representatives in Berlin and Moscow during the 1970s–1980s was addressed mainly to Xenia Proskurnikova, the CSW's vice-president (see, e.g., GARF 3 3693). While Tereshkova had a more representational role, Proskurnikova seems to have been more involved in the internal problems and conflicts in the federation, and to have been its real decision-maker. It is interesting that Proskurnikova's leading role in issues connected to the WIDF is somehow confirmed in the memoirs of Argentinian Communist and WIDF's general secretary from 1972 to 1978, Fanny Edelman (1996). Edelman wrote that she enjoyed many conversations with Valentina Tereshkova, and that they were usually shared by the company of her colleagues Xenia Proskurnikova and Zinaida Fedorova (Edelman 1996, 125). It could be implied that, while Popova had travelled and met international women's leaders alone, Tereshkova was not seen by the Soviet leadership to be qualified enough to do the same kind of work as Popova. Proskurnikova's role in the CSW and the WIDF is worthy of a further analysis considering her remarkable biography. According to the dictionary published by Elena Tonchu in 2004, Xenia Proskurnikova had an important career as both a diplomat and an intelligence officer. After finishing professional school in Chemistry in 1933, she entered the German language department of Moscow Pedagogical University. From 1937, Proskurnikova worked in intelligence, and in 1943, she was sent to Iran as a Soviet security officer (Tonchu 2004, 361). After the end of the Second World War, Proskurnikova worked in the Soviet occupation zone in Austria, and also for the KGB in Moscow (Tonchu 2004). Thus, it is possible to suppose that Xenia Proskurnikova became the main person responsible for the realization of the "Soviet-line" in the WIDF after 1968.

Kuusinen's election as WIDF president led to several conflicts within the WIDF Secretariat, as well as in Finland. The Soviet representative at the Secretariat in Berlin at that period, Zuhra Rahimbabaeva, described the first visit of Hertta Kuusinen, in her new role as president of the WIDF, to the federation's headquarters in Berlin, from 8 to 15 September 1969 (GARF 3 2122, pp. 63–73). According to Rahimbabaeva, the main aim of her visit was to get to know the activities of the federation and the work of the Secretariat. However, Kuusinen was received quite coldly by some of the representatives of the Secretariat, particularly the French women who used to work with Cotton. Cecile Hugel, the representative of the French women's organization, and the WIDF's general secretary at that time, stressed that Kuusinen's visit was a working visit of the new president and that, thus, it should not be marked by any special "celebrations" (GARF 3 2122, p. 63). Indeed, the report of Rahimbabaeva to Moscow shows that Kuusinen complained to the Soviet representative at the Secretariat in Berlin about the bad organization of the practical arrangements around her visit. In particular, she said that her housing in Berlin was too far from the centre, and that she received too little money from the federation to cover her stay in Berlin (GARF 3 2122, p. 73).

According to Rahimbabaeva, Hugel intended to teach Kuusinen the working style of the former WIDF president, Cotton. Hugel also seemed to be constantly comparing Kuusinen with Cotton, who, according to Hugel, drove herself up to the age of 80, while her personal secretary was a well-known member of the French Women's Union, Yvonne Dumont (GARF 3 2122, p. 65). However, it was Kuusinen's personal secretary, Vika (most probably, Viveca Hedengren), whom she brought with her from Helsinki to Berlin whom Hugel was particularly unhappy with:

> This young woman – said Hugel – is not a communist. Neither is she a member of a women's organization. She finished film school and worked as a director of the modern theatre in a capitalist country. And we know quite well how these kind of intellectuals can think.[25]
> (GARF 3 2122, p. 65)

Hugel further complained that this young secretary was present at all the meetings attended by Kuusinen, and it "made it impossible to discuss many problems of the internal life of the federation".

After Kuusinen left Berlin, in her private conversation with the Soviet representative, Rahimbabaeva, Hugel informed her of her own plans to travel to Helsinki (together with the WIDF's financial administrator) in order to discuss several issues connected with Kuusinen's new role with the Finnish Women's Democratic League (SNDL). In particular, she stressed that she should speak with the head of the league, Anna-Liisa Hyvönen. In spite of the coldness with which Kuusinen was met at the WIDF's headquarters during her first visit, and the open hostility of some of the older members of the Secretariat like Hugel, the letter from the Soviet representative,

Rahimbabaeva, confirms that Kuusinen was Moscow's choice to become the federation's president, and that she had its full support:

> Kuusinen as a candidate for the WIDF's presidency was a surprise for the Democratic League of Finnish Women; anybody has asked their opinion about it. Everything was decided at the meeting in Moscow. Thus, Kuusinen is an imposed figure for the Democratic League of Finnish women. And Hertta's relationships with women's organizations in Finland became complicated.
> (GARF 3 2122, p. 67)

Moscow's nomination of Kuusinen is also confirmed by Kuusinen's own words, given in a summary of Rahimbabaeva's two short conversations with Kuusinen. According to the Soviet representative, during these conversations, Kuusinen expressed her gratitude to the CSW, and also personally to Valentina Tereshkova and Xenia Proskurnikova, for their support. "It is good that I have been there because I hope for support mainly from the Soviet Women's Committee" (GARF 3 2122, p. 67).

After Kuusinen's sudden death in 1974, the WIDF, according to a letter from the Soviet representative in Berlin, Valentina Titova, experienced similar problems and insecurity with regard to their next leader (GARF 3 3414, p. 78). According to Titova, heated discussions concerning candidates for the next president were taking place at the WIDF's headquarters. As the Soviet representative, however, she seemed to have been advised to abstain from participation. However, she described some of the proposals that were discussed inside the Secretariat, and also offered her own suggestions (GARF 3 3414, p. 78). According to the letter, the WIDF's then general secretary, Fanny Edelman,[26] named several persons who could replace her at her post, among them Freda Brown and Tara Reddy from India. Titova, in her turn, wrote that Freda could probably be made president, while Reddy could be general secretary. She also disclosed her doubts with respect to Reddy, which were not so much ideological or individual, but rather geopolitical: Reddy was from the same country – India – as the general secretary of the Peace Council, Romesh Chandra[27], and "it is not clear if this country really is convenient" (GARF 3 3414, p. 78). Thus, she implied that the Soviet allies have to represent geographical breadth, and it would be inconvenient to have the head of one of the Soviet's Cold War ally organizations, the International Peace Council, and also the general secretary of another one, the WIDF, from the same country.

The letter Titova sent to Moscow on 14 November of the same year, after the meeting of the WIDF council in Tihany (Hungary) dedicated to preparing for the Congress in Berlin in 1975, and the UN International Women's Year, shows that the nominating decision had already been made. Titova wrote that "Freda Brown is ready to work in her new position" (GARF 3 3414, p. 276). The letter also shows, however, that Brown had her own ideas concerning the development of the Federation, and was unsure of the reaction Moscow and the countries of the Soviet bloc would have to some of them. In particular, she considered it important to develop cooperation with different women's transnational and international organizations, some of which, like ICW, had earlier been declared by the WIDF to be enemy organizations, rather than real defenders of women's rights. Titova wrote that Brown was aware that these organizations "usually are not defined as 'democratic'" (GARF 3 3414, p. 276). It is interesting that, in this situation, according to Titova, Brown hoped for Moscow's support in her internal discussions within the federation, while expecting a particularly negative attitude to her ideas from the representative of a Soviet ally state, the WIDF vice-president from the GDR, Ilse Thiele. Indeed, while Brown saw the position of Moscow as being more flexible, she had doubts regarding the political flexibility of Thiele (GARF 3 3414, p. 276). Finally, Titova's letter indicates that the role of Fanny Edelman, a long-standing Soviet supporter in the federation, should be seen as important for realizing the policies decided in Moscow. Edelman had promised her help and encouragement to Brown so she could feel supported in her new role (GARF 3 3414, p. 276).

This letter discussing the situation around the WIDF's new president, Freda Brown, suggests that while Moscow continued to play an important role, and its support was crucial for the president of the federation, the new president, similar to the previous ones, depended on complex alliances and existing conflicts inside the federation's leadership. On the basis of these letters, it is also possible to see several changes in the style of reporting about the power dynamics in the WIDF and CSW cadre politics, compared to the earlier period. First, the Soviet representative in Berlin seems to have achieved a higher status in the Soviet women's organization. The CSW seems to have expected that its representative should not only help fulfil the decisions made in Moscow (and approved by the CPSU), but also show her initiative and work more as an expert than an obedient employee. On the other hand, the politics of cadres led from Moscow seem to have become more complex, with more factors involved than before. In addition to loyalty to the Soviet Union and the Soviet bloc (that continues to be important), the factors of equal representation of different regions, including the Third World countries, and more complex Cold War alliances involving other transnational organizations, had to be considered. Finally, in the context of the further internationalization of the issues of women's rights, the Soviet representative in the WIDF was involved in many complex and multidimensional relationships, including those with UN representatives. In the context of incorporating the WIDF's programme into the UN plans, it made it increasingly difficult for the WIDF, and for the Soviet representative, to defend an isolationist position in confrontation with "imperialism" on ideological (and not simply tactical) grounds.

On the other hand, the correspondence between the CSW and its representative in Berlin, even in the later years of the work of federation, show that the WIDF's top leaders continued to consult Moscow's opinion on many aspects of the WIDF's policies, and to pay tribute of honour to the Soviet role in the federation. For example, the letters from Titova show that important speeches made in the name of the WIDF as a whole were discussed with her – for example, the presentations by Fanny Edelman and Freda Brown at the WIDF council meeting in Bucharest in 1975 (GARF 3 3693, p. 7). At the same time, it confirms the changing role of the Soviet representative in the Secretariat, who began to be seen as a knowledgeable and well-educated international worker by both the CSW and other members of the WIDF Secretariat. In fact, consultations with the Soviet representative seem to have been more akin to consultations with an expert in global women's issues, rather than to a source of ideological control. For example, in her letter to Xenia Proskurnikova of 19 May, Valentina Titova communicated that the presentation that Fanny Edelman prepared to the Bucharest meeting "looked quite good after all the reworking. But is it too long and too informative. We agreed that Fanny would not read the whole of it" (GARF 3 3693, p. 7).

Furthermore, the WIDF leaders, including Brown, continued to present the Soviet women's organization, Soviet leaders, and Moscow as having a special symbolic meaning for the WIDF. For example, the protocols of WIDF bureau meeting in Berlin from 12 December 1980, show that the special role of the Soviet Union in the WIDF's history was stressed in the speech by Freda Brown on the occasion of the 35th anniversary of the WIDF (GARF 3 5077, p. 12; from 12 December 1980). In her speech Brown specifically stressed that while many national organizations send their congratulations to the WIDF, she "had an honour" to participate in the celebration in Moscow organized by the CSW (GARF 3 5077, p. 13).

During the 1970s and 1980s, the CSW continued to play an important role in the WIDF's cadre politics, through securing finances for its allies there. Decisions regarding financing particular events continued to need the approval of the CC of the CPSU. For example, in her letter from 1975, Titova wrote about the $25,000 promised by the Soviet Union for organizing a congress dedicated to the International Women's Year in Berlin (about this congress, see Donert 2014). She also noted that "this sum was agreed upon when we were at the Old Squire", the last being CPSU headquarters (GARF 3 3693, p. 10). At the same time, the CSW seems to have become much freer with respect to using money allocated to its ordinary activities, for example, for giving fellowships to representatives of women's organizations from the Third World countries considered to be the WIDF's allies. It also seems to have established routine travel arrangements for the WIDF's leaders: free trips by Aeroflot are mentioned frequently in the documents in connection to discussions of the travel routes for both the WIDF's representatives and guests. For example, the already quoted letter by Titova from 1975 communicated that the American Peace Association invited a WIDF delegation to New York for participation in seminars and a trip around the country. While representatives of 25 countries were chosen to join the delegation from the WIDF, its leaders, Fanny and Freda, decided to travel to

New York via Aeroflot from Moscow, and that the CSW would be responsible for arranging their return tickets (GARF 3 3693, p. 9).

Finally, the CSW continued the practice of inviting women with important positions in the WIDF to spend their holidays, and to undergo medical treatment, in the Soviet Union. For example, in 1983, the Soviet representative in Berlin, Valeria Kalmyk, was informed by the CSW that Mirjam Vire-Tuominen, the WIDF's general secretary at that time, arrived in the USSR for medical treatment, and had a meeting with some of the CSW's top leaders (GARF 3 5871, pp. 8–9). The meeting offered the Soviet leaders an opportunity to get Tuominen's first-hand views on the situation in Finland, and in the WIDF's Secretariat. In particular, Tuominen informed the leaders of the CSW on the growth of anti-Soviet attitudes in Finland (GARF 3 5871, pp. 8–9). After her visit to the USSR, on 23 August 1983, Tuominen also sent her personal letter of gratitude to Tereshkova, which is preserved in the archive. In the letter, Tuominen wrote that she and her daughter spent one month in the sanatorium on the Black Sea coast, and thanked Tereshkova for the chance to improve her daughter's health:

> I would like to express my gratitude to you, and with your help – to other colleagues from the CSW. Thank you for the excellent holiday that you have organized for me and my daughter at the sanatorium in Sotchi [...] I hope very much, my dear Valentina, that you and your dear daughter, Alenka, also had as great a holiday as we had.
> (GARF 3 5870, p. 3)

Conclusion

The materials explored in this chapter show that the Soviet leadership saw the WIDF as a transnational organization that could be useful in attracting the attention of those who were interested in the issues of rights and justice for women and children, as well as of those who defended peace and opposed militarism. The ACSW (and CSW after 1956) was supported by the CPSU primarily as an organization that is responsible for safeguarding these Soviet interests in the WIDF and among women abroad. However, it seems that the status of this work, not the least due to its association with "women's issues", was relatively low: the Soviet leaders considered the WIDF to be only one of many organizations that could contribute to spreading the Soviet interests abroad. The low status was also connected to the lack of well-trained cadres among female CPSU's workers.

The internal correspondence of CSW with its representative at the WIDF's headquarters and with the other party and Soviet organizations preserved in the archives in Moscow shows that, in spite of the intentions of the Soviet centre to direct and control the development of the transnational organization, it was not always easy to organize in practice. In particular, during the early period of the WIDF it counted with prominent international female leaders – communist and non-communist ones – who enjoyed respect within their own countries and were often ready to express their opinion about WIDF's ideology, strategies, and tactics. Their views sometimes resulted in discussions and conflicts inside of the WIDF's leadership.

The WIDF's Secretariat – first in Paris and after 1951 in Berlin – was a central body where the preparation of the most important decisions and documents was taking place. It was this body that seems to be the special focus of Moscow's attention: the employees of CSW working in the WIDF's headquarters had to report on the individual members of the Secretariat, including information on their political views, plans and health. At the same time all of those working at the Secretariat and in the WIDF's high leadership positions during the whole period under research could enjoy the same privileges as did the Soviet state and CP *nomenklatura*. As time passed and the WIDF and its governing bodies (council, bureau and Secretariat) grew, the CPSU's leaders seem to concentrate their attention more on the highest leaders of the WIDF (president, vice-presidents and general secretary). The nomination of women who would be "friendly" to the Soviet Union and would show open support to its, often very contradictory and frequently changing, foreign policy to these higher positions in the WIDF was closely observed by Moscow during the late 1960s–1980s.

Notes

1 The hierarchically organized bureaucrats with Communist Party membership. See more in Kryshtanovskaia (1995).
2 According to David-Fox, the travellers influenced Western perceptions of what was going on in the Soviet Union and, on the other hand, were used by the Bolshevik ideologists as a mirror for comparing Soviet progress with that in the West (David-Fox 2012; see also Gradskova 2018, pp. 151–159).
3 She was the head of the Committee of Soviet Women until 1968, and the head of the Friendship Societies Organization (reorganized VOKS) until 1976.
4 VKP(b) – *Vsesoyuznaia Kommunisticheskaia Partiia bolshevikov* – was the official name of the CPSU up to 1952.
5 A humanitarian organization active during the Second World War when the USSR was the USA's important ally.
6 See for example, eight volumes of published archival documents "Classified information to Stalin about situation in the country" (*Sovershenno sekretno* 2001–2005).
7 According to the Cominform resolution from 28 June 1948, Yugoslavia was expelled from the socialist bloc for "national deviation" – Bonfiglioli (2012, 151).
8 I will discuss more about the position of the representatives of Asia and Africa in the WIDF leadership in Chapter 6.
9 1961 was the year when the Berlin Wall, separating the Soviet part of Berlin from West Berlin, was built.
10 In the 1960s–1980s, other countries of the Soviet bloc also seem to have offered such opportunities for those working for the WIDF.
11 The dictionary contains biographical information on only one Soviet representative, who worked in Berlin during the later years, Valeria Kalmyk (secretary from 1977 to 1986). After 1991, Kalmyk worked as the Russian ambassador to Costa Rica (Tonchu 2004, 197–199).

12 The name of Gurina is also present in the discussed above list of the participants of the WIDF founding Congress . There, she was presented as an engineer.
13 In her previous letter, Goroshkova suggested to publish in WIDF's media the letter sent by Eleanor Roosevelt, UN representative from the USA, that declared that the Soviet accusations supported by the WIDF about use of bacteriological weapons in Korea are false.
14 The translated variant of the letter preserved in the archive is addressed to "Fr." And it is possible to suppose that the Soviet translator was not allowed to know the addressee. However, the letter itself and other documents from the file suggests its addressee is Ovsiannikova.
15 Wächter meant the pogroms in imperial Russia, before 1917.
16 The Soviet government introduced fees for higher level of school education in 1940.
17 Here she probably has in mind both the WIDF and its member from Germany, the Democratic Union of Women, of which Wächter was president.
18 Most probably, Ibarruri meant that as a representative of the women's organization from Spain known by her heroic past, Ibarruri could be more convincing for Andreen than the Soviet women connected to the state apparatus.
19 The member of the Communist Party of India and one of the founding members of the National Federation of Indian Women. In the 1970s, she was one of the WIDF's vice-presidents.
20 They included representatives from Iran (Shakhnaz Alami), Japan (Eiko Saito), Iraq (Mary Daud), Cuba (Hortencia Gomez), Brazil (Izula Gerhard), Italy (Maria Luisa Floreniani), and West Germany (Helga Dikkel).
21 The report stated that due to her status as an exile living in France, Urriz was disconnected from the women's movement in Spain. At the same time, because of a lack of travel documents, she could not visit the Latin American countries she was responsible for in the Secretariat.
22 The report was written during the period when relationships between the Soviet and the Chinese communist parties, and also between China and the USSR, were deteriorating very fast. This conflict had important implications for the work of the WIDF (the biggest conflict observed corresponded to the 1963 Congress in Moscow). However, the most important consequence of this conflict for the WIDF was connected with direct competition between the USSR and China for influence in the Third World during the 1960s (Hasegawa 2011).
23 According to Kotila, Kuusinen was one of the few representatives of the older generation in the party to vote against the Soviet intervention in Czechoslovakia. However, she managed to preserve her good relationship with the Soviet Union (Kotila 2006, 70–75).
24 WIDF received the status of non-governmental organization at the UN in 1967.
25 Here, it is important to consider that it was 1968, the year of the student revolution and feminist radical activism, thus, Hugel's mistrust of Vika could be explained not only by her desire to preserve Cotton's traditions of leadership, and French influence inside the Secretariat, but also by her worries in connection to young people's worldwide activism. According to Kotila, Kuusinen was known in Finland for her closeness to the leftist youth (2006, 50–53).
26 In her letter, Titova indicated that Fanny Edelman, WIDF general secretary at that time, announced her decision to return to Argentina after the World Congress of Women in 1975, in order to resume her duties in the leadership of the Argentinian Communist Party.
27 Romesh Chandra (India) from 1953 was the general secretary of the World Peace Council, in 1977 he was elected as its president.

3 Protecting peace, mothers, and children

WIDF's ideology and activities in its first decades

Defending peace, mothers, and children was the federation's initial task. This chapter gives a close examination of the interconnections between these goals, and how priorities among these goals changed between 1945, when the WIDF was established, and the early 1970s, when it became involved in transnational activities surrounding the UN's Decade for Women.

Peace as the main condition for women's and children's rights

Scholars researching the WIDF's history have already shown that the WIDF began its activities in 1945 as an anti-fascist organization aimed at protecting peace (Ilic 2011; Pieper Mooney 2013a). As I mentioned earlier, Mercedes Yusta suggested that this organization had already begun to be set up in 1934, when a congress of leftist women against war and fascism was organized in Paris by Gabrielle Duchêne, the leader of the WILPF and a Soviet sympathizer. This 1934 Congress created the Women's World Committee, but its activities were interrupted by the Second World War (Yusta 2016, 167–186).

While the prevention of war and the defence of peace had been a prominent aspect of the women's movement since the late nineteenth century, often in combination with demands for social reforms and/or franchise for women, scholarship on the protection of peace has indicated that such a combination of goals led to many contradictions and conflicts (Yuval-Davis 1997, 112–113; Oldfield 2000, 210–211; Yukina 2007, 409; Egefur 2020, 202–203). Late nineteenth-century peace congresses that were organized in Europe frequently connected female biology with both caring for children and a special interest in the promotion of peace (Egefur 2020, 206). At the same time, according to Yuval-Davis, not all of the supporters of the women's peace movement agreed with the biological approach to femininity (Yuval-Davis 1997, 112–113).

With regard to the WIDF in its earlier years, Celia Donert (2016) has stated that for an organization created in 1945, the perils of war were not abstract ideas, but a personal experience that most of its leaders and members had lived through. Most of the WIDF's leaders during its first 20 years were victims and/or participants in the Second World War. The president of the federation, Eugenie Cotton, as well as its then general secretaries, Marie-Claude Vallaint-Couturier and Carmen Zanti, had served in the resistance movements of France and Italy, respectively; other leaders and activists from Yugoslavia, Albania, Italy and France were also in the resistance; and many had lost relatives and friends during the war. Many representatives of the German, Hungarian, and Japanese women's organizations, as well as those from some other countries, were victims of the totalitarian and authoritarian regimes in their countries (see, e.g., Lilly Wächter, vice-president from Germany, discussed in Chapter 2) and lost relatives and friends. Nina Popova, the head of the ACSW and WIDF's vice-president, was responsible for evacuating people and enterprises from Moscow in 1941. It was also widely known that Popova lost her beloved partner, who perished in combat; this fact was used by Popova to show herself as a person who could not be indifferent to the possibility of a future war (Grigorieva 2010). Finally, some other WIDF leaders, such as Andrea Andreen from Sweden, were well known for their anti-war activism (Larberg & Andreen Sachs 2015). These personal experiences, which the WIDF leaders readily exploited in their speeches and communication with women from around the world, gave a personal credibility to many of the early WIDF's anti-war events. Obviously, however, this shared personal experience of suffering during the war, fighting fascism, and defending peace, disappeared with the passage of time; it was not as prevalent in the late 1960s–1970s, when a younger generation of women became leaders of the WIDF.

The WIDF documents usually presented the protection of peace as being linked to the federation's two other fundamental goals – the protection of mothers and children and the promotion of the rights of women. All of these goals were related to each other in the WIDF's documents, and in its leaders' speeches. For example, the WIDF president, Eugenie Cotton, who had a PhD in Physics,[1] in her speech at the opening of the World Women's Congress in Copenhagen in 1953, stated that the delegates of 80 countries had gathered at the WIDF congress in Copenhagen "in order to together find concrete answers to the questions that are important for all women". These issues, according to Cotton, included the protection of peace, the protection of children, and the promotion of women's rights (*Za ravnopravie*, 1953, 7). Following the approach of pre-First World War peace movement (see Egefur 2020, 202–203), Cotton insisted on the obvious interconnection between the war and the violation of the rights of women and children: while every war endangers a child's happy future, the money spent on war preparations also deprives children of the education they need. When women lack rights, this prevents women from acting on behalf of the children, i.e. defending their rights. Thus, according to Cotton, the fight for women's rights also implies fighting for other goals, and she added that this was an important reason for organizing congresses like the one in Copenhagen (*Za ravnopravie* 1953, 8). Further, Cotton stressed that the congress has to show "that more and more women of different beliefs [*ubezhdenii*] can understand each other and act together" (*Za ravnopravie* 1953, 7); this implied that organizations like the WIDF were important because they were able to bring together women from different countries. Thus, the importance of women's rights in this construction did not seem to be central, per se, to the federation's work; rather, it was seen as a condition for preserving the rights of children and for maintaining peace. I will return to this triple goal of the federation in the next section, when discussing the WIDF's maternalism (see Pieper Mooney 2013b).

This combination of goals, bringing together the values of peace, children, and women's rights, as well as the need for an organization to defend them collectively, is found, in one form or another, in many WIDF official documents and publications, but it was particularly on display in the WIDF's initiative to create a special organization of mothers for protecting peace in the mid-1950s. The founding meeting of this organization took place in Lausanne, Switzerland, in 1955; the Congress of Mothers was fully supported by the WIDF. The WIDF promoted a Swedish peace activist and a WIDF's vice-president, Andrea Andreen, a medical doctor and in the past an active participant in a women's group providing civic education for Swedish women (see Rydström and Tjeder 2009) as the head of the new organization. Durable peace, in the documents of the Lausanne congress, was stated to be an important condition for a happy childhood, and for preventing the suffering women endured during the Second World War (archive of IISH). The documents of the Congress explained the importance of peace, and reminded the readers that wars endanger motherhood, as many sons would perish on the battlefields. This line of argument aimed to convince women that they should protect peace, and become politically active to achieve this goal. Thus, the WIDF followed other women's organizations, like the WILPF, in viewing women as "natural" peace-lovers (see Rupp 1997, 88–89), as opposed to men. In the words of another participant at the congress, Argentinian communist and future WIDF general secretary Fanny Edelman, the delegates of the constitutive assembly of the congress of mothers were sure that mothers "who give the life, should defend the life" (Edelman 1996, 142).

The Moscow archival materials show that this approach to protecting peace secured a lot of support from women across Europe, North America, and Japan. It reflected the feelings of many of these women, who worried about the outbreak of a new war. For example, in a 1952 letter, British activist Evis Clark expressed her fears regarding the dangers of a possible war while discussing the celebration of the WIDF-promoted Children's Day in Birmingham:

> I think that the next several weeks will be decisive in the fight against the Third World War. Support for peace is growing from day to day. Sometimes when you read the newspapers or listen to the BBC, or when you go to the cinema, you start thinking that this crazy arms race will be successful, but when you get to know public opinion, how it was this

Saturday, you understand that people aspire to peace and friendship with other countries.

(RGASPI 17 137 816, pp. 199–202, in translation to Russian)

Thus, peace politics were seen by the WIDF leaders, and many local activists, as genuinely significant. However, growing hostility between the former Second World War allies, and new local "hot" wars of the Cold War era, made the WIDF's advocacy for peace quite difficult. Sometimes, WIDF's peace activism appeared quite provocative, especially when considering that the WIDF often engaged in hard accusations on behalf of one side in the conflict.

In the early 1950s, the federation had already become involved in several controversies because it offered full support only to one side, the Soviet one, in the growing number of international conflicts. One of the earliest, and probably the most significant with respect to its consequences for the federation and for the Cold War as such,[2] was the WIDF's involvement in denouncing war crimes during the Korean War (1950–1953). The war started when (pro-communist) North Korean troops invaded South Korea in June 1950, but, according to Donert, the war soon became a "humanitarian crisis of enormous proportions" (Donert 2016, 320–321). In 1951, the WIDF sent a delegation to North Korea and then published a report in 12 languages, *We accuse* (1951). This accused American troops (stationed in Korea under a UN mandate) of committing a number of cruel war crimes against the peaceful population. These accusations were denied by the Americans, and, soon afterwards, the US government created a commission on anti-governmental activities that investigated the US member of the federation, the Congress of American Women (Weigand 2001). As a result of this investigation, the American organization was declared a "foreign agent" by the commission and forcibly disbanded. The US government also exerted pressure on the United Nations (UN), where it exerted particularly power in the early years of its existence (for US policies towards the UN during the Cold War, see Mazower 2008). As a result of this US pressure, the WIDF lost its official status at the UN in 1954, and fell under constant Central Intelligence Agency (CIA) surveillance. A declassified CIA report from 1956 shows, as an example of this surveillance, that all of the WIDF's leaders, as well as leaders and prominent activists from all member organizations, were known to the CIA (CIA report, 1956).

In general, the WIDF's position on several other "hot" episodes of the Cold War was similar to the one taken during the Korean War; the Soviet Union and the state socialist countries were portrayed as the peace-lovers, and the Western countries were guilty of endangering peace. The WIDF's publications and documents showed the USA and other Western countries as producing arms, building military bases, testing atomic weapons, and starting military operations in different parts of the world in order to spread their influence. The WIDF insisted that, on the contrary, the Soviet Union was mainly interested in defending peace, and the WIDF as a transnational women's organization was always ready to denounce those who "prepared a new war", i.e., the imperialist countries. After 1956, the Soviet proposals of détente made by Khrushchev were added to these declarations, leading to further accusations against the Western countries, who continued to be presented as preparing for a new war by building military bases and producing more and more weapons of mass destruction (see, e.g., ZM 1959, 7: 10–11; 1959, 11: 19–21; 1961, 10: 4–5).

At the same time, beginning in the 1950s with the Korean War, many Western women's organizations began to believe that the Soviet Union and Communist China were primarily responsible for the escalating confrontations, and were threats to peace. The Soviet intervention in the 1956 Hungarian revolution reinforced doubts regarding Soviet détente policies experienced by many women around the world.[3] This made the WIDF's work "for peace" very difficult, and led to conflicts inside the organization, and around its activities in many Western countries.

The WIDF's position during the Korean War, along with its exclusively positive description of the role of the Soviet Union during the Second World War, and its "peaceful" policies in the aftermath of the war, raised suspicions among some European female activists about the WIDF's peace activism. For example, the archival documents show that preparations for the conference on the protection of children that the WIDF planned to organize in Vienna in 1952 were met with negative reactions from some French activist women. A classified letter sent by Nina Popova on 21 February 1952 informed Georgii Malenkov, the member of the Communist Party Central Committee responsible for foreign policy, that while discussing the document for the conference, some female participants suggested a need to:

> discuss the project on constructing shelters for children due to the fact that war is imminent and measures of protection against air bombing should be taken in advance. The leader of one of the scout organizations, a member of the permanent council for protection of children was against diminishing spending for war with the motivation that France has to update her weapons to protect itself from attack by the Soviet Union.
> (RGASPI 17 137 818, p. 14)

On the other hand, some of the WIDF leaders doubted whether the struggle for peace should be the principal aim of all the WIDF's activities. Others felt that protecting the rights of children should not be combined with other causes, and should be a separate goal in itself. A 1952 classified letter from Goroshkova, the Soviet representative in the Secretariat, described a conversation she had had with Carmen Zanti and Marie-Claude Vaillant-Couturier in the Secretariat, during which Vallaint-Couturier defended the movement for protection of children as "an independent movement that has the protection of the interests of children as its main goal". It seems that Couturier considered children's rights to be an autonomous direction of the

WIDF's work (RGASPI 17 137 818, pp. 221–224). However, the general tone of the Soviet correspondence leaves no doubts that this position was not accepted by the Soviet female leaders.

In the early 1960s, the WIDF's peace activism was often met with suspicion and resistance in different countries where women expressed objections to Soviet policies, especially in connection with the USSR's weapons production and nuclear tests. For example, a letter from Lebedeva from 1961 informed the leaders of the CSW of multiple protests in Western Europe against nuclear weapons testing in the USSR:

> During these days we received a lot of information about protests organized in several European countries by the national women's organizations against our country resuming tests. Some meetings and demonstrations took place and appeals to the government were signed.
> (GARF 4 149, p. 148 – letter from Lebedeva to Popova, Petrova, and Fedorova, 20 September 1961)

The WIDF's strategies for protecting peace and dealing with military conflicts and their consequences often provoked tensions in the federation's relationships with women activists from European countries. Clara Maria Fassbinder is one such case (RGASPI 17 137 816, p. 196). In her conversation with Goroshkova in Berlin (21 October 1952), Fassbinder, a university professor and member of the German organization "Women for peace", asked several questions that Goroshkova did not like. They included the possibility of discussing the situation of some German female prisoners of war in the Soviet Union, and the possibility of organizing a conference of European women that would bring women of the "East" and the "West" closer together, including those from Yugoslavia. Instead of reflecting on these proposals, at the end of her letter, Goroshkova wrote that Fassbinder gave the impression of being an "insane person" (RGASPI 17 137 816, p. 199). Thus, it can be assumed that Fassbinder's ideas were never discussed seriously by the federation.

The Soviet creation of a separate German state in the Soviet occupation zone and, later, the construction of the Berlin Wall in 1961, was another issue that complicated the federation's work for peace, and also led to internal conflicts inside the WIDF. The conflicts intensified after the construction of the Berlin Wall. For example, the letter sent from the CSW to its representative in Berlin on 10 July 1961, which I discussed in Chapter 2, shows that Carmen Zanti, the WIDF general secretary at the time, during her visit to Moscow, stated that it was important to cooperate with women of different political views in order to make WIDF bigger, and the movement of women for peace stronger. She considered the problem of Berlin to be particularly important, and suggested among other things that it would be better "if two groups of women – those from West Germany and those from GDR, could meet" (GARF 4 149, p144). While Zanti's suggestion looks quite logical from the perspective of a women's organization fighting for peace, the CSW leadership were against any such kind of meetings. Most probably, it contributed to deepening the conflict between the Italian women's organization and the WIDF.

However, the danger of war, and the presumed responsibility of women-mothers to stop it, continued to be used by the WIDF as a slogan for inviting more women's organizations to become the WIDF members. For example, in 1963, the WIDF invited organizations that were not members of the federation to attend the Congress it was holding that year and stated that there was a need for women to be together when a war was threatening to commence. A draft "Appeal to all the international and national women's organizations that are not members of the WIDF" that the Congress planned to adopt stressed:

> We are living in a very tense time. Humankind is standing in front of the danger of a new war. In a time of atomic weapons, none can hope that he/she would escape the war fires, or could avoid the consequences of the nuclear catastrophe. Thus, the responsibility of women for preventing this catastrophe is as high as never before.
> (GARF 3 795, pp. 170–171)

One of the four keynote presentations at the WIDF Moscow Congress 1963 also had peace as its main theme: "Contribution of women to the struggle for peace across the whole world, for disarmament, for spending military budget funds on peaceful programmes, for friendship among people, and for the peaceful coexistence of states with different social and economic orders" (GARF 3 794, p. 11 from 4 to 5 December 1962). However, the issue of peace provoked heated discussions at the preparatory bureau meeting. Due to a number of the delegates being involved in anti-colonial and liberation movements (including Cuba and Algeria, see Chapter 6), and the new course of the Chinese government, who saw the fight against imperialism as its main goal, the possibility of "peaceful coexistence" became one of the disputed themes. In fact, the Chinese delegation insisted on the impossibility of a détente policy (which was defended by the Soviet Union and the majority of the WIDF leadership – see GARF 3 794). For example, Ko Chen, China's representative at the WIDF bureau, spoke of the impossibility of coexisting with imperialism due to its aggressivity: "We have to inform the masses where the threat to peace is coming from" (GARF 3 794, pp. 46–55). Later, she also posed a rhetorical question to the audience: "Do we have to bend our knees in order to ask the imperialists for peace?" (GARF 3 794, p. 48). However, she was confronted by several other WIDF members, including its general secretary, Carmen Zanti. In order to convince other participants, Zanti mentioned the solidarity that Italian women showed to Cuba during the American intervention in 1961; according to Zanti, women in Italy organized powerful demonstrations against American aggression and "did not ask for peace while on their knees" (GARF 3 794 p. 56). Nina Popova, the Soviet representative, in her response to the Chinese representative, also supported the WIDF policy line; she, however, stressed women's special interest in peace:

> I cannot agree with the proposal that was made yesterday at the meeting of the Commission by our friend who said that a world without weapons would exist only after the full victory over imperialism, colonialism, and human exploitation. I must ask how would it be done? Shall we wage a war [against imperialism]? It is not our task. The people would not agree to it, and, first of all, the women would not accept it.
> (GARF 3 794, p. 74)

Anti-war activism also continued to be important for the WIDF during its later period. For example, an article by Fanny Edelman, "Social consequences of disarmament", was published by the WIDF in the same issue of the WIDF journal where the declaration adopted by the UN conference in Mexico City was published (*WWW* 1975 4: 9–11). The article mainly continued with traditional WIDF rhetoric:

> The world movement of defenders of peace, of which the democratic women's movement is an inseparable part, and which actively stimulates friendship among the peoples, the development of the most varied contacts and economic cooperation between different countries, detent and disarmament, will have to intensify its efforts for implementation of the UN resolutions on renunciation of the use of force and the definitive prohibition of the nuclear weapons.
> (*WWW* 1975, 4:10)

Thus, in concluding this section, it is possible to say that "peace" was formulated as one of the important goals of the WIDF at the moment of its creation, and continued to be present in its activities during the Cold War period. In the WIDF's essentialized vision of women and femininity, female peace-loving was much stronger than that of men due to women's experiences of motherhood. In the next section, I will continue to explore the WIDF's interpretation of women's global political roles and duties in connection with their specific feminine qualities.

Women need rights in order to fulfil their duties as mothers

As stated at the beginning of this chapter, in the WIDF's ideology, the protection of peace was closely related to the wellbeing of children; while the federation rarely mentioned fathers, mothers were seen as naturally interested in the protection of children. This attention to the situation of children was one of the goals of the Lausanne congress of mothers in 1955, and in 1951, the federation also declared the establishment of a special day for the protection of children – 1 June – that was celebrated by its members with street fests, demonstrations, and exhibitions. The letter I quoted above that mentioned one such celebrations in Birmingham shows that its author took inspiration for future activism through participation in that activity. Another example can be found in a letter from Venezuela that was sent to the WIDF that same year, 1952. While the end of the letter informed the WIDF that some of the organizers of the celebration in the capital, Caracas, were arrested and accused of being Communists, the first part of the letter vividly described how well-attended the celebration was. The Union of Girls of Venezuela prepared special posters, organized concerts and games for children on the streets of the proletarian district of the city, and many children and their parents took part in the celebration. Alongside entertainment for children, the celebration also included the distribution of political information for adults, a presentation about the international conference for the protection of children in Vienna organized by the WIDF, and information about the war and the bacteriological weapons that endanger the lives of children in Korea (GRASPI 17 137 818, pp. 123–124).

Why did the WIDF specifically stress the role of mothers, and how did the federation relate women's rights to this status? Historically, as we know, many female activists and women's organizations used the argument of motherhood in order to demand political rights for women. These arguments can be found in works by female activists advocating women's suffrage in the first half of the twentieth century (see, e.g., Florin 2006, 47; Jo Plant et al. 2012). Maternalism was also used by the peace movements and by many women's organizations with Catholic and other religious orientations, particularly on the American continent (Molyneux 2001; Nari 2004). According to Molyneux, for example, at the beginning of the twentieth century, motherhood became politicized in Latin America, and women's roles as mothers began to be employed as a means of defending their civil rights (Molyneux 2001, 168–169).

Thus, the WIDF's programme during its earlier years can be seen as one that followed this direction of conceptualizing woman's role in society, and society's responsibilities towards woman, as based around woman-as-mother. However, the WIDF differed from most other organizations that declared woman's role as mother to be the most important role in society. First, the WIDF always declared that it welcomed women of all religious beliefs but, at the same time, the organization never used any religious arguments in its publications. Second, and more remarkable, the WIDF strongly advocated for the right of women to work for a paid salary, as well as the right to childcare for children of working mothers. On the contrary, the WIDF never supported the idea of woman staying home and being a housewife (the last is particularly visible through very positive images of happy women in the Soviet Union and other state socialist countries, see Chapter 5).

The relationship between women's roles as mother and women's rights was probably best expressed by Andrea Andreen, the WIDF vice-president from Sweden, in her speech at the 1953 congress in Copenhagen:

> One of the conditions for the real equality of women is their active participation in economic life on parity with men. [...] But women's rights in economic life in many countries are very limited. Women are cruelly

exploited and discriminated against on many occasions [...] The principle of equal pay for equal work is not applied even in those countries where it is declared.

(*Za ravnopravie* 1953, 11)

Further on in her talk, Andreen also connected a women's lack of work security to the lack of nurseries and kindergartens for children (*Za ravnopravie* 1953, 14). At the same time, Andreen stated that women's rights in different countries are often not enforced, especially in countries outside Europe. As an example, she noted the differences in salaries that White and Black women in the USA received for the same work, as well as the differences in salaries between indigenous majority women in the colonial countries and the salaries of the European women there (*Za ravnopravie* 1953, 13). Andreen also brought attention to problems that female workers have that male workers don't. According to her, in Iran, the birth of a child causes many problems for a woman who works at a factory, in many colonial countries women have very bad working conditions and are repeatedly subjected to attacks, and, in some cases, even suffer physical punishment (*Za ravnopravie* 1953, 15).

Thus, using this talk from 1953 as an example, it is possible to say that the WIDF was ready to demand social protection for working mothers, and was aware that working women in the colonial countries faced more difficult conditions than in Europe. Even if, later in her talk, Andreen also mentioned various old customs and traditions that were "supported by the colonizers" that "make women's situations much more difficult and convert her into a real slave" (*Za ravnopravie* 1953, 19), it is interesting that bad working conditions for women and the lack of social security for working mothers are presented in her talk as if those problems are the most serious ones when the colonial situation is discussed. Thus, women were assumed to be workers first, and were expected to claim their rights as such. While the lack of civil rights for women in many countries was acknowledged, this problem was attributed mainly to a lack of interest on the part of the colonial administration to improving the situation of the female workers, and to fighting the remnants of feudalism. Indeed, Andreen said that "in the countries where the remnants of feudalism are preserved, women are living as slaves and do not have any civil rights" (*Za ravnopravie* 1953, 18). At the same time, some of Andreen's ideas seem to have an Orientalist flavour. Andreen's vision of polygamy in Egypt, where men can beat their wives and have as many wives as they please (*Za ravnopravie* 1953, 18), does not seem to differ much from how representatives of other transnational women's organizations described the problems of colonial women (for IAW head Hanna Rydh, see Gerdov 2019).

Opposing the negative examples of the lack of women's rights in countries outside of Europe, Andreen mentioned the positive experience of women's rights in the Soviet Union and other state socialist countries. She stated that the Soviet women have rights in all spheres of life, and noted that women in China, Poland, and the GDR were also starting to build new lives (*Za ravnopravie* 1953, 21–22).

As previous scholarship has already shown, the Copenhagen conference adopted a Declaration of the Rights of Women (*Za ravnopravie* 1953, 254–255) that became a globally influencing document (de Haan 2012, 13). The declaration demanded crucial changes in the "economic, political and civic situation of women". According to the WIDF, the problems women faced in many parts of the world included lower pay for equal work with men, lack of legislation for pregnancy and childbirth leave, lack of childcare facilities, as well as employment legislation that made women more likely to be fired than men in cases of low employment levels. These problems, according to the declaration, were further aggravated by the lack of civic and political rights, and by the threat of a new war (*Za ravnopravie* 1953, 254–255). Thus, it was the right to work and choose a profession that occupied the first and the second place among the demands presented by the declaration. These demands were followed by demands for the state protection of maternity, and social security for mothers, the rights of rural women and, finally, close to the end of the document, the declaration demanded the right for women to take part in political life, and to form "democratic" organizations (*Za ravnopravie* 1953, 254–255).

The WIDF presented, in its official publications, its work for women's rights as being much more in the interests of women than the work of other transnational women's organizations. For example, a pamphlet on the WIDF published by Lidiia Petrova in Russian stated in its introduction that:

> old international women's organizations – feminist, pacifist, and cooperative – were also interested in the problems of women's rights, and the improvement of the situation of children; they also pronounced to be for peace. However, these organizations approached and continue approaching these issues only partially, and have a limited vision of their solution.
>
> (Petrova 1956, 4)

Further, Petrova continued by pointing out the differences between the WIDF and the "old women's organizations". The latter, according to her, had only a limited conception of equal rights, which included the right to vote in an election, and the right to an education. Such a programme, according to Petrova, expressed the interests of the bourgeoisie (Petrova 1956, 205). However, in further stating how the "old" women's organizations obviously disagreed with the WIDF, she also added that the leader of the IAW, Hanna Rydh, claimed that equal pay for equal work was already achieved (Petrova 1956, 209).

In opposition to those "old" women's organizations, the WIDF claimed that the protection of women's rights as mothers is particularly important, and that such a protection opened the possibility for the involvement of women in political and social organizations. From there, the possibility of defending women's political rights also opened. Thus, in its protection of women as mothers, the WIDF, from its earliest years, relied on a "human rights" discourse and widely used rights-relevant rhetoric denouncing "violations of rights" and demanding legislation in the interests of the "rights of women and children" in its official speeches and publications.

It is interesting to note here that, according to Samuel Moyn, "human rights" weren't used by the anti-colonial movements and the Western women's movement until much later on (Moyn 2010). According to Niamh Reilly, human rights ideology was employed by the women's movement before then, but it was by the predominantly liberal women's movement (Reilly 2009, 19). However, the WIDF's documents show that communist and leftist women were already eager to use this concept in defending women's rights during the 1950s–1960s, and even published a special bulletin about it in French (see more in Chapter 4).

The WIDF also cited the importance of the UN's Universal Declaration of Human Rights for its activities on other occasions. For example, a circular letter from the Secretariat of the WIDF sent out by Rosa Jasovich-Pantaleon, the WIDF general secretary, in August 1963, informed the WIDF member organizations about a letter from UNESCO reminding recipients about the 15th anniversary of the Declaration of Human Rights on 10 December 1963. She continued that:

> The WIDF that always was acting on the basis of, and struggling for, human rights, constantly defended the need for the realization of the declaration in practice and in all countries. The WIDF has given a lot of space to this problem in its publications and is happy to support the realization of this important idea.
>
> (GARF 3 1020, p. 61)

Furthermore, although the WIDF didn't recover its status as a non-governmental organization at the UN until 1967, it continued to actively participate in several meetings and events organized by the UN. For example, the protocols of the 1965 WIDF council meeting in Salzburg state that the WIDF took part in two UN commissions' meetings, discussing the participation of women in public life: the 8th session of the UN Commission on the Status of Women that was held in Teheran, and the meeting on women's participation in public life organized by the UN Commission on Human Rights in Ulan-Bator. That same year, the WIDF also participated in the 49th session of the International Labour Organization (ILO) where a recommendation on the "Employment of women with family responsibilities" was adopted. After reporting on the WIDF's participation in these high-level international discussions on women's rights at the WIDF council meeting in Salzburg, Rosa Jasovich, the WIDF general secretary, suggested that the WIDF should prepare and distribute a special pamphlet on women's rights (GARF 31396, p. 26).

The idea of "rights" was also central at most of the WIDF's congresses. While the 1953 congress in Copenhagen adopted the Declaration of Women's Rights, the 1963 WIDF Congress in Moscow included a keynote speech on the rights of women in the family and society (GARF 3 1020, pp. 15–17). The issues of rights became even more pronounced at the 1975 WIDF congress in East Berlin (archive IISH, see also Donert 2014).

Nevertheless, from time to time, some internal discussions in the WIDF showed that some of the WIDF leaders, in particular the Soviet ones, warned against too big a focus on rights that they believed to be characteristic of the "feminists". Instead, the Soviet approach to rights, where they were tied to obligations and responsibilities, was argued. For example, in her speech at the preparatory bureau meeting for the WIDF's 1963 Moscow congress, Popova stated that even "old international women's organizations" started to understand that "the focus of the activity of the international women's organizations moves from questions about the situation of women and their rights (even if these questions continue to be important) to the issues of the responsibilities of women and their participation in the life of the society" (GARF 3 790, p. 72, from 30.05.62).[4]

Despite ideas of that sort being expressed from time to time, the discourse on rights continued to be strong in future years. This discourse became especially remarkable after 1967, when the WIDF regained its official status as a non-governmental organization at the UN,[5] and when the WIDF became an important actor during the 1975 International Women's Year (see more in Chapter 8).

Conclusion

This short overview of the WIDF's ideas on defending peace, mothers, and children demonstrates that they constituted the core of the WIDF ideology's from its beginning and, in spite of all the changes during its history, the federation preserved these ideas but, at the same time, their interpretations were modified in connection with new problems and concerns. For example, the claim to protect peace, first expressed as working to prevent a repetition of the Second World War, in the context of the development of movements for national liberation and independence, began to be used when denouncing imperialism and colonialism. On the other hand, the protection of mothers and children was not limited to the demands of welfare for mothers, but incorporated women's rights to work and get an education. Thus, the WIDF could fruitfully use its early ideas on the protection of mothers and children to cooperate with the UN and ILO on broader issues of gender equality in the spheres of politics, work, and education, including demands for equal pay and non-discrimination. The defence of the rights of mothers and children also worked well in later years when the Eastern bloc confronted their Cold War adversaries' propaganda promoting fertility control as a solution to Third World developmental problems (see more in Chapter 8).

At the same time, the biological explanation of women's special role in the protection of peace, and the maternalist perspective on women's rights, limited the ability of the WIDF member organizations to imagine women's rights outside of the essentialist paradigm. Thus, akin to the perspective of the state socialist countries, the WIDF did not question women's "natural" predestination to be mothers, in a heterosexual framework, nor did it demand equal rights for women serving in the army, or participating in military opposition. This led to the federation having difficulties in understanding and communicating with representatives of grassroots organizations in Europe and other countries who, during the 1970s, raised demands for sexual and reproductive freedom, and criticized naturalist interpretation of femininity (see Alvarez 1994, 237–240 on Brazil and Latin America). Along with its pro-Soviet position, this contributed to a sharp decrease of the WIDF's popularity among West European feminists in the later part of the Cold War.

Notes

1 Eugenie Cotton was a pupil of Marie Curie.
2 According to some researchers, the quick escalation in Korea functioned as an alarm for all involved parties, clearly indicating the threat, and causing all those who participated in the Korean conflict to become more restrained in future conflicts (Hugh Lee 2011, 98–121).
3 Correspondence between Nina Popova and the Soviet representative to the Secretariat from 1956 shows that the WIDF had to make special efforts in order to refocus the attention of the WIDF's council meeting that year from the problem of evacuating Hungarian children who suffered during the Soviet intervention to the "more important" attack on Egypt by the UK, Israel, and France (GARF 4 115, pp. 1–5; p. 10).
4 She referred here to the decision of the congress of social democratic women.
5 The events surrounding the WIDF readmission to ECOSOC were explored in BA-thesis by Khadejah Al Harbi, University of Amsterdam, 2019.

4 Anti-colonialism, anti-racism and social rights

This chapter analyses how the problems of women from the countries of Africa, Asia and Latin America were addressed in the WIDF's official documents, and how some of these problems were discussed in unofficial correspondence and Soviet reports. Despite initially attempting to attract women around the world by using the ideas of maternalism and peace protection, the growth of anti-colonial movements in Asia and Africa, particularly from the late 1950s onwards, caused the WIDF to expand its agenda and introduce changes into its work practices. In particular, I pay attention to what role the WIDF's forced relocation to East Berlin in 1951 played in the changes of the federation's work; I also analyze the political effects of the WIDF's ideological involvement in the Korean war. This chapter explores how the WIDF established contacts, and how it cooperated with female activists from countries outside Europe.

The WIDF's understanding of the problems of women in Asia, Africa, and Latin America

The Second World War had an enormous impact on developments in the colonies; mass mobilizations, famine, and military operations took place in many colonial and dependent territories, and contributed to the active development of the anti-colonial movements in different territories of Asia and Africa, including Vietnam, Algeria, Indonesia, India, Malaysia, and many other places (see, e.g., Drew 2014; Melasuo 2019; Embong & Abdulla 2019). The WIDF, from its beginnings, was interested in spreading its influence to women from all continents, including those in dependent territories. This interest was shared by both the WIDF's leaders, and also its membership in different countries. The organization's engagement with women in colonial countries and dependent territories began in a situation where the colonies were still an ordinary part of the world system; the improvement of the situation of women could be discussed mainly within the colonial setting, while any clear plans for a post-independence world order could not be made at this time.[1] Furthermore, according to research on the China–Soviet post-war relationship, the Soviet leadership and Stalin himself often prioritized geopolitical interests over ideological ones (on Soviet–China relationships, see Friedman 2015, 26). Thus, the WIDF accepted the geopolitical status quo in many parts of the world.

Yet, even though fighting for women's rights in colonial and dependent territories was not the main task of the WIDF, it was very important already during the earlier period of its activities. For example, classified documents that the ACSW passed to the Central Committee of the CPSU in 1947 suggest that, in order to better organize its work, the WIDF Secretariat in Paris created three permanent commissions (GARF 4 7, p. 36, from 8.01 1947[2]): the Commission on the protection and education of children; the Commission on the social, economic and legal situation of women; and the Commission on the situation of women in colonial countries.

The statutes of the Secretariat' Commission regarding the situation of women in colonial countries indicate that it had very impressive goals. These included helping women in colonial and dependent counties win economic and political rights; collecting information about women's lives in the colonial countries and maintaining contacts with women's organizations (and also with youth groups and trade unions in these countries). The commission was also to prepare proposals on improving the situation of women in these countries for the UN, international trade union organizations, and other transnational bodies. The commission supported the equality of rights for women with men, and the right for women to be elected and to take part in elections; it also expressed that women should have the right to occupy administrative positions independently of their economic situation and race. Further, the WIDF advocated that women in the colonial countries and dependent territories should be able to establish cultural and educational societies, and participate in the activities of democratic organizations. In their family life, all women should have the right to preserve their citizenship after marriage, to choose a spouse, women should have the right to a monogamous family, and equal rights with men in case of divorce. The document also demanded the establishment of equality of father and mother with respect to their children, and equal right to property. In addition, the statutes demanded the prevention of discrimination against women in connection to their economic status and customs, and the criminalization of trafficking women and children, as well as of the forced marriage of underage girls. Other demands included the realization of the right to work, and to support the provision of work for women, elimination of unemployment and its consequences (extreme poverty and prostitution), the right of women for equal pay for equal work with men, introduction of a social security system by the state and employers that would guarantee a minimal subsistence level for women in all cases where they did not, or could not, work (unemployment, illness, disability, old age). The statutes stated that women of all professions should have at least two weeks of yearly leave, and also maternity leave – six weeks before and six weeks after delivery. Special breaks for breastfeeding mothers, and social support for mothers of many children, should be introduced by the state. Finally, the document stated that it is the responsibility of the state and of the employer to organize crèches and kindergartens, demanded the recognition of the equal right to a mandatory, free, and complete education, the possibility of all kinds of professional training, and state support for fighting illiteracy in the adult population (GARF 4 7, pp. 42–44).

As one can see, the commission's programme required fundamental changes in the social and political systems of the dependent territories. In the late 1940s, when this document was created, women in many countries across the world, not only colonial ones, lacked equal rights in case of divorce, equal access to professional education, or equal pay for equal work with men. At the same time, this programme allows to see that the federation elaborated its ideas while mainly having in mind a society with a modern social structure (where women get a professional education and engage in gainful employment). Thus, it did not consider the complex social hierarchies and inequalities that existed in different societies, and were often normalized through the period of colonial rule. It is easy to suppose that the fulfilment of all the points of the commission's statutes required not only substantial reforms of family, work, and social security legislation, but also a lot of financial investment, for example, for organizing kindergartens. In general, it is possible to say that the realization of such a plan was hardly possible in the context of the preservation of the colonial system, as such.

Another classified document from the same file, in this case addressed directly to Stalin and several other members of the Central Committee of the CPSU, also exposes the WIDF position as being a radical one (I already mentioned it in chapter 2). The materials of the February 1947 WIDF council meeting in Prague show that there was a discussion around a presentation made by Alice Sportisse (an Algerian communist and member of the French Parliament) about the situation of women in colonial and semi-colonial countries, and a presentation by Philipps (USA) about the situation of African-American women. The report of the Soviet representatives in the WIDF informed the Soviet leadership that the federation discussed the colonial question in connection with the defence of peace:

> Alice Sportisse in her speech correctly posed the question indicating that the situation of women in colonies and equality of their rights with men depends on the general solution of the colonial problem. In her presentation, Sportisse made an analysis of the colonial question and its connection to the problem of the establishment of durable peace.
> (GARF 4 7, p. 52 classified letter from 20 March 1947)

Thus, it is possible to see that the colonial question was seen to some extend as a part of the problem of peace, while the situation of women was expected to be improved not so much through the results of women's activism in the colonial territories, but rather after the "colonial question" had been solved by governments. Thus, while on the one hand, the WIDF sought a radical solution to the "colonial question" – the end of colonialism and through this, the end of wars for colonies – on the other hand, the

WIDF seems do not pay special attention to the role that different aspects of the colonial past could play for the struggle for women's rights in the future. The documents do not seem to consider that experiences of dependencies, deprivations, and traumas that women from the colonized countries were exposed to could influence their specific needs, problems, demands, and forms of action. Neither do they seem to pay attention to the role of different religions that could be seen by women in the Global South as an important spiritual resource against foreign cultural domination. Thus, this vision ignored the grounds for the growth of nationalism, which became an important factor in the implementation of gender ideologies and legislation in the post-colonial countries (see more in Yuval-Davis 1997).

Some other documents show, nevertheless, that the WIDF made important attempts to learn about the situation of women in the colonies, and to establish contacts with women's organizations there. In particular, a few years after founding of the federation, the WIDF created a special commission to study women's lives in colonized countries. The Commission's activities, and a following congress in China in 1949, has already attracted researchers' attention (see McGregor 2016, 932–933; Armstrong 2016, 311–315). Both accounts praise the WIDF's efforts to support the anti-colonial struggle. However, using the documents from the Moscow archives, I want to problematize and nuance a further description of these events.

The archival documents show that in August of 1946 Jeanette Vermeersch wrote a letter to Nina Popova, the head of the ACSW, in which she suggested that the WIDF should create a special commission to visit several colonial countries; her proposal also mentioned that a French delegation could probably apply for money from the French government (GARF 1 5, 46–47). However, Vermeersch noted that some of the representatives of the federation would most probably meet with difficulties in accessing the colonial territories as a part of the commission. In particular, she meant those women from colonial territories, for example, the representatives of the Indian women's organization. Thus, it is possible to understand that the WIDF's first attempt at meeting the needs of women from the colonial countries had to be realized in the colonial framework, when participation in the commission was more likely to be open for white European women.

The commission was created in September 1947 at the WIDF's executive committee meeting in Stockholm. It planned to visit India, Vietnam, Burma, Malaya and Indonesia, but due to the French and Dutch governments' refusal to issue visas to their overseas territories for its participants, the Commission could visit only three countries, and could not visit Vietnam and Indonesia. The visit occurred in February–April of 1948, and was reflected in a detailed report (GARF 1 97). The Commission consisted of Simone Bertrand, French representative to the WIDF and a member of the French Parliament, Dr. Pat Miles from the UK, and Professor Tamara Morozova from the ACSW. During the Commission's stay in India, Miss Bacon, representative of the Federation of Australian Youth, joined the Commission. The report stated that Miss Brant (USA), who initially was planning to serve on the Commission, could not travel to India – according to her, she was hindered by the US government. The representative of China was also hindered and could not obtain a visa for India (GARF 1 97, p. 6). In spite of these difficulties, the final report of the Commission was prepared by a broader collective of authors, including the representatives of the Soviet republics of the Central Asia (Kazakhstan and Kyrgyzstan), as well as representatives from North and South Korea, Albania, China, India, and Mongolia.

With reference to the UN Charter adopted in 1945 in San Francisco (article 73), the commission stated the importance of women's rights, and the obligations of the countries that signed the charter to protect the interests of people in the non-self-governed territories (GARF 1 97, pp. 4–5). Thus, one of the aims of the Commission's visit was to compare the responsibilities that the colonial powers took upon themselves according to the UN document with what was actually happening in those territories. The report described the situation of women and children, with a focus on women's work and their rights, as well as women's and children's health and education (from a perspective similar to that discussed above in the example of the statutes of the permanent WIDF commission in the Secretariat). These goals defined the choice of institutions that the Commission decided to visit; jute factories, tea plantations, tobacco and textile industries, and coal mines (GARF 1 97, p. 7). The report is mainly centred around difficult working conditions, the poor health of workers, differences in the salaries of men and women, violations of the rights of pregnant women and mothers, lack of social security, and children beginning to work at the age of 7 or 8 (GARF 1 97, pp. 8–14). Many pages of the report were dedicated to the working conditions of workers of both sexes, and a comparison of prices with salaries. The report states that the leadership of the main organization of Indian women, the All-Indian Confederation of Women, did not support the idea of joining the WIDF. However, the report expressed hope that the left wing of that organization might be interested in cooperation with the WIDF (GARF 1 97, pp. 28–30).

In the case of India, the Commission's visit took place during the transition period from British colony to independent country. However, the Commission began its report by stating that "the situation of workers did not become better with the coming to power of the national government" (GARF 1 97, p. 7). The report contained many critiques of the Nehru government, for example, with regard to tea plantation the Indian government's policies were defined as "anti-worker" (GARF 1 97, p. 18), and the government was accused of repressing demonstrators (GARF 1 97, p. 32). The poverty of a large part of the Indian population, however, was described as "a tragedy of colonial people" (GARF 1 97, p. 14). The members of the Commission were particularly impressed by their visit to a workers' settlement in Kolkata:

> The workers were following us on the streets, and as soon as we stopped, they made a circle around us and stretched out skinny hands

with paddy in their fists (paddy is the worst type of raw rice); they said that a small amount of such a rice is their only food, that it is difficult to cook this rice, and that both children and adults are sick from it. Thus, they demanded help from the Commission.

(GARF 1 97, p. 13)

According to the Commission's conclusions, the whole settlement was an example of "deep poverty (*nishcheta*)" (GARF 1 97, p. 14).

The administration of Burma, which was then still a British colony, obstructed the work of the Commission, and prevented its members from meeting with local women. After a few days of work there, the Commission had to leave – "our Commission was under permanent and open snooping, at every moment the civil servants showed their extremely unfriendly attitude towards our commission" (GARF 1 97, p. 33). Still, the report mentioned that the members of the Commission were able to establish a relationship with Burma's Women's Congress, and that organization expressed interest in becoming a member of the federation (GARF 1 97, p. 34).

In the conclusion of the report, the authors stated that, in the process of its visit, the Commission found confirmation of the "crimes of British imperialism that are taking place in British colonies and the so called 'independent countries'" (GARF 1 97, p. 41). Thus, it is possible to state that the WIDF Commission was quite critical of not only the colonial policies of the European powers, but also of independent India's policies towards women.

The Commission's work in Asia was particularly important to the WIDF because it had to prepare ground for the WIDF's Asian conference and, at the same time, to expand the WIDF leadership's knowledge regarding the situation in the region. Initially, the WIDF planned to organize its conference in India; as we know, however, the WIDF's Asian conference took place in Beijing from 10–18 December, 1949 (GARF 1 99). In her speech before the WIDF's Executive Committee in April 1949, Lu Tsui, one of the organizers of the Beijing conference, reported that the Indian government refused to allow the WIDF's conference to be held in Kolkata because it wanted to organize its own conference in New Delhi, with representatives of 16 Asian countries, focusing on solidarity with Indonesia. This conference, according to Lu Tsui, did not allow participation of guests from the USSR, Mongolia, North Vietnam, or China, and was rather an attempt at creating "a reactionary Asian bloc serving British and American imperialism" (GARF 1 99, pp. 35–36). Lu Tsui further stressed that, in this situation, revolutionary China felt itself obliged to organize the Asian conference itself, even though the situation in China was not very convenient for such an important international meeting. Lu Tsui emphasized that China did not have diplomatic relations with many countries, resulting in visa and travel problems for some conference participants (GARF 1 99, p. 43).

According to a report by another Chinese organizer, Bai Yun, prepared for the meeting of the WIDF's executive committee in Helsinki after the conference, 197 delegates from 23 countries attended the Beijing conference (GARF 1 99, p. 141). 14 of these countries were Asian (including the Soviet republics of Kyrgyzstan and Kazakhstan, as well as North Vietnam and North Korea). Representatives from European countries (France, Netherlands, Great Britain) as well as from Czechoslovakia, Algeria, Cuba, and Madagascar also attended. The Soviet delegation included Nadezhda Parfenova, one of the key figures of the ACSW, and Asia Atanapesova, minister of social provision of the Turkmen SSR. The delegates from the poorer Asian countries had their lodging and travel expenses covered by the Chinese government, according to this document.

The conference materials contain the archived draft of the keynote speech by Simone Bertrand, representative of the Union of French Women (UFF). According to her speech, titled "The Struggle of the Women of Asia and Africa", Bertrand emphasized the economic importance of the region, the lack of rights for women, and the growth of women's organizations in Asia and Africa (GARF 1 99, pp. 1–31). As in the report of the Commission that visited colonial countries in 1948, discussed above, the main problem with colonial rule that Bertrand discussed was the economic exploitation of the population, including working women. However, she also stressed that women in Asia and Africa were starting to play a more important role in the "struggle for independence, better life, and peace". Bertrand added that "women of the whole world support this struggle of their sisters" (GARF 1 99, p. 1). Thus, the Western European "sisters", the women from the colonial countries, were called upon to help their "sisters" in Asia and Africa obtain rights. At the end of her talk, Bertrand said:

> Women in the imperialist countries have a major responsibility with respect to oppressed women [in other parts of the world], they have to energetically help in their struggle; the French women should effectively help the women of Vietnam, Dutch women should help the women of Indonesia, women of England – the women of Burma, Malaya, Palestine, and the USA's women should help the women of the Philippines and other dominated countries. They have to help their sisters not only out of a feeling of justice, but also because the struggle of women in dominated countries against their oppressors is part of our common struggle for democracy and peace.
>
> (GARF 1 99, pp. 30–31)

Thus, the WIDF's vision of the development of relations between European women (women from Western Europe and the Soviet bloc constituted a majority in the WIDF and in its leadership) and women from the Global South was based on assumptions of common goals, but at the same time, it supposed a certain hierarchy between the two groups of women, expressed through the idea of "help". The Chinese and Soviet representatives mainly agreed on this interpretation. For example, Bai Yun, in her report on the conference for the WIDF Executive Committee meeting in Helsinki after the conference, stressed the emotional closeness of the delegates from European and Asian countries:

> The scenes of exchanging gifts between French delegate, Jeanette Vermeersch, and the Vietnamese delegates was particularly touching. When they hugged each other expressing love and friendship, many women had wet eyes.
>
> (GARF 1 99, p. 142)

Most probably, the relations between the French and Vietnamese delegation were seen as the kind of relations that were expected from women who were members of the federation; women defending peace and women's rights should be able to cooperate in spite of their unequal statuses. On the other hand, Bai Yun's report suggested that this unity was inspired by communist ideals and rhetoric, the slogans "Van sui" (Long live), "Stalin", "Mao Zedong" and "Hurra" were mentioned as those with which all of the delegates were familiar (GARF 1 99, p. 142). Furthermore, the example of the emancipation of women in Soviet Central Asia was another important belief that was shared by the participants, and contributed to unity. In her speech at the conference, the Chinese representative Den In Chao stressed that "if Chinese women are only starting to be emancipated, women in the Asian republics of the USSR have been totally free for a long time" (GARF 1 130, p. 55). At the same time, the independence of countries such as India, Burma, or the Philippines was classified as "false independence"; such political changes, according to her, did not bring changes to the situation of women (GARF 1 130, p. 56).

In concluding this section, it is possible to say that the WIDF's leadership mainly saw women from the colonized countries as "working women" who were more exploited (when compared to women in the imperialist countries) due to the pressures of the colonial administration. Thus, the common fight for social reforms was seen as an obvious reason for acting together, for both women from the colonizing countries and also those from the colonies. The WIDF's leadership, consisting predominantly of (West- and East-) European women, would have an especially important role of organizing help and support to the women's organizations in Asia, Africa, and Latin America.

The WIDF meets the anti-colonial struggle and decolonization

In this part of the chapter, I explore how the WIDF reacted to the declarations of independence by many Asian and African countries in the 1950s–1960s, as well as to the growing importance of women's issues and activism outside Europe. I also explore how these changes influenced the WIDF's programme, structures, international position, participation, and leadership.

Anti-colonialism, anti-racism and social rights 85

If we consider first how these changes were presented in the WIDF's publications in English and Russian, it is possible to see that the WIDF's support for women from the Global South was regarded as obvious and non-problematic. For example, a pamphlet published on the occasion of the WIDF's 40th anniversary in 1985 stated that in 1956, a WIDF delegation went to Egypt to show its solidarity in the face of the aggression by France, Great Britain, and Israel (*WIDF 40*, 1985, 24). It also mentioned that in 1961, the WIDF sent international missions to Cuba, Mexico, Brazil, Mali, Guinea, Nigeria, and Ghana (*WIDF 40*, 1985, 25), and in 1962 the WIDF sent a delegation to Johannesburg (South Africa) to study the situation of women and children under Apartheid. In 1969, the WIDF started construction of a centre for mothers and children in Hanoi, while the World Congress of Women in Helsinki that same year adopted a resolution on peace in Vietnam. In 1970 and in 1971, the WIDF organized seminars in Khartoum and Delhi for training female cadres to combat illiteracy among women. In 1971, the WIDF also sent a delegation to the liberated parts of Angola (*WIDF 40* 1985, 27). At the same time, all these activities are presented intermixed with other activities, including those dedicated to the protection of peace and children, while the role of women's organizations from the Global South is not specified in this commemorative picture.

Aside from this official representation of cooperation, the archival materials allow us to explore some problems and conflicts around the WIDF's activities in the newly independent countries of Asia and Africa. Thus, in this subchapter, I explore different – and not always successful – interactions of the WIDF with women and issues connected to the process of decolonization; among other issues, I pay attention to unrealized intentions and problems.

Anti-colonial struggle, the Cold War, and the WIDF's relocation

Previous scholarship on the WIDF has already shown that the WIDF was forced to move out of Paris as a result of growing Cold War tensions, and in connection with the wars in Korea and Vietnam (Ilic 2011; McGregor 2016). The Moscow archival documents and circular letters preserved in the archive ARAB in Stockholm allow us to explore further the development of the situation around the WIDF at the moment of its relocation, as well as connections between relocation and the anti-colonial struggle.

In particular, the documents from the Moscow archive suggest that the situation around the WIDF's headquarters in Paris had already started to become tense in the early 1950s. At that moment, the WIDF had made a public call for the independence of Vietnam, and showed its support for the movement led by the Communist leader and old ally of the Soviet Union, Ho Chi Minh. Nevertheless, the correspondence between ACSW and its representative in Paris shows that neither the WIDF leaders nor the ACSW were prepared for this development of the situation around the WIDF's Paris headquarters. The Soviet representative to the Paris Secretariat, Zinaida

Gurina, wrote to Nadezhda Parfenova, vice-chair of the ACSW, on 14 February 1950, that a "visa war" is being waged against the Soviet representatives of the WIDF in France (GARF 4 45, p. 52). This made Parfenova's planned arrival in Paris on 19 February highly doubtful. Giving examples of other WIDF Secretariat employees from the Soviet Union who were refused visas, Gurina concludes "The French government is so angry with the Soviet Union due to its recognition of Vietnam that is using every possible reason for retaliation" (GARF 4 45, p. 52). The Vietnam campaign led by the WIDF was framed as an "anti-war" campaign, and it was also the French women's organization, the Union of French Women (UFF), the WIDF member, that seemed to provoke a strong reaction from the French government. In a letter from May 1950, Gurina informed the Soviet authorities that Mme. Cotton, the president of the WIDF and one of the leaders of the UFF, was informed by the French authorities that a legal process had been initiated against her, due to a poster produced by the UFF reading "You are not going to sign this contract" against recruitment into the French Expedition Corps to be sent to Vietnam. According to the letter, Cotton had to attend a court hearing that evening (GARF 4 45, p. 128). A WIDF publication in Russian produced in 1956 also supports this assumption, and gives another example of the struggle that the WIDF was proud of; in February 1950, a French activist, Raymonde Dien, put herself on the rails in order to stop a train carrying ammunition for the war (Petrova 1956, 162–163).[3]

Several circular letters from 1951 found in the archive of the Swedish section of the WIDF, the Swedish Women's Left Union (SKV), also indicate that it was the WIDF's independent position that led to the decision of the French government to close down the federation in France:

> Today, 26 January 1951, the official Gazette of the French Government announced the official dissolution of the women's International Democratic Federation. This decree is signed by Mr. Henry Queille, Minister of Interior, who refers – among others – to the Law of July 27th, 1940, i.e. a law passed by the Petain government at the time when France was occupied by the Hitlerian fascists, with the logic of banning the existent democratic organizations.
> (ARAB, 3340, letter in English signed by Vaillant-Couturier & Cotton, Paris, 26 January 1951)

Thus, the decision on relocating the WIDF to Berlin seems to have been made drastically. On a standard form, but with the WIDF address in Paris crossed out, Vaillant-Couturier wrote from Berlin on 14 March 1951:

> After the unqualified measure of the French Government against the seat of the WIDF, the Council charged the Secretariat to proceed with finding a new place for our office. Considering the importance of Germany for the peace problem, the Secretariat has decided to accept

the offer of the German Democratic Women's Union to establish our seat in Berlin. Our address is 13, Unter den Linden, Berlin, NW7.

(ARAB, 3340)

The WIDF widely diffused information about this French government's decision, and accused it in acting against UN norms and legislations. For example, the WIDF's council, meeting in Berlin 1–6 February 1951, published an *Appeal to women of the whole world*. The *Appeal* addressed its readers as "Dear sisters", and ended with a resolution protesting against the decision of the French government to prohibit the activities of the WIDF in France (*Prilozhenie k zhurnalu*, 1951 2: 3). The resolution informed the participants of the WIDF council meeting in Berlin that it would appeal to the UN ECOSOC in protest against the French government:

> The council meeting protests this ban and asks it to be cancelled immediately because it denies the human rights and civic freedoms guaranteed by the UN Charter. The French government promised to respect them. This meeting declares that the WIDF is a non-governmental organization having the consultative status of category "B" in accordance with paragraph 71 of the UN Charter. The WIDF has sections in 59 countries, they unite 91 million women.
> (*Prilozhenie k zhurnalu Sovetskaia zhenshchina*, vol. 2, 1951, 3)

The *Appeal* continued by indicating that the WIDF is working for the realization of principles that could be found in the UN Charter, in particular, working on economic and cultural issues, and activities that guarantee equal status for women in political, economic, and social life. However, as we know, this *Appeal* did not have any effect, and the WIDF was forced to continue its activities from Berlin for the rest of the Cold War.

At the same time as the WIDF became involved with the war in Vietnam for independence from France, the federation also became embroiled in conflict with the United States concerning developments in Korea. In this case, the WIDF clearly took the side of the Democratic People's Republic of Korea (DPRK) and thus openly placed itself on the pro-Soviet and anti-American side of this hot battle of the Cold War. On 25 June 1950, North Korean troops, supported by the army of the People's Republic of China (and with approval from Moscow), entered the territory of South Korea below the 38th Parallel,[4] and were confronted by the US army operating under a UN mandate to keep peace; the American troops would cross the 38th Parallel and march north in the fall of 1950. The Korean War is described by researchers as one of the most acute crises of the Cold War period (see Paik 2010, Hajimu 2015). At the same time, according to Masuda Hajimu, this war cannot be seen just as a result of pure East–West confrontation, but had a more complex nature, and was used by governments on both sides to realize their internal political goals (2015, 285).

Unlike in Vietnam, in the case of Korea, the WIDF created a special commission consisting of the representatives of the UK, Denmark, Italy, China, the Soviet Union, Cuba, Algeria, and from some other countries, that visited the military conflict zone in the northern part of Korea in May 1951, and published a pamphlet *We accuse* later that same year. This pamphlet had the same title that the French intellectual Emile Zola used as a slogan when defending Alfred Dreyfus from anti-Semitism in the well-known, so-called "Dreyfus affair" at the end of the 19th century. The WIDF pamphlet was published in 12 languages and distributed widely. As Donert has already shown, the pamphlet was based on the stories of women who were victims of crimes committed by the American troops (Donert 2016).

The publication used harsh, Second World War-style rhetoric and spoke about the "extermination" of the Korean people:

> The people of Korea are subjected by American occupants to a merciless and methodical campaign of extermination which is in contradiction not only with the principles of humanity, but also with the rules of warfare as laid down, for instance, in the Hague and the Geneva Conventions.
>
> (*We accuse* 1951, 3)

The pamphlet described the American crimes in Korea, and compared them directly to the Nazi crimes: "These mass tortures and mass murders surpass the crimes committed by Hitler's nazis in temporally occupied Europe" (ibid., 3). Using Second World War-style rhetoric allowed to the WIDF to present the pamphlet as being a part of the anti-war activity declared in its programme, while anti-colonial rhetoric, got little space. Still, "independence" was used by some of the representatives of the WIDF from Korea, the Korean delegate, Che Den Zuk, addressed the WIDF council in Berlin on 1–5 February 1951: "In the name of the Korean people who are fighting for the independence, freedom and unity of Korea against the American aggressors" (ARAB 3340).

Later on, the wars in Korea and Vietnam were often present in the WIDF's publications as similar events that required broad solidarity actions from women "of the whole world". For example, Abassia Fodil, representative of the Union of Algerian Women and a member of the WIDF commission behind "*We accuse*", in her presentation at the WIDF congress in Copenhagen, stated that the women of Algeria "fight for end of war in Korea and Vietnam" (*Za ravnopravie* 1953, 154–155).

The WIDF's international report – *We accuse* – was later succeeded by the report of another commission with which the WIDF was involved, this commission investigated the use of biological weapons in Korea by the US Army. Unlike the first one, the second commission consisted of professional medical doctors and biologists. The WIDF was represented there by Andrea Andreen – the WIDF's vice-president and a prominent Swedish medical doctor and peace activist. Together with other members of the commission,

Andreen signed the report accusing the USA of using biological weapons (Andreen 1974).

Both reports on the Korean War became the subject of an intense Cold War ideological battle, and they led to the political persecution of the members of the commissions, and also the federation. In her article, Donert gave a detailed analysis of the court process started by West Germany against the German member of the WIDF commission, Lilly Wächter (Donert 2016, 329–331). Soon after the report of the second commission was published, Andreen became a focus of a strong Swedish campaign accusing her of communist activities (Larberg & Andreen Sachs 2015, 75–76). Furthermore, Eleanor Roosevelt, the spouse of the former US president, and head of the UN Commission on Human Rights, published a special letter denouncing the WIDF's accusations as false (answer of the WIDF to Eleanor Roosevelt, 3 September 1952, ARAB, 3340). The WIDF's unprecedented involvement in one of the "hot" conflicts of the Cold War seriously affected its international reputation, and made all of its activities easy targets for accusations of "Communism". As I have already detailed in the previous chapter, this accusation on the part of the US government led to its American member organization, Congress of American Women, being accused of anti-American activities, which finally led to the dissolution of the American organization. The WIDF was also deprived of its non-governmental organization status at the UN's ECOSOC between 1954 and 1967. The years that followed the WIDF's relocation and expulsion from ECOSOC were probably the most difficult years in the federation's history; it, and its members in different countries, were often accused of communist activity and disseminating propaganda, while all of the members of the WIDF's leadership, and the leaders of its member organizations, were on the CIA watch-list (see CIA 1956).

On the other hand, while the WIDF never denied the importance of national independence for achieving women's rights, an analysis of its documents and publications shows that up until the late 1950s, it mainly continued to stress suffering of women from war and colonialism, paying less attention to the promotion of national independence. Pointedly, the *Declaration of the Rights of Women* adopted by the Copenhagen WIDF Congress in 1953 did not have a special point on independence, while Cotton and Andreen's speeches at the Congress continued paying attention to a bigger exploitation of women in colonies, and to anti-war activism, rather than to women's pro-independence activism as such (*Za ravnopravie* 1953, 7–39). At the same time, published materials of the 1953 Copenhagen Congress expressed support for the women of Korea and Vietnam. The publication emotionally described that, while the Vietnamese and Korean representatives could not attend the conference due to the Danish government's refusing to issue visas for them, Eugenie Cotton went to Berlin and had a special meeting with them there instead (*Za ravnopravie*, 1953, 244–245).

On the other hand, the WIDF's growing international isolation, and geographical dislocation, resulting from its support of Vietnam and Korea, not only led to a forced relocation of the WIDF headquarters to the (Communist) East, but also made it even more likely that the federation would be used by one of the sides of the Cold War, the Soviet one, for foreign policy purposes. Nevertheless, it could be assumed that after being forced from Paris, and in the context of the growing Cold War polarization and the development of the anti-colonial movements in Africa and Asia, the WIDF's appeals, agenda, and anti-colonial stances probably became more attractive to some political forces aiming for national independence in Africa and Asia, as opposed to when the WIDF was based in Paris.

Growing women's activism in the Global South and new challenges and opportunities for the WIDF

The escalation of the Cold War in the early 1950s led to growing suspicions of the WIDF's activities, as well as to more difficult political conditions for its member organizations in different parts of the world. For example, documents from the Moscow archives indicate several acts of repression occurring in Latin America. A March 1952 letter by Carmen Zanti, general secretary of the WIDF, for example, informed the Secretariat that the main organizer of activities for protecting children in Cuba, a medical doctor named Augusto Castellanos, was called to the American embassy in Havana three days before the conference on the protection of children that was to take place in Cuba (RGASPI 17 137 818, p. 43). After that meeting, he withdrew his signature from the appeal for the protection of children, and called the planned conference a "Communist enterprise". The same archive folder contains the letter from Venezuela that I have already mentioned; on 18 June 1952, Dr. Marcario Coello, the main organizer of the celebration of Children's Day in Caracas, was arrested and accused of taking part in a conference organized by foreign forces hostile towards the country (RGASPI 17 137 818, p. 184).

However, the situation inside the WIDF, and around it, underwent critical changes at the end of the 1950s. The growing anti-colonial movement in Africa and Asia further coincided with the beginning of de-Stalinization in the Soviet Union, which led to reforms in many Communist parties across the world. These processes influenced the WIDF's agenda and tactics. The changes are visible in the federation's periodical publications; in the mid-1950s its journal changed its design, and, at least partly, its main focus. It started to publish more information about the context of women's activism in different countries. In the late 1950s, the journal also published much more material about non-European countries, and in several different forms.

For example, issue 7–8 from 1958 published a long article on women's protests against Apartheid, and on the women's march on Pretoria in 1956. For the first time, the article explained to its readers what apartheid was and why that system violated the rights of African women (ZM 1958 7–8: 17–19). In 1959, the journal started to experiment with its cover, now featuring the colour photos of female faces, in many cases the faces of prominent women from Asia and Africa. For example, issue 3 from 1959 had on its cover Mme. Sékou Touré, the spouse of the president of the Republic of Guinea, while issue 9 from 1959 had Rojan Vidjevdar, described as a dancer and master of Indian classical dance, on the cover. These pictures were in addition to pictures of the Soviet Asian woman Tajihom Jumahodzhaeva, an engineer in Tashkent (ZM 1959, 11), and a young Chinese worker on the cover of issue 3 from 1960. The same tendency continued for several years, until 1965, when the cover design changed again and started to include collages, objects etc.

Along with the portraits of prominent women, in 1958–1959 the journal experimented with more a popular style that was closer to commercial women's magazines and featured fashion and culinary recipes. However, unlike Western commercial or fashion magazines, the fashion pages of the WIDF's journal published a combination of traditional ethnic clothes, "socialist fashion", and "western fashion". For example, an issue from 1959 showed Swedish (modern European) clothes together with traditional women's clothes from Bethlehem (part of Transjordan at that time) (ZM 1959 9: 35).

However, other aspects of representing women from the Global South in the journal changed more slowly, particularly in terms of the voices of women from countries outside Europe. For example, the same issue that published the article on the women's march on Pretoria lead with the report on the WIDF congress in Vienna (ZM 1958, 7–8, 5–9). The article report stated that the Congress focused on two issues, "the protection of peace and the problem of the struggle against colonialism", and noted that the congress was attended by women from 70 countries. The presentation of anti-colonialism, however, did not leave much space to discussion of the building of the new nation-states or to women taking part in the building of the national ideologies and political institutions. But the colonial exploitation and domination received a sharp critique at the Congress (Petrova 1959, 17). Issues from later years increased the number of articles and reports on events in the countries outside Europe, and those written by the representatives of non-White activists. An article by Eslanda Robeson,[5] "Africa for the Africans", published in 1959, presented its author as "a representative of the independent press of America" in Russian version (and "the Negro press of the United States" in the English one); in it Robeson shared her impressions from visiting the All Africa People Conference, held in Ghana in 1958. This article radically defended the struggle for independence, stating that those who participated in the conference wanted to join their efforts together in "order to end colonialism and to achieve independence". Robeson continued that people that were represented at the conference "decided to establish an African Personality in order to exert their special influence on world affairs. They decided that, as from now, Africans must rule Africa and that foreigners remaining in Africa must submit to African rule or go home" (*WWW* 1959 3: 10–11). Geeta Mukherjee, the Indian representative at the WIDF's Secretariat, also shared her impressions from the same conference (*WWW* 1959 3: 12). Issue 1, from 1960, published an article by Bani Dasgupta,[6] who, as a WIDF representative, attended the first congress of Iraqi women that took place on 8 March 1959 in Baghdad (ZM 1960 1: 11).

At the beginning of the 1960s, the WIDF used the UN language of human rights in its support for the anti-colonial struggle quite extensively. The Moscow archive preserved the bulletin *For the Defence of Human Rights* ("Pour la defense des droits de la personne humane") that was published in France by the WIDF during the early 1960s. The bulletin was dedicated to the rights of women, but often approached the issues of war and political freedoms by using Cold War rhetoric. For example, issue 4 from 1962 published an article about the suffering of South Korean women caused by the American army and the local "fascist regime". The article stressed that one out of every 100 Korean citizens was arrested, and the situation of women and children was getting worse (GARF 3 801, p. 21). The same issue contained material against repressions in universities in Guatemala, and the WIDF's solidarity with Guatemalan women (GARF 3 801, pp. 23–24). In the bulletin's issue 6/7 from 1964, it states that in South Africa, power belongs to the "racists", and they use it against the black population (GRAF 3 1043, p. 43). The bulletin also mentioned that after demonstration by the Black population, many participants were arrested; in some families both parents were arrested, and their children were left to live alone. The journal called for solidarity with South African activists. Thus, it is possible to state that this bulletin was bringing together different cases of discrimination against the rights of women, many of them made visible the abuse of women's rights in the colonial countries, and also racial discrimination. The role of women as mothers, whose children are suffering, for example, in the case of their arrest was usually stressed and, most probably, was aimed at making the WIDF's message stronger.

Nevertheless, the documents suggest that the WIDF had limited financial and human resources, and in spite of a wide solidarity campaign, in some cases it could not prevent the closing down of its member organizations (including those connected to Communist parties) that encountered a hostile environment in their countries. A letter sent in 1962 by Branca Fiala, the leader of the Brazilian women's organization, to Carmen Zanti revealed the persecution and indifference that Brazilian women who were members of the WIDF's organization met at home:

> In spite of all the efforts of a small group of very loyal women, the Women's Federation of Brazil ceased to exist. We had many difficulties and could not overcome them. The Catholic women were against us, because the Church is fighting against us and has declared us to be communists. Bourgeois women are afraid to cooperate with us; the police have closed down our federation (even though the federation is legal again). I do not know why the Communists do not want to work with us, probably, they are afraid to compromise themselves. Thus, only 4–5 women remain in our organization. Without members, without people,

we cannot work. That is why we have to declare that our organization does not exist anymore.

(GARF 3 803, p. 79, from 16 June 1962)

In spite of the problems in some national organizations, in the late 1950s–early 1960s, the federation became more well-known in the countries of the Global South. In those years, the federation tried to keep track of the participation of women from different Asian and African countries in its events (GARF 3 799, pp. 5–8), and started to receive more and more letters from women's organizations in different countries. The authors of the letters hoped that the WIDF would help them distribute information about their problems, and organize solidarity campaigns. For example, women from Jordan created a committee for the defence of political prisoners and those exiled from Amman, they described the torture in prisons, and concluded that they are sure that the federation was also worried about what was happening in the prisons (GARF 3 803, p. 6, 15 March 1962). The Union of Women of Cameroon, in exile in Ghana, sent from Accra their complaints about the situation in the country, "the women from Cameroon who do not support the policies of the current marionette government are persecuted, thrown into prisons, are exiled, or hide in the forests". The letter finishes with "we hope that all of the women's organizations will hear our cry – help to us to break down the chains of domination and our dominators" (GARF 3 803, p. 116, 4 June 1962).

The letters between the Soviet representatives to the WIDF and members of the CSW show that the growth of the political and social movements in the countries outside Europe allowed the WIDF to increase its solidarity activities dramatically. The demand for solidarity became so strong that its systematization and mechanization took place. A letter from Lebedeva sent in 1961 stated, for example:

> Due to the need to show solidarity with one or another group fighting for its freedom and national independence, apart from the bulletin, we decided to produce a special template that we could use every time, when necessary. This template will have the form of a letter and will be accompanied by an epigraph about the people's struggle. In every case, this letter should be sent to corresponding addresses and to the national committees.
>
> (GARF 4 149, p. 15)

Lebedeva wrote that such letters were sent to the women of Cuba, to women of the Congo, and to the wife of Patrice Lumumba.[7]

Furthermore, the WIDF became active in sending representatives to different regional events organized by the women, governments, and independence movements in Asia and Africa. As I already mentioned in Chapter 2, the WIDF general secretary, Carmen Zanti, was very active in establishing contacts with women's organizations in newly independent countries.

The leadership of the CSW also considered establishing contacts to be very important: "one of the WIDF leaders should visit Africa. The movement is on the rise there and establishing contacts is of much importance now" (GARF 4 134, p. 120).

In practice, establishing good relationships with the new women's organizations was not always easy, and the Cold War confrontations and alliances played an important role here. For example, the WIDF was invited to take part in the conference of women of Asia and Africa, held in the spirit of Bandung, in Cairo from 14–21 January 1960. However, even though the organizing committee included a representative from the WIDF, the Egyptian activist Ceza Nabarawi, who was also one of the federation's vice-presidents, she communicated to the Secretariat that she could not greatly influence the organization of the conference (GARF 4 134, p. 180). According to Nabarawi, the president of Egypt, Gamal Abdel Nasser, wanted the conference to correspond to his expectations, and he did not want to give the WIDF too much visibility. Thus, Nabarawi suggested that the WIDF should be particularly careful when selecting the members of its delegation to Cairo, while the Nasser government wanted to avoid discussion of political issues at the conference, the WIDF should send delegates that would be able to do it (GARF 4 134, p. 180).

In other cases, the European origin of the organization, and its famed pro-Soviet position, negatively influenced the WIDF's reception in Africa. For example, the participation of a WIDF delegation at an African conference in Tanganyika (Tanzania) at the beginning of 1963 (GARF 4 169, p. 29, 13 February 1963) indicated the complexity of the WIDF's situation when communicating with Africans. According to the report of the Soviet representative at the Secretariat, after coming back from Tanganyika, Carmen Zanti organized a small informal meeting for secretaries at her home. There, she stressed first that "almost the whole of Africa was present at that conference" and that this conference was very important for the WIDF. She also conveyed that the conference was held under difficult circumstances, and representatives of several African countries could not be there. At the same time, Zanti's report showed that in spite of the fact that the representatives of WIDF (along with those of the World Peace Council) were the only international delegates present, the WIDF delegation had observer status and could not take part in any commission, including the one dealing with women's issues, nor could it make a presentation. She also noted that she learned there that the organizers had difficulty deciding whether the WIDF delegation should be invited at all. According to Zanti, the Chinese delegation (this was when the Soviet–Chinese split was growing) was responsible for the problems:

> [the Chinese delegation] was working with African delegates according to its strategy, using the unthinkable arguments that only enemies could use. For example, they were trying to convince some African delegates that the Russians could not understand and truly support the struggle

of African people, because they are "white" and the Whites always were exploiting Africa and Asia.

(GARF 4 169, p. 29)

Thus, it is possible to understand that many African politicians, both men and women, had been informed about the WIDF's special relationship with Moscow, and some of them saw the organization with suspicion because of this. At the same time, it is possible to suppose that the whiteness of the WIDF's top leadership could constitute a problem in post-colonial Africa, even without the special efforts of the Chinese delegation.

However, Zanti finished her report on the conference quite positively, stating that the conference delegates were happy to receive issues of the WIDF journal, as well as pamphlets and other materials, such as postcards and buttons that were produced for the upcoming women's congress in Moscow (GARF 4 169, p. 30). Hence most of the meetings between the WIDF leaders and women from the newly independent countries were quite challenging for the WIDF's European leaders; while African female activists could be interested in broadening their contacts with transnational organizations, their tactics were influenced by considerations grounded in the local political contexts, and embedded into the experiences of colonial injustices.

In addition to participating in events organized by African and Asian women's organizations, the WIDF also attempted to bring the WIDF's activities closer to the countries of the Global South, and to organize its own conferences and other events there.

One such attempt was the organization of the first WIDF bureau meeting outside of Europe, in Jakarta, Indonesia, in 1960. However, as the documents show, not all (European) members of the WIDF's leadership were particularly satisfied with this decision, because the organization of such a meeting demanded changing established patterns, and confronting WIDF leaders with the difficult conditions endured by women living outside Europe. For example, a secret report by the Soviet representative in Berlin, Maria Skotnikova, from 23 March 1960, informed Nina Popova:

> After coming back from Indonesia, Carmen Zanti informed the Secretariat about the meeting of the WIDF's Bureau and its decisions. She stated that in spite of the shortcomings of having a meeting of the Bureau in Indonesia, it is a positive moment for the development of the women's movement in the Asian countries, in particular, for the women's movement in Indonesia. At the same time, the members of the Bureau would be able to better understand the problems of women in Asia and Africa.
>
> (GARF, 4 142, p. 52)

Besides indicating the dissatisfaction of some bureau members with meeting in Indonesia, the passage also implies significant differences in the standards of life and working conditions of the representatives of WIDF in Berlin with those they had to adjust to in Indonesia.

Two years later, in 1962, the WIDF organized one more WIDF bureau meeting outside the European continent – in Bamako (Mali). The bureau sent its special greetings to all African women who were liberated from colonialism (GARF 3 789, p. 1). The WIDF also took an active part in organizing the first conference of Latin American women, which took place in Santiago de Chile in 1959, with the participation of Eugenie Cotton, the WIDF president (ZM 1960 2:2). Due to the victory of the Cuban revolution (January 1959), and the success of the first conference, the WIDF also planned to send a delegation to several Latin American countries, including Cuba, Mexico, Venezuela, and Brazil (letter by Lebedeva to Popova from 8 February 1961; GARF 4 149, p. 13). According to this letter, however, the federation had financial difficulties in practically realizing the plan.

As time progressed, the WIDF came to be increasingly recognized as an important organization that had expertise with respect to women's rights, and, in some cases, its participation in regional seminars and other events in newly independent countries was supported by the local governments. For example, in a letter, the head of the Council of Ministers of Senegal, Mamadou Dia, invited the WIDF to take part in a colloquium on the advancement of women in Africa (organized with support from UNESCO) that was held in Dakar from 20 to 30 November 1962. The invitation stated that Senegal's government was interested in discussing issues concerning the education of women in the post-colonial situation, and promised that the government would take upon itself all the costs connected with the time the WIDF delegation would spend in Senegal (GARF 3 803, p. 200 from 29 August 1962).

Conclusion

The material considered in this chapter supports the findings of previous scholarship (see Pieper Mooney 2013b; McGregor 2016; Armstrong 2016) regarding the importance of the WIDF's early attention to the rights of women in Asia, Africa, and Latin America. However, the first part of this chapter shows that despite the WIDF having defended the rights of women "in the whole world" from its beginning, its main focus was always the social rights of women in colonies and dependent territories, and their right to live without war. Thus, if we use Mohanty's critique of the "First World" feminists who judged economic, religious, and familial structures in the "Third World" by "Western standards" (Mohanty 2003, 40), it is possible to say that the WIDF also had a quite unified vision of the situation of women in countries outside Europe, as well as a singular vision of emancipation for woman (mainly according to the state socialist or "Second World" standards). I will further discuss these standards in the next chapter.

The right of self-determination for the colonial territories was important in the WIDF's vision of the future of the colonial countries. At the same time, however, the women's struggle for independence did not occupy a central place in the WIDF's publications and official documents regarding the protection of women's rights until the late 1950s. This resulted in the federation being unprepared for the mass participation of women in anti-colonial and national movements in Asia and Africa. The archival documents studied here also show that in the late 1950s, the WIDF had to restructure its work in order to give more space to the problems and concerns of women in different countries of the Global South in its main periodical publication, at its official meetings, and in its solidarity work. This adjustment, however, was not always an easy one.

On the basis of the studied documents, it is possible to conclude that in the 1950s–1960s, the WIDF expanded its membership, and broadened its geographical influence, due to the participation of the new women's organizations taking part in the anti-colonial struggle. This expansion, particularly the geographical one, reinforced the political confrontation of the federation with the West. The WIDF's isolation from political participation in transnational bodies following its fierce support of the anti-Western side in the Cold War's "hot" conflict in Korea, and its forced relocation to East Berlin, contributed to its further involvement in the struggles and problems of women in Africa, Latin America, and Asia.

Notes

1 It is important to note here that at the end of the Second World War, the Soviet leadership hoped to obtain some of the former colonies of its war enemies, especially the Italian territories in Northern Africa, as mandate territories from the UN (see Mazov 2008, 9).
2 The letter is addressed to the department of foreign policy of the CPSU, to Comrade Suslov, M.A. The sender was the responsible secretary of the ACSW, Lidiia Petrova.
3 A recently published book by Jessica Franzier on women's anti-war activities during the Vietnam War years gives an impressive picture of women's anti-war activism. However, the WIDF is not discussed in her book (Frazier 2017).
4 After the end of the Japanese occupation of Korea in 1945, its territory became divided between the Soviet occupation zone in the North (where the Communist state of the DPRK was established) and the US occupation zone in the South. The division line was on the 38th parallel.
5 Eslanda Robeson and her husband, Paul Robeson, were Black American civil rights activists and longtime sympathizers of the Soviet Union.
6 Bani Dasgupta (1924–2012) was a member of the Indian Communist Party and one of the leaders of the Federation of Indian Women (https://www.outlookindia.com/newswire/story/cpi-leader-bani-dasgupta-dead/771001).
7 One of the Congo's independence leaders, assassinated in 1961 as result of the post-independence civil war.

5 The state socialist model of women's emancipation as an example to follow for the "Whole World"

As its name implies, the WIDF presented itself not only as an organization for protecting peace, mothers, and children, but also as a democratic organization. In using the definition "democratic", the federation wanted to indicate that, in contrast to its Cold War adversaries, the WIDF campaigned for a broad (democratic) accessibility of rights for all women. It is important to note here that the adjective "democratic" was also widely used by other transnational organizations over which the Soviet Union had a particular influence, as well as in the official names of several countries of the "Eastern Bloc" – such as the German Democratic Republic (GDR) or the Democratic Republic of Vietnam (DRV).[1] Interpretations of "democracy" and "democratic politics" were at the centre of the confrontations of the Cold War period, and women's rights constituted only one of aspects of the cultural Cold War competition, where the state socialist countries insisted on their outstanding achievements in the field of democracy when compared to the "capitalist countries".

Furthermore, previous research has already shown that the image of the Soviet system as the best and the only possible variant of socialism was an important element of Soviet propaganda in many countries, particularly those that had acquired their independence during the 1940s–1960s (see Mazov 2008 on Africa, for example). At the same time, previous research on the Bandung movement, and on independence movement in countries such as Algeria or Indonesia, indicated that, in several cases, the leaders of the independent countries were interested in alternatives to liberal capitalism, and in learning more about state socialism (Lee 2010a; Roman 2011; Byrne 2016; Eslava et al. 2017, 211–212; Kalinovsky 2018; Mark et al. 2020). However, some parts of the "Second World" were more important than others when being presented as showcase examples of successful modernization.

The Soviet "borderlands" – territories that were formerly colonial, and inhabited by a non-Russian/non-Slavic population – from the 1930s onwards had already become a notable showcase object for displaying a positive example of Soviet cultural transformation and the emancipation of women (Gradskova 2018). According to Rasulov, the Soviet borderlands, and in particular the Central Asian republics, were one of the "most important ideological points of reference", with regard to the success of alternative modernizations, for those who met in Bandung in 1955 (Rasulov 2017, 215).

Thus, this chapter focuses specifically on the representations of Soviet achievements with respect to women's rights, and explores how they were encountered by women from Africa, Latin America, and Asia. In the first part of this chapter, I explore how the benefits of state socialist women's emancipation were demonstrated and explained in WIDF documents and publications, with the help of the example of women's emancipation in Soviet Asia. The second part of this chapter is a reflection about some impressions and effects of encountering the state socialist reality, and Soviet women, in practice.

State socialist equality and "women of colour" from the Soviet borderlands

Distribution of positive information regarding the achievements of the state socialist countries, with respect to the involvement of women in industrial work outside of the home and in politics, was seen by the WIDF as a very important aspect of its activity. The WIDF had several methods of distributing its messages: information bulletins in several languages, its own journal, and, at least in the 1960s, radio broadcasting in eight languages – French, English, German, Spanish, Italian, Serbian, Greek, and Swedish (ZM 1963 1, 10). As opposed to the liberal feminists' claim on the need to do away with the patriarchy around the world, the WIDF's critique of the problems of women's and children's rights in capitalist countries implied that women who lived in the "socialist countries" were in a much better situation, and already enjoyed most of the rights. Thus, a positive image of the Soviet Union and other state socialist countries was an important part of the information transmitted through WIDF's different channels, and was experienced by some female activists who were able to visit the Soviet Union or other countries of the "Eastern Bloc".

The WIDF on the happy lives of women in "people's democracies" and Soviet republics

As I already noted in Chapter 2, the Bolsheviks implemented important reforms in the realm of women's status in the first few years after the 1917 revolution (Engel 2004). However, during the Stalinist period, some of these new rights were taken away – abortion, for example, was banned between 1936 and 1956, and divorce was made difficult to obtain during the same period. As for equality in work, towards the end of the USSR's existence, women were represented in equal proportion among university students and in the workforce, but their salaries were still lower than those of men. This was also connected to the infamous double burden – until the end of state socialism, women in the Soviet Union and, to a lesser or greater degree, in all the countries of the "Eastern Bloc", had a double responsibility – taking care of home and children and working in the state economy (Engel 2004, see also Asztalos Morell & Gradskova 2018, 3–14). Thus, combining care duties with work outside of the home often influenced their professional choices, and hindered their promotion. The situation was different from country to country, for example, according to Uzbek researchers, the changes sponsored by Moscow in Central Asia were quite limited. While most women were fully involved in work outside of home by the 1940s, family life continued to be patriarchal throughout the entire Soviet era (Tokhtakhodzhaeva et al., 2002, 9). Shortcomings of the state socialist emancipation, in most cases, could not be discussed publicly within the state socialist countries without falling under the danger of being accused of anti-socialist and anti-Soviet activity.

The WIDF's main periodical publication, *Women of the Whole World*, followed the same uncritical approach when describing the situation of women in the state socialist countries as that offered by the media inside the bloc; women were mainly shown as enjoying their equal position in society. This message was communicated through different forms, reports on important WIDF events taking place in one or another state socialist country, descriptions of changes in women's living and working conditions in one or another Soviet region, accompanied by pictures of happy and smiling local women, as well as interviews with politicians, scientists, and activists from the "people's democracies". Letters from female visitors sharing their impressions after travelling to the Soviet Union and Eastern Europe were also published. In many cases, publications about the achievements of women under state socialism were written by reporters from countries outside of the Soviet Bloc; this was designed to encourage foreign readers to trust that the pro-Soviet picture of women's lives was accurate. While an analysis of all these representations can constitute a study of its own, I will only discuss several examples of this material, with a focus on the representations' main themes and rhetoric.

One of the first issues of the WIDF's periodical publication available to me is issue 2 from 1953. This issue of *Zhenshchiny mira* was published soon after the death of Stalin, and dedicated several pages to commemorating him (ZM 1953, 2: 3–4). In particular, the journal quoted Stalin speaking about the possibility of avoiding a war with the USA, thereby demonstrating the peaceful character of Soviet foreign policy contributing to women's peaceful lives (ZM 1953, 2: 3–4). The next issue from the same year contained articles by Hilda Neiman, a member of the Association of Jurists-Democrats, stating that women jurists in the Soviet Union and the other people's democracies often occupy very high positions (ZM 1953, 3: 8). The same issue also published an article on China with the optimistic title "Everyday our life is becoming better and richer" (ZM 1953, 3: 10).

Publications from after the beginning of de-Stalinization mainly continue to show the achievements of state socialism with regard to women's rights. For example, issue 7–8 from 1958 was dedicated principally to the

WIDF's Vienna congress, and published the speech made at the congress by the Soviet vice-president of the WIDF, Nina Popova. Popova stressed that "Soviet women are proud to be members of the WIDF", and that women of all professions supported the decisions of the WIDF's congress in mass meetings (ZM 1958, 7–8: 6). Thus, Popova wanted to demonstrate the political activism of Soviet women, and their interest in the federation. The journal also published the words of another guest at the same congress – Alicia Musialova, the head of the League of Polish Women. Musialova stressed the importance of supporting formal equality through social reforms: "it is not enough to give women equality guaranteed by Constitution and protection of the State", as realization in practice requires further efforts (WWW 1958, 7–8: 7). Even though the quote from her speech was left very short, it was possible for the reader to understand that Poland was on the way towards the practical achievement of equality.

During the late 1950s, the period of de-Stalinization and détente, the WIDF's periodical publication tried to attract a higher female readership and, as written in earlier chapters, there were significant changes in both the format and content of the journal. For example, the journal introduced fashion pages, while some issues even included culinary recipes. At the same time, the journal never stopped publishing materials that allowed its international readers to learn about specific positive experiences of women's lives in the state socialist countries. Thus, issue 9 from 1958 discussed the work of the Fashion Congress in Bucharest, and showed examples of fashion garments for women produced by designers from Czechoslovakia, Poland, Romania, and other Eastern European countries (ZM 1958, 9 :28–29). Issue 2 from 1959 published a long article about a Kyrgyz woman, Kerimbyubyu Shopokova, who was a delegate at the 11th CPSU Congress, and a member of the Supreme Soviet.[2] Titled "Two gold stars", the article presented Shopokova as a person of humble origin coming from a peasant family in the mountain region of Kyrgyzstan, who was also the widow of a Second World War hero, as her husband had died heroically defending Moscow. In spite of this tragedy, Shopokova was shown in the article as an active and successful woman; she worked planting sugar beets, and was an exceptionally good worker. Shopokova also took part in political life, and was sent to represent Kyrgyzstan in the Soviet governing bodies in Moscow (ZM 1959, 2: 9–11). In the same year, the journal published several other articles describing the happy lives of women and children in the state socialist countries. Two of them, by Maria Gallo, were dedicated to the Soviet Union: one described the leisure centre for children – the Palace of Pioneers in Leningrad (ZM 1959, 8), while the second one described the transformation of Uzbekistan (ZM 1959 12: 18–20).

Many articles dedicated to the Soviet Union and the other state socialist countries compared the current achievements of women with the situation that existed in one or another particular region/country before the beginning of the socialist transformations. For example, issue 8 from 1965 published an article by Musa Selimkhanov about Baku, the capital of Soviet

Azerbaijan. Describing a modern and comfortable city, the author stressed that the life of the Azeri woman changed after the 1917 revolution, and that these changes required a lot of effort (ZM 1965 8: 22–23). An article signed by Leyla, "I have seen, I have heard, I have learnt", which was published by the WIDF's journal in 1963, informed readers about a seminar dedicated to the education of women in Africa that was held in Tashkent in 1963. The article's author demonstrated her knowledge of Russian literature by beginning her text with a reference to a nineteenth-century Russian writer, Saltykov-Shchedrin, describing Tashkent as a place where there were no libraries or educational centres. The author continued by contrasting the "old" and the "new" Tashkent:

> The same town less than half a century after the October revolution has become one of the largest industrial and scientific centres of the Soviet Union.
> (WWW, 1963 1: 9)

After the Soviet–China split in the early 1960s, the WIDF journal published much less material about China. In the 1960s–1980s, it was the Eastern European and other countries that were assumed to follow the socialist direction were used as examples of the positive transformation of women's lives, and of women gaining access to their rights. Issue 3 from 1965 published an article by Renata Urban about the promotion of women in the GDR (ZM 1965 3:16–17). In a 1981 journal issue, Elena Lagadinova discussed how state socialism had led to great changes in the status of women in Bulgaria (ZM, 1981, 4: 24–26). Finally, a number of articles on countries outside Europe that were considered to be "building socialism" were also published. For example, issue 1 from 1966 was specifically dedicated to women's rights, and published graphical material about the achievements of women's rights in the DRV under the title: "The numbers that speak for themselves" (ZM 1966 1: 30–33).

The ideas expressed in the WIDF journal were repeated in many other WIDF materials. For example, a package aimed for distribution to participants of the commission number 3 (dedicated to development) at the 1975 WIDF World Congress in Berlin stated:

> the experiences of the socialist countries show that constitutional principles can become reality; men and women have the right and indeed the duty to participate in the economic, political, social and cultural life of their countries irrespective of sex, nationality, race, religion and social class. An expression of this is the large proportion of women elected to government.
> (WIDF documents in IISH, p. 14)

The positive experience of the state socialist countries in dealing with women's rights was often also demonstrated during international conferences and seminars organized by the WIDF; these conferences almost always included the participation of the Soviet representatives and also, in several cases, representatives from other countries of the "Eastern Bloc". The archival materials show, for example, that the Soviet and Cuban experiences in the spheres of education and the elimination of illiteracy were of particular interest to governments and women's organizations from Africa and Asia in the 1960s. The Soviet delegation shared their experience of organizing women's education in the USSR at the January 1961 conference of women of Asia and Africa in Cairo (GARF 3 402, pp. 209–210), while the Cuban delegation presented its experience of eliminating illiteracy at the 1962 colloquium for the education and promotion of women in Dakar, Senegal (*ZM* 1963 3: 22–24).

However, the most powerful presentations of the achievement of the Soviet republics and the "Second World" in the field of women's rights were probably given through inviting women from different countries to visit the state socialist countries and observe everything on the spot. Documents from the earlier years of the WIDF show that trips to the Soviet Union and other "Eastern Bloc" countries were seen by their organizers (the CSW was one of them) as a means of convincing visitors of the political, economic, and social benefits of state socialism. The trips organized by the CSW were thus quite close in their aims to those described by David-Fox for intellectual visitors from the "West" to the Soviet Union in the 1920s–1930s (David-Fox 2012). The visitors were expected to observe the part of Soviet reality that was carefully chosen for them, and to make a dutiful report of the positive image when they returned home.

For example, documents from the file on the ASWC's contacts with women in Italy in the 1950s that I discussed in Chapter 2 indicate that the Italian women visiting the USSR were expected to participate in different public events and publish articles and pamphlets praising Soviet achievements. Thus, a short report on the trip made by Renata Antonicelli, a female activist from Turin, to the Soviet Union in 1952, which was preserved in the Soviet archive, stated that after her trip she actively worked in the Soviet–Russian friendship society, and that she enjoyed a lot of respect in her circle (GARF 2 1773, p. 49; from 18 February 1956). Antonicelli obviously fulfilled her hosts' expectations. At the same time, another Italian participant in a similar trip, the writer Anna Maria Orteze, received a negative evaluation from the ACSW; according to a letter by an ACSW employee, Blinova, to Maria and Ema Cercero in Italy, after her return, Orteze published a book and newspaper article about her experience, and both were critical of the Soviet Union (GARF 2 1773, p. 53). Blinova stated further that the ACSW did not like Orteze's article: "her story is not objective, and facts and episodes only partly correspond to reality. It contains a lot of fantasies and sick imagination".[3] It is interesting that Blinova partly attributed Orteze's lack of objectivity to her bad tourist habits; according to her, Orteze, "who claimed to be exhausted and afraid of flying, did not see that much of our country" (GARF 2 1773, p. 57). Thus, it is possible to say that visitors' critical comments, or their interest in aspects of Soviet life that were not included in the visit's programme, were not welcomed.

As the archival materials show, the ACSW not only invited foreign women-activists to visit the USSR on their own, but also used the WIDF's congresses, and other WIDF events in Europe, to invite women's delegations to visit the Soviet Union. For example, a classified letter from Nina Popova sent to V.G. Grigorian (Molotov's administrator in the CPSU Committee on Foreign Affairs) in 1952 communicated that the Union of Australian Women asked about the possibility of visiting the Soviet Union in connection with the conference on the protection of children in Vienna organized by the WIDF (RGASPI 17 137 818, 49–50, letter from 22 March 1952). The ACSW further suggested sending the Australian delegation to Leningrad and Tbilisi, and providing their food and accommodation in the "Intourist" hotel. Letters with similar requests were also sent by Popova regarding delegations from China (RGASPI 17 137 818, 56), and from Latin America (representatives from Panama, Argentina and Chile – RGASPI 18 137 818, 65). Thus, it is possible to say that with the help of the WIDF, the Soviet Union received more chances to showcase the Soviet experiment (David-Fox 2012) to new groups of visitors in the middle of the acute period of the Cold War.

During Khrushchev's Thaw, there was an increase in the number of invitations from the WIDF for foreign guests to come to the Soviet Union. This often occurred at conferences and seminars the WIDF organized for women from the Global South on Soviet territory. The usual destinations for the guided tours of women from foreign countries included visits to factories and meeting female workers, as well as visits to schools, libraries, and kindergartens. For example, the detailed programme of a Cuban women's delegation to the USSR in 1965 shows that three representatives of the Federation of Cuban Women (Federacion de Mujeres Cubanas, hereafter FMC) spent about three weeks in the Soviet Union and visited Moscow, Leningrad, Kyiv, Crimea, and Volgograd (GARF 3 1468, p. 1). The programme combined cultural tourism – circuses, theatres, art galleries, city tours – with meeting representatives of women's councils (*zhensovet*) at a car plant in Moscow, female activists from the city of Yalta, and visiting a nursery in Leningrad (GARF 3 1468, pp. 1–4).

In some cases, visits of foreign guests could also include institutions that, as a rule, were not object for showcasing. For example, one of the archived files from the period of de-Stalinization (1956) described such a visit – to the female section of one of Moscow's prisons (GARF 2 1678 from 21 September 1956). The report stated that the participants of the international seminar on the "Equality of the rights of women in the USSR" visited Butyrskaia prison in Moscow. The delegation included Anastasia Valkova, observer of the UN commission on women from Bulgaria, Zhanna Fucar from the Belgian member of the Association of Women-Lawyers, Eugenie Rzapantirana from the Society for Improvement of the Situation of Prisoners from Ceylon, and several women from Iraq, the UK, and Syria. According to the archived documents, the guests had the opportunity to visit the prison's facilities and ask several questions to both the administration and the prisoners. The questions the visitors asked included questions about food, the physical workload that female prisoners perform, and their remuneration. The answers by the administration informed the visitors that the female prisoners constitute only a small percentage of the inmates, and that the prisoners are delivered everything they need by the state, that they also have access to books if they want to study, and that they can use the bath-house and hospital. The female inmates, according to the report, did not express any complaints, and were ready to explain to the guests their reasons for being sentenced (small theft, not coming to work for three months and then refusing to work in the detention centre – GARF 2 1678). Thus, the way this visit – occurring at a time when the GULAG system was not yet fully dismantled – was organized and documented can probably help us imagine how the visits of female guests were usually structured, and what part of the Soviet reality the guests were expected to see.

Soviet Central Asia as an example of women's emancipation

In the first part of this chapter, I showed that the showcasing of Soviet achievements with regard to women's emancipation and rights included a large variety of geographical locations, and women of different ethnic groups. Therefore, I decided to dedicate this section to a closer exploration of these representations, using the example of Central Asia in order to better explore the role of the Soviet borderlands in the WIDF's work with women from the Global South.

The concept of the borderlands in connection to the former Soviet space was used by Madina Tlostanova, who defined them as regions that were colonized by the Russian empire and populated by non-Slavic and non-Orthodox people, in other words, not belonging to the "core" population of the Soviet state (2010). As I wrote in the introduction, the term "women of colour" first appeared in critical Black studies, and was influenced by postcolonial thinking about non-White subjects of feminism (hooks 1989; see also Anzaldúa 1991). I think that the use of this concept contributes to an understanding of the specific embodied experiences and political in-betweenness of women from different national autonomies in the Soviet Union. As I show elsewhere, non-Slavic/non-Russian women were marginalized by the Soviet narrative of bringing culture and emancipation to the "backward women from the periphery" (see Gradskova 2018), these women were also often "othered" on the basis of their ethnicity and looks and, thus, could be addressed as the Soviet "women of colour". The application of this concept to Soviet history also helps make visible the specific marginalization of those women who did not belong to the Russian/Slavic majority, as well as to establish their alleged similarities vis-à-vis the (White) majority of the Soviet women – in spite of differences in their ethnicity and religion.

The women from the Soviet republics to the East and South of Moscow were important in representing Soviet achievements and, in particular, for women from Africa and Asia, from quite an early time. The WIDF documents already indicated the importance of the participation of women from "Soviet Asia" when planning the first Asian women's conference in 1949 (GARF 1 99). Several high-ranking female representatives of the Soviet Central Asian republics, for example, a minister of the Turkmen Soviet Republic, Asia Atanapesova, were present in Beijing. It was at this first Asian women's conference, organized by the WIDF, where the special importance of Soviet Asia for other Asian and colonized women in other countries was stated by the conference hosts. In her speech at the conference, the Chinese representative Den In Chao said:

> We know that the Asian republics of the Soviet Union before the October Revolution were colonies of Tsarist Russia, and in that time there was the same oppression, the same cultural backwardness, the same poverty and economic backwardness as in India today. The life of a woman was even more hard. Women [in the territory of today's Soviet Asia] not only did not have any rights but were totally illiterate. They were slaves and only slaves.
>
> (GARF 1 130, p. 55)[4]

Hence, by describing the achievements and advancement of women in the Central Asian republics, and inviting visitors from the newly independent states or dependent territories of Asia and Africa there, the Soviet authorities and the WIDF leaders expected them to learn about the possibilities of economic development and the improvement of women's status in those formerly "backward" parts of the country. As I showed above, as early as the early 1950s, several foreign delegations visiting the Soviet Union in cooperation with the WIDF were invited to spend time in different parts of the Soviet Union, and the delegations from China and Latin America taking part in the Vienna conference were invited to visit the non-Russian parts of the Soviet Union (RGASPI 17 137 818, p. 56, p. 65). However, it was the Central Asian republics that became particularly central to the Soviet discourse of "overcoming backwardness" and thus, the chosen destination for delegations from the Global South.

The centrality of Central Asia in Soviet showcasing practices can be attributed to a variety of factors, including the idea of Muslim woman being more "enslaved" compared to other national minority women (Gradskova 2018), and taking into consideration the adherence of many women in Asia and Africa to Islam. Also, the special role of Tashkent – as Soviet Asia's most modern city – became important in the late 1960s.[5] Tashkent became a place where many conferences, festivals and other cultural events for Asian and "Third World" intellectuals[6] were held, and it also became the place where the seminar on education for the women of Africa was organized by the WIDF in 1962.

The archive in Moscow preserved the protocols of this seminar from 9 to 15 September 1962. Alongside the main discussions in Tashkent, the seminar included trips to other Central Asian republics, and the final meeting in Moscow. The seminar was prepared in cooperation with UNESCO, and its representative, Ruth Lasarus, took part in the event. High-level Uzbek female representatives of the Soviet *nomenklatura* were invited to meet the foreign guests, and to show Uzbekistan's achievements. For example, Shakurova, the head of Uzbekistan's committee of friendship with foreign countries and Uzbekistan's Department of the Soviet Society for Friendship with the People of Africa, proudly presented all the achievements of Soviet politics in Central Asia:

> Women of Uzbekistan were happy to tell their friends about their life. They told you that in Uzbekistan, where before the revolution the population was totally illiterate, there is a wide network of schools and professional educational institutions and research centres and that we have our national professional cadres now. [...] You could see how the problem of education for women is solved in Uzbekistan and what results we have. You could also see that women in Uzbekistan work successfully in all the spheres of the economy. We will be happy if your visit was useful for you, dear friends.
>
> (GARF 3 776, p. 27)

As I already said, women from Central Asia holding high-level positions were often shown in publications dedicated to the Soviet Union in the WIDF journal. For example, the Kyrgyz woman delegate of the communist party congress, Shopokova, featured in the 1959 article, expressed her pride and happiness in being a Soviet woman:

> Where could you find a similar country where I could work like this and also take part in governing the state? We, the Soviet women, have equal rights with men, and not only on paper.
>
> (ZM 1959 2: 11)

The active use of the image of Central Asia as a modern and developed region, and of the images of highly-positioned Central Asian women, also continued later on. For example, the issue dedicated to the 60th anniversary of the Bolshevik revolution in 1977 contained an article by Wanda Tycner, a journalist from Poland, called "The new life began in October" – dedicated to the "new life" of the Uzbek women. At the heart of the article are several interviews with Uzbek women who had achieved high-ranking positions in the Soviet hierarchy. One of them is Sadykova, the minister of Social Welfare in Uzbekistan. With the help of the events of her own life, Sadykova shows the enormous changes that happened in the lives of Uzbek woman over several decades: born in 1914, Sadykova attended the Muslim school for girls and had to wear whole-body-covering clothes. She also confessed that girls in the "old life" were often forced into early marriages – sometimes as young as 9. Another person interviewed, a writer and the editor of an Uzbek-language women's magazine, *Saadat*, told readers the story of the Bolshevik attack on the subordination of women and about the unveiling campaign – *hujum*. Although in recent years the *hujum* campaign has provoked a lot of interest and criticism from researchers, as it resulted in multiple women dying after being attacked by the conservative opposition (see Northrop 2004; Kamp 2006), the journal presented this campaign as a glorious achievement – a "heroic and special period". According to the interviewee, the *hujum* was a rather peaceful campaign: "I remember how, in my family, my brothers liberated their wives in dignity and solemnity by removing the *paranja* ans *chachvon* themselves" (WWW 1977, 3:18–20).

However, the most crucial method of building an attractive image of state socialism through demonstrating the advancement of women in the Soviet Asian borderlands was probably the nomination of one of the "new Uzbek women", Zuhra (Zahra) Rahimbabaeva, as the Soviet representative to the WIDF Secretariat in Berlin in the late 1960s, in the midst of decolonization in the Global South. Born in Uzbekistan in 1923, Rahimbabaeva defended her dissertation on the history of the Soviet emancipation of women in Uzbekistan and its importance for women of other countries in the East in 1954, and was the author of several publications in Russian that praised Soviet policies in Central Asia. For example, in her book published in 1949 – *Women of Uzbekistan on the way to Communism* – Rahimbabaeva stated that the "happiness of the Uzbek woman is unlimited":

> the Great October has given her equal rights with men in all the spheres of economic, state, and cultural life, it waked up her talents and her creativity that had to sleep for centuries before that. Together with her Russian sisters and with women of all the Soviet nations, she started to work for the new life.
>
> (Rahimbabaeva 1949, 3)

During her career, Rahimbabaeva occupied important positions in the CPSU and government structures of Uzbekistan; at various times, she was the head of the Department of the Central Committee of the Communist Party of Uzbekistan, vice-minister, and then the minister, of culture of the Uzbek Soviet Republic.

Rahimbabaeva's work in Berlin was similar to the work of many other Soviet employees whom I mentioned in this book (Ivanova, Goroshkova, Titova, etc.): taking part in meetings, following the instructions from Moscow and reporting on events and people in the Secretariat. However, it is possible to suppose that Rahimbabaeva's presence in the Secretariat had a rather special and unique effect, as she could be seen as an embodiment of the Soviet woman from the borderlands, a non-white woman who was educated and emancipated and, who, obviously thanks to the Soviet policies of women's rights, could go so far as to represent all Soviet women in the WIDF Secretariat. Thus, her image not only could help oppose the "Chinese propaganda" (as it was described in the Soviet report) claiming Soviet women were not able to understand African women because they were white and European (see Chapter 4), but she could also inspire many women from the Global South to admire the achievements of the Soviet Union and the advancement of its women from the former borderlands.

Rahimbabaeva was one of the organizers of the important WIDF seminar on overcoming illiteracy in Africa and Asia that was held in Khartoum in 1970. As the Soviet representative at the Secretariat, Rahimbabaeva dealt with the financial aspects of the seminar, and she authored a detailed financial report to Moscow regarding travel expenses for the seminar participants (GARF 3 2122, pp. 103–107). However, she also was one of the keynote speakers at the seminar, in her pages-long presentation at Khartoum, Rahimbabaeva shared her knowledge of the history of women's emancipation in Uzbekistan, defended the importance of *hujum*, and proudly stated the achievements of the Soviet educational system (GARF 3 2421, pp. 29–44). For example, she stressed that in Soviet Uzbekistan, "there are many times more students for every 10,000 people than in France, Italy, and West Germany" (GARF 3 2421, p. 30). Rachimbabaeva also described in detail the steps on the way to these achievements; the growth of separate women's schools by 250% from 1926 to 1928, then the *hujum* in 1927, and the further steps towards mandatory primary education in the 1930s (GARF 3 2421, pp. 33–34). Instead of the usual Soviet way of addressing other members of the federation as "friends" (*podrugi*), in her speech in Khartoum, Rahimbabaeva addressed her audience – mainly African women – as "dear sisters" (GARF 3 2124, p. 44). It is possible to suppose that, though not only because of Rahimbabaeva's addressing her audience as "sisters", but a combination of this way of addressing them along with her being a Soviet women of colour made her audience listen the WIDF ideas as voiced by her with more attention, and more sympathetic to them.

Encountering state socialism and its women – impressions, personal connections, and memories

While the Soviet Union and other countries of the "Eastern Bloc" widely distributed information about the benefits of the Soviet model of women's emancipation and showcased the achievements of state socialism at all events organized on its territory, it is more difficult to explore the impression that guests received from such demonstrations. Could they see contradictions in these positive images? How well were they convinced of the benefits of the state socialist system for women? While this book cannot answer all these questions, in this subchapter, I want to analyse several examples of how the Soviet achievements were approached, evaluated, and used by the participants of the meetings with women from the "Eastern Bloc", and by the guests of the events organized by the WIDF.

Previous scholarship on Latin American participants in the WIDF has already shown that trips to the socialist countries were seen in positive terms by many women. In her chapter dedicated to women in the Uruguayan communist party, published in the book *Queridas Camaradas*, Ana Laura de Giorgi showed that the Soviet model of women's emancipation was an important reference point for the periodical publication of the Uruguayan women's organization *Nosotras* in the late 1940s–early 1950s (Giorgi 2017, 221). Members of the Uruguayan organization attending the WIDF's 1953 Congress in Copenhagen also took a trip through the USSR after the end of the conference; one of heads of the delegation, Grecia Campistrus, published an article after her return, describing the Soviet Union as "an authentic democracy" where men and women have equal rights and good living conditions (Giorgi 2017, 226). Laura Bier, in her article on a women's magazine in Egypt during the 1950s–1960s, wrote that the magazine informed Egyptian women about the progress of women's rights in different countries, including reports on travels to the Soviet republics, Uzbekistan and Azerbaijan, showing the progress of women together with their involvement in the preservation of the national culture and traditions (Bier 2010, 162). Ghodsee, in her recently published book, demonstrates that Zambian women who attended forty-day-long summer courses for women, organized by the Bulgarian women's organization with the support of the WIDF in 1980, were also very impressed by the success of socialism and the progress of Bulgarian women (Ghodsee 2018, 190–191).

On the other hand, research on international students in the USSR (Matusevich 2012; Katsakioris 2019) and workers in the GDR (Rabenschlag 2014) suggests that, as opposed to short visits to the state socialist countries, students, workers and long-term visitors from the Global South frequently encountered a lack of understanding, and even hostility and racism. Considering the fact that during the 1960s–1980s, the CSW, for example, was offering several fellowships for female students from the Global South to study in Soviet universities (GARF 3 1396, p. 32), it is possible to understand that different kinds of visitors connected to the WIDF could get rather different impressions.

The experiences of female visitors to the state socialist countries differ widely, depending on the sources available to me. Travel accounts published in the WIDF's journal mainly follow the logic of showcasing socialist achievements, while the archival materials and memories suggest a more complicated picture. All of these documents, however, are quite contradictory, and have many limitations, not least due to the practices of censorship and self-censorship connected to all visits of "Soviet friends" (see, e.g., the book by Bechmann Pedersen & Noack on Cold War travel 2019). When thinking about the self-censorship of the members of the WIDF, it is possible to suppose that even the authors of the personal letters found in the archive, and not aimed for publication, had, most probably, important motives for presenting a mainly positive side of their experiences, rather than a negative one. Reasons for this could include, for example, hope for future collaboration with Soviet and East European women, dependence on financial support from the WIDF for future trips, or just politeness and gratitude towards the hosts. Finally, memory accounts, even those written in a period after active participation in the organization, and after 1989, could also be influenced and guided by a set of different contexts and feelings.

As I already shown in Chapter 2, some visitors to the Soviet Union, including those who were considered to be not only "fellow travellers", but also co-workers and fellow members of the WIDF's leadership, experienced their travel to the state socialist countries in a way opposed to what was expected by the organizers. Lilly Wächter, a German activist and Soviet sympathizer, who spent some time in Moscow with the aim of receiving medical treatment in the exclusive party hospital, became convinced that Stalin was guilty of multiple crimes and that there was social inequality in the Soviet Union. She got these ideas through conversations with another patient in the same hospital, an "old communist", as she carefully presented her in her letter (see Chapter 2). However, such a revelation could be seen as a unique case, rather than as a common way of experiencing the Soviet Union. Still, the example of the Italian woman Orteze (see above) shows that some visitors did not like the Soviet reality. After her trip in 1952, Orteze would go on to publish a book that was critical of the Soviet Union.

The letters of, and interviews with, the African and Asian visitors that were published in the WIDF's journal in the 1950s–1960s mainly demonstrate an admiration of the Soviet educational and maternity care system, as well as of Soviet gender equality, and are practically free of any criticism. A letter from a Cameroonian female leader, Marthe Ouandié,[7] published in issue 11 of the WIDF's journal from 1958, is a good example of such a publication:

> It was very interesting for me to visit factories, schools, maternity welfare clinics, the museums, the historical places and the mausoleum where the founders of the USSR are resting, as well as the villages where they were born. I very much like the Russian and Georgian cooking.
> (*WWW* 1958, 11: 21)

The article authored by Leyla, dedicated to the Tashkent seminar on education for African women in 1962, is in a similar style. She described the women of Soviet Uzbekistan, with a particular focus on their achievements in education, culture, and political participation. For example, she wrote about her meeting with one of the Soviet Uzbek women:

> [the president of the Uzbek republic] The charming and intelligent, Yadgar Nasriddinova, meting the delegates said: "hundreds of kilometres separate us from you but one goal unites us all: the preservation of peace in the whole world".
> (*WWW* 1963 1: 13)

Leyla seemed also to be fascinated that the taxi driver in Tashkent spoke good English, proudly stating at the same time that it was young Uzbek women who were his English teachers (ZM 1963 1: 9–13).

Some letters from women of the Global South found in the archival files are similar to the published ones, in terms of their acceptance of Soviet discourses. For example, a letter from an Indian activist, Gita Banerjee, to Nadezhda Parfenova from the ACSW, written in 1952, starts by expressing gratitude to Parfenova for her letter, and for the magazine of the Committee of Soviet Women – *The Soviet Woman* (RGASPI 17 137 816, 187). Banerjee further described her difficulties in organizing work among women in India, considering that "almost 100% of them are illiterate". As an example of her activity, Banerjee described the "week of protection of peace in Asia" that was inspired by the WIDF, and included an exhibition about people's lives in the Soviet Union and China:

> You would be very happy to see how much hope was in the eyes of workers when I was telling them about your five-years plan, and about all the success that the socialist state has. The pictures and magazines sent by your Committee were a big help to us. We also plan to create a magazine for middle-class women; thus, the WIDF's ideas can be distributed by our own democratic press.
> (RGASPI 17 137 816, 189, letter in translation to Russian)

A letter from another Indian female activist, Kapida Khandwala from Bombay, written a decade later, in 1962, described her visit to the Soviet Union and the GDR after Khandwala took part in a meeting of the WIDF council in Budapest. Khandwala proudly informed the CSW that after her return to India, she spoke at 17 meetings and in front of more than 3000 people. In order to support her report, the author sent copies of articles she wrote about the WIDF, and about her visit to a Moscow factory, the Moscow Children's hospital, and the Pioneer Palace. At the end of her letter, Khandwala stated that she was trying to organize a women's committee in Bombay (GARF 3 803, p. 60, 23 May 1962).

The already-mentioned protocols of the seminar on education of women in Africa held in Tashkent that same year list the presentations of many African guests. It seems that in this case their attention was particularly focused on differences between the realities of their home countries in (partly still colonial) Africa and the achievements of the Central Asian republics and their women. Participants from the African countries mainly voiced the problems that women there met with on the way to getting an education, and the legacy of colonialism was mentioned as one of the biggest hindrances. For example, the representative from Cameroon said that under colonial rule, woman was seen as a "working machine" and as a "machine that produces children" (GARF 3 776, p. 4). Manhala Lestela, from Bastawland in South Africa, mentioned that in spite of the level of women's education in her country being one of the highest in Africa, it is still too low; furthermore, her country remained a colony and women's organizations could not be established there due to the colonial legislation (GARF 3 776, pp. 51–52). These, along with similar experiences and assumptions, made the participants of the seminar impressed by the women and educational institutions of Tashkent. Each of the participants of the seminar also had the chance to visit another Central Asian republic, and the meetings after the trip showed that the participants were very satisfied. Ramantulayte Bagura from Guinea, for example, said that during her trip to Tajikistan, the seminar participants could visit libraries and the medical university in Dushanbe. It was there that she noted "that half of the students there were young women" (GARF 3 776, pp. 48–50). This was very different from her home country, and thus, probably, the most important item in her "gaze" at Soviet reality during her short visit to Tajikistan.

As for published memoir accounts, unfortunately, most active members of the federation did not leave memoirs, while other memoirs were not accessible to me due to problems of availability or language. Yet I would like to include a few words about how the state socialist countries and their women were presented in two memoir accounts published after 1991. The first author, Fanny Edelman, the WIDF general secretary during the 1970s, and a member of the Argentinean Communist Party leadership, visited the Soviet Union and other countries of the Eastern Bloc many times, beginning in the 1950s. In her book, she mainly follows the discourse of the official publications of the federation, but she pays special attention to the female leaders and activists. For example, in her description of the congress of mothers in Lausanne, Edelman stressed that everybody were moved by the mother of Zoya Kosmodemianskaia, the Soviet Second World War heroine.[8] After losing both of her children in the war, the only thing that was left for her was to love others' children (Edelman 1996, 142).

Edelman's excitement regarding the achievements of the Soviet Union and GDR (1996, 234–235), with the state socialist welfare system and women's rights, is not problematized and seems to be naturally included in her position as a communist and women's rights activist. Remembering her multiple visits to the Soviet Union in the 1970s, Edelman specifically stressed the modesty of Valentina Tereshkova, the world-famous female cosmonaut and the leader of the CSW (Edelman 1996, 125).[9] Describing seven years of her life in the East Berlin as a WIDF general secretary, Edelman does not mention any problems or contradictions in East German society, nor does she give an exact description of the conditions of her life there. Indeed, her story moves easily from the picturesque streets of Berlin's "working class district" to description of museums and, then, to the equality of women's rights that were realized in practice in the GDR (1996, 234–235).

The memoirs of the Cameroonian activist Marthe Moumié (2006) are mainly dedicated to the anti-colonial struggle in her country, and to her husband, murdered during this struggle in 1960, in Geneva. Moumié gave only a brief account of her participation in the trip to the GDR and Czechoslovakia in 1957 (organized by the Asian and African People's Solidarity

Organization) and the conference organized by women from the GDR in 1959.[10] It was then when she visited the Second World War memorials and genocide camps (Moumié 2006, 119). However, Moumié wrote little about her encounters with ordinary women in any of the countries she visited. She did, however, notice the differences between East and West Berlin; when, during this trip, the Cameroonian women arrived in West Berlin "we felt ourselves as foreigners from the East" (Moumié 2006, 119).

Thus, it is possible to say that, unlike the memoirs of Edelman, a confirmed friend of Moscow, Moumié does not seem to give special importance to her meeting with state socialist reality, and nor does she provide details of her meetings with Soviet or East German women. The most emotional pages of her memoirs instead were dedicated to the leaders of the Global South, like Ho Chi Minh (Moumié 2006, 123) or Algerian president Ahmed Ben Bela. It is easy to suppose that there were many other women from Asia, Africa, and Latin America for whom a trip to the European countries of the "Eastern Bloc" did not constitute a particularly memorable experience outside of the ordinary tourist one.

However, the Moscow archive also preserved some individual letters that were different from those reporting accomplishments, or expressing gratitude for an interesting (and free) trip through one of the state socialist countries. These were personal letters written by WIDF collaborators to their colleagues and friends in the state socialist countries. One such letter, written by the Chilean representative to the Secretariat in Berlin, Emperatriz Villaroel, was sent to one of the employees of the CSW, Liudmila Balakhovskaia. The letter was signed informally, by only the first name, Emperatriz.[11] The author of the letter, a member of the Chilean Communist party, described her experience of moving to Berlin in order to work at the WIDF Secretariat in early 1970. The letter suggests that Emperatriz was very happy with her life in Berlin, wrote about her satisfaction with her work and good health, but that she was suffering from missing her country, her female colleagues and friends, and her partner back in Chile. At the same time, her work at the federation was very different from how she used to work in Chile; it involved a lot of new forms and methods of work, many different languages, and people of different races (GARF 3 2440, pp. 108–109).

The letter suggests that representatives of Latin American, African, and Asian countries coming to work at the WIDF Secretariat were guaranteed, according to GDR measures, a relatively high level of living standards, and social security protection. Emperatriz wrote that she had started learning German, and had the possibility of bringing two of her adolescent sons to the GDR. Further, she happily wrote that her sons already started their education in Germany, and that after three months of intensive language courses in Dresden, they could start a preparatory programme for technical education – "what we need most in our underdeveloped country".

In her letter to her Soviet colleague, on several occasions Villaroel expresses her admiration of the Soviet people, showing examples of heroism in the struggle against imperialist domination in Latin America, and ended her letter confirming that she is a Chilean woman who can appreciate the "daughters of Lenin". Together with these elevated political utterances, and a short discussion on the tense situation in Chile in connection with the general elections, the author expressed a lot of warmth and friendly care for her addressee. Villaroel invited Liudmila, her daughter Tania, and their relatives to visit her in Berlin, and to stay in her apartment; she also promised to show them the city. Villaroel also warmly writes about Liudmila's daughter, and promises to send her wool that she brought from Chile in order to knit a dress for Tatiana (or even to knit a dress out of it herself) (GARF 3 2440, pp. 108–109).

The letter is interesting, not only because it helps us understand how the members and collaborators of the Secretariat from different countries felt in Berlin, what the arrangements for their families were, and what difficulties they encountered, but it is also interesting due to its informal character, which helps us understand what kind of extra-work relationships could exist inside the federation, including with a CSW employee.

The personal and friendly tone of this letter, sent to a colleague, is similar to that of another letter sent to the CSW that same year (GARF 3 2772, p. 27). This letter was sent by Salwa Zayadeen, a Jordanian activist who worked at the Berlin Secretariat for about ten years. Unlike Villaroel, Zayadeen (who most probably lived in Berlin under the pseudonym Leyla, see Chapter 7) and her two little children were forced to leave their country due to the threat of arrest. Salwa's husband spent many years in prison, while she was working in Berlin, and the letter sent by Zayadeen to Moscow in October 1970 was on the occasion of her return home from exile, and the reunification of her family (GARF 3 2772, p. 27). In the first part of her letter, Zayadeen sent her greetings for the anniversary of the Great October Revolution to all her "multiple friends in Moscow, Uzbekistan, other republics, and to all good people". She also expressed her strong belief in the coming common victory "over imperialists and Zionists", and stated that "your moral support, your wise politics, and your friendship has for us [meaning, most probably, Jordanian women] not less of an importance than the large material aid you offer". In the second part of her letter, Zayadeen expressed her happiness to be home, and stated that everything was going well for her and her husband "unlike so many other people here". Zayadeen finished her letter with a less formal expression of love to all the people she met during her years of working in the organization (GARF 3 2772, p. 27).

Thus, on the basis of these two letters, it is possible to say that in spite of the ideological dogmatism of the federation's rhetoric, which is repeated in the letters sent by its journal's readers and visitors from different regions, the everyday contacts of the representatives of the Global South with the state socialist reality and people allowed some space for shared emotions and friendship.

The contacts with state socialist reality seemed to be an interesting and complex experience for many women coming from the Global South.

However, while some of the guests could get more a multifaceted picture of women's lives in Moscow, Prague, Berlin, or Tashkent, many of the participants of the short trips, most probably, had no other choice but to follow the guidelines on how they should see the "socialist women's life" as conveyed by the official programmes and tours.

Conclusion

The improved status of women in the society was an important part of the representations of the achievements of the Soviet Union and other state socialist countries during the Cold War. The state socialist countries proudly presented themselves as "democratic" countries that cared for their citizens and gave them many more rights than the "capitalist" countries. As opposed to how it was in the past, women in "socialist" countries were presented as enjoying the right to work, to political participation, and to get an education. At the same time, their rights as mothers were protected through the social security system. The rapid changes in the countries of Africa, Asia, and Latin America during the post-war years, and the mass political mobilization of women there, opened new possibilities for exporting the state socialist experience of the solution to the "women's question", and the WIDF could offer both educational activities in the region, with the participation of guests from the "Eastern Bloc", and seminars and educational trips to the state socialist countries. The "emancipated women" of the "Eastern Bloc" welcomed their "sisters" from the Global South to visit their workplaces, nurseries, and educational facilities, while women from the former colonial countries were particularly welcomed to visit the Soviet borderlands with a colonial past, like Central Asia.

The material analysed in this chapter supports the conclusion made in previous studies on the special role of Central Asia in the Soviet politics during the Cold War (see Rasulov 2017; Kirasirova 2018). It shows the special importance of "Soviet Asia" in spreading Soviet influence to the countries of the Global South. Having a Central Asian (Uzbek) woman represent the WIDF in important international forums for women from Africa and Asia, and bringing multiple delegations of women to study modernization and rights based on the example of Central Asian developments, did indeed add credibility to the WIDF's picture of the great achievement of state socialism.

Due to the ideological censorship of the WIDF's official publications, as well as to a personal interest in glorifying the achievements of state socialism by some of the politically engaged authors of reports and memoirs (like Edelman 1996), many visitors' accounts demonstrate conformity with the hosts' self-presentation. They reproduce the picture that the state socialist countries wanted their guests to see. However, everything the female visitors wrote about cannot be explained only as due to ideological control. In particular, it is important to pay attention to the locus of the gaze of the guests from the Global South. The African participants at the 1962 Tashkent seminar, for example, observed striking differences between the possibilities for education for women in their countries, and in the republics of Central Asia. Thus, even if we do not know how much information they had about, for instance, the violent and, at the same time, limited character of the Soviet emancipation of women in Central Asia, it is possible to suppose that this contrast was quite remarkable. Therefore, it is possible to say that some of the achievements of state socialism could be seen as quite impressive by the female visitors from the Global South; some of them were convinced of the benefits of the Soviet emancipation, and came to believe in the promises of state socialism.

Finally, personal letters preserved in the archives indicate that some women from Latin America and the Middle East who were closely involved in the WIDF's work established good personal relationships with women from different countries, including women from the state socialist countries. Thus, my examples partly support Ghodsee's observation of personal friendship between representatives of the "Second" and "Third" worlds (2018). However, it is important to consider that good personal relationships, in the case of Villaroel or Zayadeen, were a part of the framework of their rather privileged life in the GDR.

Notes

1 Many of the federation's early member organizations also had the word "democratic" in their names (for example, the Democratic Union of Cuban Women – member of WIDF before the 1960 reorganization after the Cuban revolution, Chase 2015; Democratic League of Finnish Women – 1944–1990, etc.).
2 Most probably, this article was published only in the Russian version of the journal.
3 I am grateful to Monica Quirico for finding information that Orteze left the Italian Communist Party soon after her trip to the Soviet Union.
4 On the centrality of this thesis for Soviet propaganda and the limitations of such interpretation of women's lives of in Central Asia before 1917, see Gradskova 2018.
5 For more about the role of Central Asia and Tashkent, in particular, in the propaganda of Soviet modernity, see works by Kirasirova 2018, 53–66; Djagalov & Salazkina 2016.
6 African American intellectuals were also guests of such events – see Audrey Lorde on her trip to the writers' conference in Tashkent in 1975 (1984, 13–55).
7 For more on Oundié and Cameroonian women, see Terretta 2016.
8 Zoya Kosmodemianskaia was widely known in the Soviet Union as a heroic partisan and Second World War martyr.
9 I will return to Edelman's memoirs in Chapter 7.
10 The Union of Cameroonian Women joined the WIDF in 1958.
11 I am very grateful to Maria Fernanda Lanfranco, a Chilean researcher, who helped me to identify this person.

6 Women from Asia, Africa, and Latin America make themselves visible in the WIDF

This chapter continues the analysis of the changes within the WIDF related to decolonization and the increasing participation of women from Asia, Africa, and Latin America in the federation's activities. Unlike the previous chapters that focused on the WIDF's visions and actions in connection to the growing role of women from Asia, Africa, and Latin America, and on showcasing the achievements of state socialism for women from the Global South, here I explore the growing involvement of women from countries outside of Europe in the WIDF. Thus, I focus on the concerns and demands of the women from the Global South through an analysis of their interventions at meetings of different WIDF governing bodies, and comments made in private conversation that can be found in the archival materials. What expectations and concerns did they voice, and what was reaction of the WIDF's leadership?

Discussion on the WIDF's structures, leadership, and agenda

According to the WIDF's official documents, women of the "whole world" could and should be involved with the federation, and they should also be represented in its leadership. While women from some countries, like India, participated in the WIDF from the beginning, women from many countries of Africa and Asia only began to be interested in establishing contacts with the WIDF from the mid-1950s onwards. For example, Fatima Ahmed Ibrahim, a young Sudanese women's organization activist, visited the WIDF's Berlin headquarters in 1954 and stated that she was interested in cooperating with it (GARF 2 1482, pp. 1–2, 26 July 1954). According to the brief report sent to Moscow by the Soviet representative at the WIDF's Secretariat, Ibrahim described activities and problems encountered by the Sudanese Women's Union, and reacted enthusiastically to the WIDF's proposal to visit Sudan and her organization. As I show in Chapter 4, the WIDF also intensified its efforts to learn more about the fight for independence in Asia and Africa, and to establish contacts with women's organizations in these regions.

Neither the WIDF nor the Soviet Union was invited to take an official part in the 1955 Bandung conference of African and Asian countries that was held in Jakarta. However, researchers into the Non-Aligned Movement have shown that many of the conference participants were interested in socialist ideas and got inspiration from fast economic and cultural transformation of the Soviet Union (Mark et al. 2020, 7–8), and the Indonesian women's organization, Gerwani, was an active member of the WIDF (see McGregor 2013). The Bandung conference showed that the countries of Asia and Africa had become a new important player in world politics, they formed "the Third World", a new community, which challenged the worlds of both capitalism and state socialism. This new geopolitical distribution of power also implied the growing importance of women's organizations from countries outside Europe. However, while many of the WIDF's leaders welcomed the broader participation of new women's organizations from the Global South in the WIDF (see Chapter 4), most of them did not expect that many of the new female activists and leaders would bring new demands and ideas, and that their participation would conflict with the established routines of the federation.

The Moscow archive preserved several documents showing that, in the late 1950s, the overly Europe-based leadership of the federation was seen as a problem by different members of the WIDF's governing bodies, and by some representative of its member organizations. The leaders of the CSW realized the growing political importance of the inclusion of women from newly independent countries in the federation's governing bodies, including the Secretariat (see Chapter 2 with regard to the important role of the Secretariat in the WIDF). However, the process of change in this direction was rather slow. Answering a request from Popova, Zoya Ivanova, the Soviet representative at the Secretariat in Berlin, discussed the composition of the WIDF leadership in a 1957 letter:

> I want to send you some information about how different countries are represented in the Secretariat. There are nine countries represented there; Italy, France, England, China, the Soviet Union, Spain, the GDR, Czechoslovakia, and the USA (represented by an emigrant American woman). Thus, of nine countries there are seven that belong to the European continent, one country belongs to the American one, and one belongs to Asia. Latin America, Africa, and the Middle East are not represented in the Secretariat, while Asia is represented insufficiently.
> (GARF 4 115, p. 30)

The archive also preserved critical remarks on the composition of the WIDF's leadership made by Argentinian Communist leaders in 1959. In a classified letter to Nina Popova in Moscow, the Soviet representative at the Secretariat in Berlin, Skotnikova, informed her that the leaders of the Communist Party of Argentina, who took part in the celebration of the 10th anniversary of the Chinese revolution, commented that the "bureau of the WIDF has too many representatives of European countries" (GARF 4 134, pp. 135–137, from 13 November 1959). This information was communicated to the WIDF Secretariat in Berlin by Adela Betinelli, a WIDF secretary and representative of the Argentinian Communist Party who took part in the events in Beijing. Skotnikova wrote that, according "to the opinion of our Argentinian friends":

> the main role in the world democratic movement belongs to the struggles of people from Asia, Africa, and Latin America and not to those from Europe. It should be reflected in the structure of the leadership [rukovodiashchie organy] of the WIDF. According to them [Argentinian friends], the fact that the federation does not give enough attention to the problems of the struggle for national independence is a result of the lack of representation of the countries of Asia, Africa, and Latin America in its leadership. The representatives of the European countries do not represent fully the demands of the people of those countries. For example, according to their opinion, the speech by Vaillant-Couturier in the name of the WIDF in China on the occasion of 10th anniversary of the Chinese People's Republic was the speech of a French woman, not one by the vice-president of the WIDF.
>
> (GARF 4 134, p. 136)

While it is not easy to understand what the Argentinian "friends" meant by the speech of "a French woman", this definition obviously indicates some conflict between the anti-colonial aspirations of those gathered in Beijing and Couturier's "Europeaness" and, probably, whiteness. As I already noted, the rhetoric of race and colour are mainly absent from the WIDF documents. Special terms indicating race (like "Negro-woman") were used mainly for describing the situation in the USA during earlier years (GARF, 1 4, 1–2), where the Black population was seen as discriminated against as a result of racist politics. However, it seems that a certain colour blindness was characteristic in the discourse regarding most of the colonial countries. Even if racial discrimination was addressed in many articles on colonialism in Africa, women fighting against racial discrimination most frequently were defined as "African" (see, for example, the long article explaining the politics of Apartheid in South Africa and describing "African" women's protests against it; ZM, 1958, 7–8: 7–19). Thus, considering a certain colour blindness of the WIDF discourse, "European" in the quote above probably implicitly includes "whiteness".

Finally, it is important to mention that the critique by the Argentinian "friends" also indicated the need for paradigmatic changes in the WIDF's leadership. With reference to Betinelli, Skotnikova wrote that, according to the Argentinian communist leaders, European women had obviously done much for the development of the international democratic women's movement, but the new demands of the time should be considered. Thus, they considered it wrong that the president and general secretary of the federation both represented European countries (GARF 4 134, p. 136).

Discontent with the representation of non-European countries in the WIDF's leadership is also visible in the protocols of the discussions from the WIDF council's meeting held in Prague on 13–15 October 1959.

Among the issues that were planned to be discussed at the meeting were a report from the editors of the federation's journal, preparation for the celebration of 8 March, and new anti-nuclear war activism (GARF 3 221). However, the problem of representation of women from non-European countries became one that involved many participants. Several of them used arguments that were quite similar to those that were expressed by the Argentinian communists. For example, the representative from Brazil, Izula Gerhard, insisted on the importance of including more representatives from Latin America in the WIDF's leadership:

> It is not correct that only two representatives of Latin America are present in the leadership. It makes it difficult to correctly understand the problems that one or another country [of this region] has.
> (GARF 3 221, p. 8)

In addition, Safira Jamila from Iraq joined the Brazilian representative in expressing the need to have representatives of the Arab countries in the Secretariat: "the WIDF still does not fully understand the problems in some countries, which is also the case of the countries of the Arab East" (GARF 3 221, pp. 39–41). The same stance was also taken by the representative of India, Bani Dasgupta, who suggested having more representatives from Asia and Africa in the WIDF's leadership, particularly in the Bureau. According to her, "the Bureau has to discuss not only general problems, but also national ones, and it is impossible without representatives from those countries" (GARF 3 221, p. 41).

Furthermore, the representative from Cameroon, Marthe Moumié, suggested that the number of non-European women in the WIDF's Secretariat should be increased. Stating that her country needed the WIDF's help, she said that the inviting the representative of Cameroon to join the Secretariat would be one possible way to improve not only the work of the Cameroonian women's organization, but also the WIDF as a whole. According to Moumié, "she [the female representative of Cameroon in the Secretariat] could be invited to join it, not only because she would be able to learn how to work, but also to provide the correct orientation on the problems of the women of Cameroon" (GARF 3, 221, p. 41).

However, many of the WIDF's leaders did not seem very happy with this situation, fearing that it might lead to a possible radicalization of WIDF's ideology. For example, Nina Popova, the Soviet representative at that meeting of the Bureau, expressed her disagreement with Moumié. Popova defended professionalism and stressed that, especially for the work of the Secretariat, having the correct qualifications was more important than the representation of different continents and knowledge of the local situation. According to her, those who worked in the Secretariat:

> ... had to be those who have a high level of development and who are able to do a good analysis of all the problems of the women's movement, who are able to analyse the activities of regional organizations

and to also make the correct conclusions from this analysis. The secretaries must be able to prepare high-quality recommendations and present them to the Bureau and to the Council of the WIDF. It would be helpful to the organization's leadership to come to the correct decisions.
(GARF 3 221, pp. 34–38)

Popova was later supported by the WIDF's general secretary, Vaillant-Couturier, who similarly stressed that the Bureau could not have too many members, and that it already had enough representatives from Africa (GARF 3 221, p. 42).

Thus, it became apparent that the most difficult problem connected to the inclusion of women from different countries in the WIDF's leadership was that such an inclusion demanded changes inside the federation itself. The representatives of women's organizations from countries of the Global South did not have the exact same views on the problems of women's rights and the work of the organization as those that the Soviet and European Communist, or leftist, women had agreed upon in earlier years.

Discussions on changes and possible new directions in the work of the WIDF continued during the late 1950s and the first half of the 1960s, as the position of women from Asia, Africa, and Latin America was voiced at WIDF meetings on different levels. The problems encountered by women from the newly independent countries in their attempts at cooperating with the WIDF were expressed most concisely in the report of the meeting of the Executive Committee of the National Federation of Indian Women, and brought by Anasuya Gyanchand to the WIDF's first bureau meeting outside of Europe, in Jakarta in 1960. The report started by stating that the WIDF had to make more efforts if it was interested in attracting women from outside Europe:

> In our opinion the WIDF, in spite of being the one international organization which had striven to its utmost to reach out to, and help women of these areas, still was not able to find out the key slogans which would appeal to the vast masses of women of the East and was not able to work out organizational forms that would correspond to the conditions of these countries.
>
> It was a fact that the women of Asia and Africa did not play a leading part in the WIDF, and that, with the exception of the Chinese and some other countries, either whole countries remained outside the sphere of our organization, or the women who were elected to the leading bodies of the WIDF did not represent the leadership of the broad masses of women in our countries, though they were in themselves prominent personalities.
> (GARF 3 410, p. 66, from
> 31 January–2 February 1960, document in English)

Thus, it is possible to say that the authors of the report saw a direct connection between the lack of representation of Asian (and other non-European) women in the WIDF leadership, and its difficulties with formulating a programme that would be attractive to women in the "Third World". This critique was similar to what had been voiced before by the representatives of Argentina, Iraq, and several other countries I discussed above. However, the report did not limit its critique by the issues of representation, and pointed out important differences in the conditions of life, and in the political situation of women, in Africa and Asia that were not paid enough attention to by the WIDF leadership.

One such problem was the different attitude of women in former colonial countries towards their men. According to the report:

> In the colonial and semi-colonial countries women fight for their rights was linked up for the fight for independence;[...] national independence could not have been won without the active participation of women; and [...] women could not be roused and mobilized for this sacred task if not the men at least formally conceded their right to better life.[1]
> (GARF 3 410, p. 67)

As shown in Chapter 3, the materialist rhetoric of the WIDF official documents and publications usually did not give any attention to men; to avoid being feminist, the WIDF publications never expressed hostility to men, but they did not defend the importance of common actions with men either. Thus, the issue of the common struggle of women together with men for independence that, according to the report, was so important for women in all countries where such a struggle was taking place, was absent from the WIDF's programme.

At the same time, the report stated that in countries that already have achieved their independence, and where women's rights are declared in their constitutions, they often only exist on paper, and, thus, the WIDF should work more to claim the practical realization of these rights.

The report of the Indian organization pointed out another important aspect of the work of the federation that was not problematized much in the WIDF's official publications – the relationships between women from the colonizing countries and from the colonized nations. In contrast to the WIDF's emphasis on the solidarity between all women, the report stated that the problem of relationships of women in (former) colonies to women of those nations that for centuries were their colonial masters is more complicated than the WIDF's idealized vision:

> how to bring home to our women the need for friendship even with those nations, who while not actually dominating over us, seem to be challenging our sovereignty and independence, is the problem for us.
> (GARF 3 410, p. 68)

Thus, while the WIDF's official and simplified version of friendship and solidarity was expected to be grounded in the rational evaluation of alliances, it totally ignored negative feelings (for feelings connected to "wounded dignities"; see Mignolo & Vasquez 2013) accumulated during the years of colonial exploitation. The experiences of being dominated and exploited by the women of the dominant nations,[2] could endanger the fragile solidarity balance inside the federation.

Further, the report criticized how the WIDF approached several specific problems of women in Africa and Asia. One of them was the problem of unemployment that affected women in many countries, and was often addressed by the WIDF's official publications. Calling the WIDF's interpretation of the problem of unemployment a "Western" interpretation, the report explained:

> we have hundreds of millions who need jobs but who are not even capable of working even if they were given the job. Thus training and education for earning a livelihood becomes a big issue.
>
> (Ibid.)

Similarly, the report noted that problems of employment for women in the countries of Asia and Africa are connected with the special situation of housewives, who need employment in order to contribute to country's wealth.

On the other hand, the report stressed that other WIDF demands that are central to its ideology when applied to Europe should probably be modified when applied elsewhere. The demand of prohibiting child labour, according to a report, was a problematic demand from the perspective of contemporary India. While the authors of the report agreed on importance of demanding support "for maternity, child welfare, and crèches", they were against banning child labour; "for if we do so what relief can we give to these whose livelihood depends on the earnings of children?" (GARF 3 410, p. 68). Indeed, following her arguments, the prohibition of child labour, before changing many other structures and institutions of society, would lead only to more suffering on the part of these children and their families.

The report also discussed the issue of the class structure in Asia and Africa, and criticized "our friends from Europe and America" for their lack of understanding of the multiple inequalities and complexities:

> we would like to point out one very glaring truth about conditions in Asia and Africa which is often not kept in mind by our other friends when planning a campaign or world wide movement for the WIDF. This is the fact that in no country in Asia and Africa are women at a uniform level of progress and development. [...]
>
> We feel that our friends in Europe and America are too used to looking at the different social strata of people as "industrial workers,

capitalists, farmers or agriculturalists". They find it difficult to understand that different levels of social emancipation exist both in the town and country-side.

(GARF 3 410, p. 69)

Finally, the report noted that "European women" do not understand that some problems, including illiteracy, marriage laws, and the lack of education and nourishment, are very serious for women in that part of the world, in contrast to Europe.

While a copy of the report is preserved in the archive, unfortunately, I did not find many comments or discussion of it from the WIDF's leadership. However, it is possible to see that some of the WIDF leaders, in particular Carmen Zanti, the WIDF general secretary, with the passing of time became increasingly convinced of the need for fundamental changes in the federation, and the meeting in Jakarta seemed to be an important milestone for Zanti's thinking.

The political situation in many post-colonial countries was changing fast, and several of them were soon involved in political turmoil or civil wars (see, e.g., Terretta 2013a, 2013b on Cameroon); unstable democracies in some other countries, including Latin American ones, could be substituted by dictatorships (as in Brazil in 1964). In this situation, the "European" (both West and East) WIDF secretaries often did not have enough knowledge regarding the context of these developments, nor about the problems of specific women's organizations in this fast-changing situation. Thus, the WIDF had difficulties in organizing informational and solidarity work. This is visible, for example, in a letter of the Soviet representative discussing the WIDF response to the situation in the Congo in 1961 (GARF 4 149, p. 1, letter from Lebedeva to Popova 19 January 1961). According to Lebedeva, in planning WIDF work for 1961, Carmen Zanti "actively insisted on support of the workers on strike in Belgium, and on help to Algerians. She did not oppose the plan of support for Cuba, but strongly insisted that at the present moment there were no condition for organizing solidarity with the Congo in Western Europe, because it is not very clear what is going on in the Congo and it is difficult to say who we support." The same letter also indicated that Zanti had profound doubts as to the usefulness of WIDF tactics and work methods in the new situation. According to Lebedeva, Zanti evaluated the discussion climate at the meeting of the WIDF council in Warsaw (1960) as an "anti-European atmosphere". In her reflection about it, according to Lebedeva, she said that she does not know "what we shall do with Africa", but also expressed the idea that the representatives of countries such as Italy and France should no longer lead the federation.

Other letters by Lebedeva from the same year also show that it was not only Carmen Zanti, the WIDF general secretary, who felt a lack of knowledge and difficulty understanding what different political actors in African and other non-European countries want, and whom the federation should support. This led to a situation where decisions concerning organizing solidarity with different women's organizations were taken slowly and provoked uncertainty (GARF 4 149 p. 15). According to Lebedeva, many members of the Secretariat were thinking; "we do not know what is happening there [in one or another 'Third World country'] in reality. It is better to wait." Thus, according to Lebedeva, only after several conversations and with the help of some particularly active members, like the representatives of Romania or Argentina "it is possible to move to some concrete actions – sending letters, telegrams or some other way of showing solidarity" (GARF 4 149, p. 15).

Finally, the growing Soviet–China discrepancies after 1956 intensified at the beginning of the 1960s, in parallel with the wave of decolonization, and grew into open confrontation, including in the Global South (see Friedman 2015). In the framework of the WIDF Secretariat, this confrontation was expressed in long, heated discussions in meetings, and the division of those working in the Secretariat between those who supported the Soviet or Chinese position. For example, in the beginning of 1963, *Pravda* published a long article criticizing the Chinese leadership. The Soviet representative in the Secretariat, Lebedeva, wrote that members of the Secretariat expressed different opinions about *Pravda*'s article from 7 January (GARF 4 169, 1963, p. 4, 16 January 1963). According to her, the Spanish representative, Eliza Urriz, "noted the importance of the article and supported all its main points", and Leyla Zayadeen, the representative from Jordan, characterized the article as very helpful for everybody involved in discussions with the Chinese. However, it is possible to understand that not all members of the Secretariat had the same position as Urriz and Zayadeen. Lebedeva considered it important to write about the Chinese representative in the Secretariat, Yan, getting into a conflict with the WIDF's general secretary, Carmen Zanti. Yan wrote a very critical letter concerning the situation of women in South Vietnam, but, according to Lebedeva, "Carmen did not accept this letter, and invited her to a meeting. However, Yan did not come to speak with Carmen up until the day when Carmen had to travel" (GARF 4 169, p. 15). According to the letters of the Soviet representative, the political confrontation went so far that everyday communication between the Soviet and the Chinese representative in the Secretariat in Berlin practically stopped: "the Chinese friends did not have any conversations with me and we do not have much contact anymore. We just meet at the lunch room".

Thus, it is possible to say that the independence of many countries in Asia and Africa, and the many new women's organizations that joined the WIDF, had a big influence on the federation. The organization created to defend women's rights in a political framework originating in Europe had to adjust not only its programme, but also its structure, leadership and style of work to the new demands. All of this further intensified internal conflicts within the federation that first became visible after destalinization in 1956 (see Chapter 2).

Thus, in the next subchapter, I am going to look closer at one of the most dramatic periods in the history of the federation, connected with the increased influence of women from Asia, Africa, and Latin America on its work: the Moscow congress of 1963 and events surrounding it.

Decolonization and women's activism in the Global South make an impact on the WIDF

Discussions around changes in the WIDF became particularly heated at the WIDF Moscow congress in 1963, and meetings aimed for its preparation during 1962–1963 in Prague and Berlin.³ These discussions, however, were not just a free exchange of opinions; the congress was strongly influenced by the growing split between the USSR and China, and discussions of the problems of women from Asia, Africa, and Latin America in the WIDF took the form of a confrontation between the majority supporting the position of Moscow and a minority who supported Beijing. "Taking sides" in this new geopolitical division seemed to influence the positions of many members of the WIDF leadership, bureau, and congress delegates.

During the preparatory bureau meetings, both the WIDF president, Cotton, and the general secretary, Zanti, recognized that after the last congress (1958 Vienna) the world had gone through enormous changes, and that issues of national independence should take more a central role in the work of the federation. Thus, Zanti stated that "we live in the new world now" and, in particular:

> There is an entire continent, Africa, where enormous changes happened almost everywhere, where women actively participated in the struggle for national independence and now are taking a leading role in building their countries. It is obvious that women did not have such a place [in their societies] before.
>
> (GARF 3 790, p. 21)

For her part, Cotton stated in the next bureau meeting that "the map of Africa has changed so much during the last years". She stressed that in reading the reports and suggestions of the national organizations, it was becoming clear that "at the present moment, one of the most important problems that women are dealing with is national independence" (GARF 3 794, p. 6).

The Moscow Congress aimed to discuss a new programme for the WIDF. Thus, meetings preparing this congress in 1962 and 1963 as well as the Congress itself became a space where women from different countries met, and where discussions were much hotter than at WIDF meetings of earlier years. The disagreements and conflicts between the congress participants related to both the organizational issues connected to the work of the federation, and also its goals and tactics for defending women's rights.

Many speakers taking part in the session of the commission on national independence stressed that a declaration of independence did not mean full independence in many countries. For example, the representative of Cameroon stressed: "in Cameroon, independence was declared only formally.

In fact, the imperialists have all the administrative, military and cultural positions" (GARF 3 967, p. 38). The representative of Laos stated that the situation in her country was getting worse[4] and suggested making the resolution of the session stronger in order to have it correspond with the real situation of countries like hers (GARF 3 967, p. 246).

Some other delegates[5] mentioned continuing colonial rule and the importance of independence for a country's social progress:

> My country is to the North from Madagascar. The regime of the French colonialists is preserved in the country. We do not have hospitals, electricity, or work. The death rate is very high and death is considered to be an ordinary event. We do not have social security or the right to create a political organization. Such organizations could only exist abroad.
>
> (GARF 3 967, p. 84)

At the same time, in her intervention at the commission on national independence, the Soviet representative, Zuhra Rahimbabaeva, conveyed that the Soviet Union not only decolonized its own territory (she presented herself as a representative of a Soviet republic that was formerly a Russian colony), but also helps "young states that are now free from the yoke of colonialism". Thus, Rahimbabaeva stressed that, unlike those who use the label of "help" to practice neo-colonialism (i.e. Western countries), the "Soviet Union takes part in the construction of 480 industrial enterprises in the countries of Asia, Africa, and Latin America" (GARF 3 967, pp. 22–23).

Issues of the national independence and neo-colonialism received major attention in the discussion of the new WIDF programme. The delegate from Sudan stressed the importance of including support for the struggle for independence in the programme:

> We want the programme of the federation to correspond to the desires of our women. We want the federation to directly say in its programme that it supports the struggle for national independence and democracy, and against colonialism.
>
> (GARF 3 970, p. 101)

The most heated discussions were probably those regarding the concept of "imperialism". The representatives of the countries from the Global South played a leading role in these discussions. This discussion started at the preparatory bureau meeting in Berlin, on the initiative of the Chinese delegation. Its representatives insisted on need to include into the text of the new WIDF programme a clear notion of who is the main enemy – of women and of the WIDF (GARF 3 1027, p. 4). In her speech, Chinese representative Ko Chen insisted that imperialism was the main hindrance to both peace and national independence: "who endangers national independence?" Dismissing concerns that the concept was too radical for many women's organizations and, thus, would prevent them from joining the WIDF (794, p. 50), Ko Chen stressed:

> We consider imperialism to have an aggressive character. It does not stop its policy of war and aggression and because of this, we should organize a very broad joint front against the policies of war and aggression realized by the imperialists, in particular, by the American imperialists.
>
> (GARF 3 794, p. 52)

The Chinese delegation, at different points in the discussion, was supported by other countries – including Indonesia, Vietnam, Albania, Venezuela, Japan, and Cuba. For example, the representative of Vietnam in her intervention at the Moscow Congress stated that "the fight against imperialism is the most important problem for us [...] and it is quite similar for many countries of Latin America. Without solving this problem [of imperialism] we cannot solve other problems" (GARF 3 970, p. 45). Thus, the representative of Vietnam not only supported the idea of specifying more about imperialism in the WIDF programme, but also suggested writing about American imperialism first:

> that is why we want it written exactly that it is American imperialism that is enemy number one of the whole world, it is the enemy of all countries fighting for freedom and national independence.
>
> (GARF 3 970, p. 45)

Further, the representative of Venezuela said:

> We need to liquidate imperialism in order to achieve peace and détente. As long as imperialism exists, fascism and militarism continue to exist as well. Some of our friends think unfortunately that if we use some particular words [for naming the enemy] we make women afraid [of our organization]. But we have fight against imperialism in the protocol of the congress in Budapest. We must explain to women what real imperialism could do. There are some countries that think that the Soviet Union is an imperialist country. Thus, we have to define exactly who is our friend and who is our enemy. Colonialism, neo-colonialism, and all the imperialist policies are the product of imperialism.
>
> (GARF 3 1027, p. 19)

However, the Italian representative, Maria Magdalena Rossi, already at the preparatory meeting expressed her disagreement with the Chinese and Venezuelan representatives, and insisted on specifying that the WIDF is a world-wide organization that is officially independent from any political party. When the representative of China demanded a write-up about imperialist aggression and noted that "to fight imperialism is the task of the communist party", Rossi made a clear distinction between the two ways of discussing: "I want you to discuss the issues how they should be discussed here, and not how they are discussed at the communist party meetings" (GARF 3, 1027, p. 24).

The discussion on imperialism also became a discussion on tactical issues. According to some representatives of the WIDF leadership, and the delegates of the congress, including "imperialism" in the programme could diminish the number of potential members of the organization due to its radical character. In the preparatory meeting, Nina Popova clearly suggested avoiding the use of overly ideological language in the interests of unity: "The federation is a mass organization and we should think about what language we are using when speaking to women, if we want them to work with us" (GARF 3 794, p. 77).[6] In the Congress, Ilse Thiele from the GDR and Ivonne Dumont from France expressed similar views. According to Thiele, "women's actions will not be stronger if we repeat the word 'imperialism' seven times in the introduction to our programme" (GARF 3 975, p. 26).

Many representatives of other European countries were also opposed to this use of language. According to the Swedish representative, Valborg Svensson, even though some women in Sweden and Norway thought "that imperialism was an enemy, most women in our countries do not think so" (GARF 3 975, p. 77).[7]

Several representatives of women's organizations from the Global South also showed themselves to be very careful with the use of the word "imperialism" in their work. For example, the representative of the Chilean women's organization insisted that it was difficult to use the "Communist language" in her work:

> Our organization wants to be a mass organization. At our first congress, we also spoke about a fight against imperialists. Women in Chile are less advanced than women in Venezuela and Cuba. Thus, we do not speak to them with the language of Communist women [ne govorim s nimi na yazyke kommunistok]. Not all of them understand what the "fight against imperialism" means. We speak with them about problems they have, this is our tactic. In order to expand the influence of the WIDF, we have to use the language that can attract women from other organizations. We have to attract them, and only then make a qualitative change.
>
> (GARF, 3 1027, p. 20)

Finally, some delegates (who did not fully support the Chinese rhetoric on anti-imperialism) considered the term useful, but for other reasons. Renu Chakravarti from India, for example, suggested that "imperialism", in Asia and Africa, could be understood by women better than the word "fascism":

> In the colonial countries, the struggle for national independence is very important. The people here do not understand the word "fascism" and

only communists use it, but imperialism is used more frequently and people understand it better.
(GARF 3 1027, p. 26)

It seems that, in spite of the usefulness of the term "imperialism" in some cases, the majority of participants rejected the Chinese proposal to place a greater emphasis on it. The representatives of the countries of the Global South made many suggestions for changing the WIDF's programme so that it would better correspond to the situation of women in their countries. For example, a representative from India suggested the following additions: the firing of married women should be prohibited; all working women should have access to maternity protections; and women in underdeveloped countries should have the opportunity to work on a part-time basis (GARF 3 795, p. 121).

Discussions at the congress concerning the programme showed that the representatives of the Global South had a lot to say. For instance, the representative from Indonesia said:

> First of all, I want to propose changes in the title of this chapter [that was under discussion]. According to the table of contents that we have here in the project that was prepared by the bureau, it sounds like "defence of women, mothers, workers," etc. We want to suggest the title "Defence of women and realization of the rights of women in political, economic social, cultural, and educational spheres". We would also like to add a paragraph dealing with peasant women. We want to include a special point on the equal rights for men and women to own and use land. I want to repeat this so that my words will be correctly translated into French: equality of women and men with respect to ownership and use of land, as well as in use of the products of the land.
> (GARF 3 970, p. 101, from 27 June 1963)

The final comment of the Indonesian representative was in support of the proposal of the Vietnamese participants "to place 'respect and recognition of the human rights of women' first, and only after that to write about respect for her in the family and society" (GARF 3 970, p. 101).

Discussions of the programme and statutes of the WIDF led to further deliberations around the WIDF's decision-making, and democracy inside the organization. During the preparatory meeting, Carmen Zanti suggested that the "upcoming congress should be prepared differently from the previous ones" (GARF 3 790, p. 20). In order to attract more members to the organization, according to Zanti, it would be important to have more internal democracy (GARF 3 790, p. 26). Further, the Indonesian member suggested that it was important to write in the statutes exactly who would make decisions regarding adding Secretariat members; she added that Indonesia had been "excluded from the Secretariat" without any special decision (GARF 790, p. 28). After all the discussions at the Congress itself, the Chinese delegates considered that they were not treated democratically when discussing the issues of national independence and the WIDF's programme: "it is discrimination with respect to China, several times we were denied a chance to intervene the discussions, we were not allowed to say what we wanted" (GARF 975, p. 268).

The Moscow Congress showed that the problems and concerns of the representatives of the countries of Asia and Africa were at the heart of the discussions, while the situation in the countries of Western Europe seemed to decline in significance. This made some representatives of these countries raise a question about a need for special meetings where West European representatives could discuss their specific problems. Thus, the recognition of differences between the problems of women in the First and the Third Worlds was one result of a situation where women from the Third World were able to speak more about their specific problems, and raise demands that did not coincide with the demands of European women. Thus, some representatives of European women, in their turn, also attempted to indicate that the WIDF's programme did not fully express their needs, either. For example, the representative of Sweden, in one of her later interventions at the Congress, suggested:

> we support the view point that was expressed here by our French friends, and by many others who spoke here, for example, the representative of Austria. Obviously, it is very important that we should exchange our experiences. For example, I mean that there are many countries in the Western part of Europe that live under similar conditions. It would be very good if we could organize a conference in Western Europe where we could discuss women's rights, what women should do, and what we should do in the future. The conference should be dedicated to this particular issue, as well as to the education of children and some other issues.
>
> (GARF 3 970, p. 224)

Thus, this suggestion indicates that, as early as the early 1960s, women from Western Europe began to feel themselves pushed to the margins of the WIDF's agenda. While the further development of the WIDF shows that there were no more large events organized by the WIDF in the "West" – the 1969 Congress in Helsinki did not specifically focus on problems of women in Western Europe – it is possible to understand that the federation did not acquire many new supporters in the "West" after the late 1950s. The recognition of differences in the problems that women from different regions face led to new solutions, such as the organization of regional centres (see Chapter 8). It is also remarkable that, in her speech, the Swedish representative indirectly complained that some of the federation's documents "did not apply to our conditions at all". However, she added that as the members of her organization were not forced to work according to this document, they would adapt it to their local conditions.

The growing differences in interpretations of developments in the countries of Africa and Asia (together with the factors of internal democracy within the WIDF and internal political developments in the Italian women's movement – see Bonfiglioli 2012) led to the end of active participation in the WIDF not only by Chinese, but also by Italian women soon after the Moscow congress. Carmen Zanti, who defended the need to bring African women to top positions in the WIDF's leadership, did not seem to receive the support of other WIDF leaders.

At the same time, the federation definitely learned some lessons from decolonization, and heated discussions with women from Africa and Asia. Along with bringing the fight for independence into the core of its official declarations, and making solidarity with the countries of Asia, Africa, and Latin America one of its main activities, the WIDF changed the composition of its leadership. During most of the 1960s–1970s, two Argentinian women, Rosa Jasovich-Pantaleón and Fanny Edelman, occupied the position of general secretary. Furthermore, while white communist women – first Hertta Kuusinen from Finland, and then, from 1974, Freda Brown from Australia – continued to occupy the post of the WIDF's president, by the beginning of the 1970s, women from Asia, Africa, and Latin America constituted the majority of the WIDF's Bureau and Council. In addition, many more non-European women also joined the Berlin Secretariat.

It is important to stress that, in the context of the WIDF's declarations of support for anti-colonial movements and women from the countries outside Europe, the WIDF's prestige started to depend more on its ability to attract important and world-wide recognized leaders of women's organizations from Asia and Africa to its events. This improved the WIDF's chances when in competition with other forces, like social democratic organizations, that also supported these countries and movements.

Conclusion

On the basis of the studied material, it is possible to say that many women from Asian and African countries were interested in cooperating with the WIDF, and in participating in its activities, in different forms. However, although their participation was very much welcomed by the federation, they met certain practical difficulties in making their ideas and suggestions become part of the WIDF's programme, as well as in being able to join the decision-making bodies of the organization. In particular, many women from Asia, Africa, and Latin America, who started to participate actively in WIDF congresses and other events from the late 1950s onwards did not belong to their countries' communist parties. Many of these women were part of women's organizations connected with broader nationalist and national liberation coalitions. Thus, many of these women were very concerned with the processes happening in their countries, but they cared less about what was going on in Europe, most of them having no experience with big transnational organizations.

All of this led to a growing number of internal conflicts inside the federation that became particularly visible around the 1963 WIDF Moscow Congress. Representatives of countries in Asia, Africa, and Latin America participated actively in heated discussions around issues like détente or imperialism, as well as about internal democracy in the organization, and representation of different countries in the Secretariat. The congress showed an increased influence of women from the Global South in the organization, but also the influence on the women's movement of the new geopolitical confrontation inside the communist bloc itself. The split between the Soviet Union and Communist China would contribute to further divisions between women inside and outside the Global South.

Regardless, competition with Cold War rivals to attract African, Asian, and Latin American women led the WIDF to expand its ideas of women's rights in order to attract and to keep women from the Global South on their side. As a result, the leaders of the federation, including the powerful Soviet member, could not control the federation to the same extend as they had during the late 1940s-early 1950s.

To conclude the analysis of the changes that happened in the WIDF in connection with decolonization, it is possible to say that by the late 1960s, women from countries outside of Europe had become more visible on different levels of the WIDF leadership. Participants from the Global South also started to receive more support from the federation with respect to their travel to different WIDF-sponsored events. However, these changes did not fully transform the WIDF as an organization; communist women continued to lead the federation, and no African or Asian woman was ever elected president or general secretary (though two Communist party members from Latin America did achieve it). While problems of illiteracy and Apartheid became the focus of many events organized and supported by the federation, all of the important issues discussed there continued to be somehow tied to the main points of the programme the federation had from its beginning: the protection of peace, mothers, and children.

Notes

1 Mohanty also notices the important role played by men in the struggle for women's rights in India – "key players in the emergence of the 'woman question' within Indian nationalist struggle" (Mohanty 2003, 63).
2 For women's role in colonial domination and economics, see Bier (2011).
3 WIDF bureau in Prague 28 May–1 June 1962 (GARF 3 790), in Berlin 4–5 December 1962 (GARF 3 794) and in Berlin in 14–17 March 1963 (GARF 3 1027; GARF 3 795).
4 It was a period of civil war in Laos.
5 The protocols attribute this speech to Ibrahim from Sudan, but it seems to be a mistake.

6 In her speech, Popova used a rhetorical form asking if she, as a Soviet representative who believes in the communist future, would suggest including "communism" in the programme (GARF 3 794, p. 76).
7 She warned that if the proposal regarding imperialism became part of the preamble, "only communist women and some progressive women would cooperate with our organization, all the others would disappear from under our influence" (GARF 3 975, p. 77).

7 Activists from the Global South and the WIDF
A biographical perspective

Unlike previous chapters that explored the WIDF's work as an organization, this chapter has a more personalized focus, and is centred around several individual women activists who played important roles during different periods of the federation's work. Following Mohanty, I am interested in further deconstructing the "woman activist" from the Global South that worked with the WIDF through looking at the WIDF activists and leaders as real and material subjects (Mohanty 2003, 19). Thus, I want to discover the context of their first contacts with the WIDF, the reasons for their interest in collaboration and, when possible, the successes and problems it generated. Of course, several thousand remarkable female leaders from different countries were crucial to the WIDF's work at different periods of its history, and even making a list of those who came from Latin America, Africa, and Asia would take several pages. In practice, as Ghodsee has already shown (2018), after the end of the Cold War, many women from different parts of the world who were active in the WIDF were forgotten (Ghodsee found this to be the case in both Bulgaria and Zambia). Considering the diversity of languages, shifting national boundaries and political identities, as well as the multiple exile experiences of female activists from the Global South, a real biographical study of their lives, most probably, would best be undertaken by a team of researchers possessing knowledge of the relevant languages and contexts. Yet, in this chapter, I make an attempt at a biographical enquiry into the lives of a select few prominent female activists from the Global South involved with the WIDF during different periods of its history. This could serve as a beginning for exploring the complexities of identities, as well as of work and life experiences, of some of those women. This exploration does not aim to reconstruct the full biographical information, but focuses on analysing how a cross-section of activists' different political, social, and geopolitical belongings and interests were mobilized through their participation in the WIDF. I am also interested in the presentations and evaluations of these activists in the WIDF's documents.

In making my choice of individual women for this chapter, I was guided by several criteria, including availability of documents on activism and collaboration with the WIDF in the Moscow archives and the WIDF's journal, geographical spread of chosen persons through different continents and regions, as well as the availability of individual memoirs, earlier research, or other secondary materials about this person. Thus, in what follows, I focus on the biographies of several women activists – from Latin America (Argentina), Nigeria, and the region of Northern Africa and the Middle East. Being aware from the beginning that the presented life accounts are incomplete, the main focus of my analysis in this chapter is on women's experiences of cooperating with the WIDF. Thus, I decided to present them by commencing with a quotation from the archival material that indicated their place in the federation and/or the place of the federation in their life. I then move on to continue reconstructing their biography using the other materials available to me.

Argentinian communist women as WIDF leaders

I start this section with several lines from a letter that the Soviet Young Pioneers (the Communist youth organization' special institution – club of friendship[1]) sent to Fanny Edelman, a member of the leadership of the Argentinean Communist Party and the WIDF's general secretary, in 1976.

> Dear Comrade Fanny Edelman!
> […]The participants of our club know that you are an important figure in the international communist movement and a promoter of the celebration of the International Women's Year. We know how much effort and how much energy you put in to get this idea supported by as many people as possible.
> (From a letter in Spanish written by the members of the club of international friendship in the city Alexandria, Ukraine, and sent to the CSW with the request to forward it to Fanny Edelman – GARF 3 3962, p. 8)

What does this letter tell us about Edelman? First of all, it suggests that Edelman was well-known in the Soviet Union, and a person who was presented to the Young Pioneers as an "important figure in the international communist movement" and, at the same time, an important person in the promotion of the International Women's Year (IWY). This presentation allows us to perceive that in the Soviet Union and, probably, in other countries of the "Eastern Bloc" and in circles of state socialist sympathizers abroad, the IWY was perceived as a part of communist internationalism – a part of the well-established social agenda on peace and friendship. It is also remarkable that, in this letter, Edelman's status as one of the leaders of the Argentinian Communist Party is placed before her position in the WIDF and women's rights activism (Edelman's affiliation with the Communist Party is mainly absent from WIDF official documents).

The name Edelman occurs very frequently in this book. She will also be named in the next chapter as the author of many important WIDF documents from the 1970s, and as a person who reported to the WIDF bureau meetings and congresses. Edelman was frequently referred to in correspondence between Moscow and Berlin as a person who was trusted by the CSW, and who had a lot of influence in the Secretariat. All of this makes her a particularly important person for my study.

None of the documents available to me, including her book published in 1996, and her extended interview to the Argentinian left-wing journalist Claudia Korol in 2001 on Marxism and feminism, point out any specific conflict or disagreement with the WIDF, nor with Soviet policies, and nor did she seem to have any conflicts with individual female activists (Edelman 1996, 2001). Thus, these books give an impression that Edelman could non-problematically combine communist ideas with her engagement in the campaign for women's rights. In what follows, I will try to show some explanations for this through analysing some small differences in her self-presentation, and by considering the biography of another remarkable Argentinian communist woman in the WIDF, Rosa Jasovich-Pantaleón, who also served as the WIDF's general secretary (in the 1960s).

Edelman's biography – *Women, Flags and Comrades* – suggests that her experiences with intersectional oppressive social orders were crucial for her becoming a leftist political activist. Fanny Edelman (1911–2011) was born into a leftist working-class Jewish family in the Argentinian province of Cordoba. Her parents had both escaped the Russian Empire's anti-Semitism and *pogroms* and emigrated to Argentina at the beginning of the twentieth century. Thus, Edelman, from her early years, was aware of both class and ethnic/racial discrimination. This influenced her early involvement in political activism in Argentina, and her membership in the Communist Party. In 1936, with her husband (who was also a member of the Communist Party), Edelman went as a volunteer to Spain alongside several other Argentinian men and women (1996). It seems that the experience of fighting against fascism in Spain had a big impact on Edelman's views of anti-fascism and contributed to her closer contacts with the Soviets. According to her memoirs, during the Second World War, Edelman was one of the leaders of the anti-fascist women's organization (Junta de la Victoria) in Buenos Aires, and collected money to help to the Soviet Union's struggle against fascism (1996, 84–85). While Edelman did not describe herself as "a feminist" in her book from 1996, she had shown herself to be a leader in the women's movement already in the 1940s. Even if her work with women, probably, was initially a party task, later on Edelman definitely saw women's work as important. Being one of the main organizers of the leftist women's organization Union de Mujeres Argentinas (UMA) in 1947, in her memoirs she stressed that "UMA was the important part of my life" (1996, 103). Many pages of Edelman's memoirs are dedicated to the "brave" female activists of the UMA. The Argentinian Communist Party had a large influence within the UMA (see Valobra 2017, 77), and UMA expressed sympathies for the Soviet Union.

For example, the Moscow archives preserved about 20 copies of a machine-typed letter from 1950 honouring Soviet women (each letter had a certain number of signatures from Argentinian women – GARF 2 709, p. 9). Thus, Edelman seems to have enjoyed political visibility through both the UMA and left activism; and she is also happy to connect her activism in Argentina with broader revolutionary activism in Latin America, not least through noticing the important roles of women. Edelman proudly wrote that on one occasion she was arrested and shared a prison cell with the mother of Che Guevara, Celia (Edelman 1996, 125). By this, Edelman, most probably, wanted to show the importance of women as mothers bringing up children who create social change.

As already mentioned above, Argentinian women joined the WIDF in 1945 and seem to have played a prominent role in the federation. The Argentinian representative, Adela Betinelli, worked at the Berlin Secretariat for many years, while two members of the UMA served as WIDF general secretaries at different times – Rosa Jasovich between 1963 and 1967, and Edelman from 1972 to 1977. Both of them were members of the Communist Party, and the descendants of Jewish emigrants. While neither of them is mentioned as an important activist in accounts of the Latin American women's movement published after 1991 (Leon 1994; Molyneux 2001), Edelman seems to be receiving more attention from researchers (see Pieper Mooney 2013b) than Rosa Jasovich. As the above letter of the Soviet Young Pioneers shows, Edelman was also probably more well-known in the Soviet Union. However, "closeness" to the Soviet Union influenced position of the Argentinian Communist party on the development of the political situation inside Argentina, and led to some criticism by a part of the left in her country. According to Argentinian historian Natalia Casola, the "moderate" position that the Communist Party of Argentina took vis-à-vis military regime in Argentina (1976–1983) was connected to Soviet trade interests in Argentina, and led to its presentation of military rule in Argentina as being more "mild" than in Chile during that same period (Casola 2015, 64–67). Thus, Edelman could be seen as sharing a certain responsibility for the lack of critique of the mass violations of human rights in Argentina during this period.

The book that I discussed above, which Edelman published soon after the collapse of the Soviet Union, is full of admiration for the WIDF, Soviet female leaders (see Chapter 5), and female activists from many different countries visited by Edelman in her capacity as general secretary. This book describes the WIDF as a great and important organization that brought together talented and inspiring women from different countries. In particular, Edelman expressed her admiration for women from Vietnam and, first of all, Nguen Thi Dinh (Edelman 1996, 159; 2001, 165). Among the other names were Ceza Nabarawi and Angela Davis (Edelman 1996, 132–133), Jeane Dambendzet from the Congo (Edelman 1996, 135), and Jeanne Martin Cissé, the head of the PAWO (Edelman 1996, 180).[2] Edelman's memoirs recorded visiting a school for peasant girls opened after the Cuban revolution (Edelman 1996, 156–157), and her travel to several countries of Africa and Asia and the female activists she met there. With the help of this memoir and names, Edelman presented the activities of women connected to the WIDF as multifaceted and global and, thus, implied both the importance of the federation and her own role within it. Thus, Edelman's memoirs mainly confirm the impression that could be drawn on the basis of the letter quoted above.

However, in her extended interview from 2001 that she gave to the Argentinian feminist Karol on issues of Marxism and feminism, Edelman spoke more about theoretical issues of feminism (that implied that she presented herself as a feminist), and dedicated several pages to the Federation of Cuban Women (FMC) and Fidel Castro. However, she also briefly mentioned the WIDF and her contacts with the Soviet Union (Edelman 2011, 164–170). In this interview, Edelman also criticized Gorbachev for bringing back the "patriarchy" to his country (Edelman 2001, 187). These changes of focus could suggest that Edelman was a very skilful politician who could successfully adjust herself (and her biography) to changing political circumstances. Probably, in order to preserve her place in Argentinian left politics, she has chosen to focus more on theoretical perspectives of Marxist feminism, rather than on the practices state socialism that were much criticized during those years.

The factors of her early involvement in both communist and women's activism, international connections, and trust of the Soviets, all seem to be important in the case of Edelman and, alongside some individual aspects, differ from the case of her predecessor as WIDF general secretary, Rosa Jasovich. Unlike Edelman, Jasovich does not seem to have been a figure of the same importance as Edelman for the WIDF or for communist women's history in Argentina (comparable with other communist female activists such as Margareta de Ponce or Irma Othar – see Valobra 2012, 2017). But, Rosa Jasovich Pantaleón became famous in Argentina during the 1970s as one of the founders of the Permanent Assembly for Human Rights in Argentina (1975). This assembly was one of the most important actors in denouncing the crimes of the dictatorship, and making a list of the "disappeared" during the military regime.[3]

However, Jasovich also seemed to have played a very important role in the WIDF. She became the general secretary at the peak of the anti-colonial movement, soon after the Soviet–China split, and after the Italian women left the federation. Jasovich was the first woman from the Global South to be nominated for this position; however, this nomination could not be made without the support of the Argentinian Communist Party. In spite of the period when she became head of the WIDF's Secretariat being crucial, according to the documents I studied, Jasovich does not seem to have been issuing special statements inside the federation, nor did she have a particularly close relationship with the CSW. The classified correspondence between Berlin and Moscow from 1963 suggests that in personal conversations, Jasovich sometimes expressed doubts as to the federation's political line (*neuverennost v tom, chto my delaem* – GARF 4 169, p. 16). A letter from Lebedeva stated that Jasovich was concerned with Fidel's words criticizing established communist parties with respect to their readiness to lead the revolution in the Global South. The same letter shows that Jasovich was very sensitive to information about the growth of anti-Semitism in Europe (GARF 4 169, p. 16). Finally, Jasovich often showed her vulnerability and sensitivity, which, according to Lebedeva, made her a person with whom it was difficult to work with.

Thus, the example of these two representatives of the Argentinian women's organization suggest the importance of paying attention to differences, and not only to similarities, among the WIDF's top leaders who formally belonged to a communist party and represented the Global South. The differences could also help us better understand the concerns and expectations the Latin American communist female leaders had vis à vis the WIDF.

Representing Nigerian women in the WIDF

I start this section with a quote from the protocols of the 1962 WIDF bureau meeting in Prague. The main aim of this meeting was the preparation of the World Women's Congress in Moscow in 1963, and the WIDF vice-president, a representative of Nigeria, Funmilayo Ransome Kuti, said:

> This Congress will be an important event. It is important that many African women come. Now, many international and other organizations want to get African women under their influence. In the case of Nigeria, the Americans are working particularly actively. In almost all the colleges and high schools are the representatives of the so-called Peace Corps. Thus, the WIDF should deal with the problems concerning women of Africa, and actively work with these problems.
> (GARF 3 790, p. 29, in Russian)

At the time of the bureau meeting, Ransome Kuti, who was elected WIDF vice-president at the 1953 WIDF Congress in Copenhagen, had already been a member of the WIDF's leadership for about 10 years. The quote shows that she was well aware of the new important role of Africa for the international women's movement, and of the main actors in the Cold War confrontation. The quote also suggests that Ransome Kuti defended the interests of the WIDF, and considered it important that the WIDF be more popular among African women than the US-supported women's organizations. At the same time, the quote also indicates that the WIDF was not doing enough for African women, and that it should pay more attention to their interests.

While post-independence Nigeria did not have a specifically close relationship with the Soviet Union (see Matusevich 2003), or other countries of the Soviet Bloc, the Nigerian activist Funmilayo Ransome Kuti became one of the first African women to cooperate with the WIDF and its first vice-president from Africa, many years before the independence of Nigeria.

Thus, in this section, I want to explore what made Ransome Kuti interested in the WIDF, and how the experience of her participation was connected to other aspects of her life and activism.

Funmilayo Ransome Kuti (1900–1978) is regarded today as being one of the most prominent women's rights activists in African history. UNESCO has published a special pamphlet dedicated to her in its series "On Women in African History". According to this pamphlet, Ransome Kuti was one of the first women's rights activists in Nigeria, and her activities are used as examples by African women's organizations today (Onajin & Ofoego 2014). The pamphlet consists of comic sketches made by Nigerian artists, and short captions accompanying them. Furthermore, two Nigerian researchers, Cheryl Johnson-Odim and Nina Mba, published a book on Ransome Kuti's activism and conducted several interviews with her at her home in Abeokuta during the last years of her life, between 1974 and 1976 (Johnson-Odim & Mba 1997, x). In spite of this book, and the pamphlet published by UNESCO, Ransome Kuti's name is relatively unknown to feminists and researchers in Europe, who may presume that she only had regional rather than global importance.

The pamphlet published by UNESCO informs us that Ransome Kuti was sent to the UK for her university studies, and that she experienced racism while she was there (Onajin & Ofoego 2014, 44). The pamphlet also shows that Ransome Kuti started to fight against the injustices of colonial oppression at a young age. Both publications praise her as a remarkable female leader, who had already started a women's club in one of the Nigerian provinces, Abeokuta, in the mid-1940s; the club demanded changes to colonial law and, later, also demanded the franchise for women. The UNESCO publication, with the help of sketches, explicitly shows the transformation of the Abeokuta organization from a charity club where urban Black middle-class women gathered together (Ladies Club of Abeokuta) to the Women's Union of Abeokuta – an organization open to women from all classes, and with anti-colonial aspirations and demands for improvements in women's rights (Onajin & Ofoego 2014).

Johnson-Odim & Mba, in their book, characterized Ransome Kuti as a "democratic socialist"[4] who fought against racial and gender oppression (Johnson-Odim & Mba 1997, 41). At the same time, they noted that, during the most difficult period of the fight for independence, her writings acquired a more nationalist tone; in 1961, for example, she advised women to temporarily "forgo their personal interests for those of their husbands" in order to help constructing the new nation (Johnson-Odim & Mba 1997, 41). Part of the book by Johnson-Odim & Mba is dedicated to Ransome Kuti's early years, and shows the importance of the Christian religion in her life at that time; she is also said to have become the wife of a priest and a school rector. At the same time, the experience of racism during her student years in Britain is said to have influenced her to drop her Christian name, and encouraged a growing interest in traditional religions and the cultures of the region (Johnson-Odim & Mba 1997).

Johnson-Odim and Mba suggest that Ransome Kuti's international contacts were first developed through her and her husband's travels to Britain, in particular, their meetings with pro-independence activists from other African countries there. However, according to the authors, Ransome Kuti was also interested in the development of social institutions in Britain itself; in 1947, she spent two months there with a delegation of Nigerian women, visiting welfare organizations, kindergartens, and factories (Johnson-Odim & Mba 1997, 135).

When discussing Ransome Kuti's international interests and contacts, none of the publications consider Ransome Kuti's participation in the WIDF to have been particularly important for her. The illustrated story produced by UNESCO, towards the end, merely informs its readers that Ransome Kuti visited the Soviet Union and in 1970 received the Lenin Prize (Onajin & Ofoego 2014, 49–50). Johnson-Odim & Mba dedicate more space to Ransome Kuti's involvement in the WIDF. They write that, most probably, Ransome Kuti met WIDF representatives during one of her trips to London around 1947 (Johnson-Odim & Mba 1997, 137). Due to the WIDF's bad fame as a Communist organization, Ransome Kuti, according to the authors, was very careful with the federation at first, and in 1949, "diplomatically" refused the WIDF's invitation to attend its congress in China (Johnson-Odim & Mba 1997, 139–141). The researchers also show that later on, however, Ransome Kuti intensified her contacts with the WIDF and visited the federation's meeting in China in 1956, in spite of the fact that the Nigerian government banned WIDF publications in the country, as publications of a "Communist organization". During the 1950s, on several occasions the Nigerian colonial authorities refused Ransome Kuti's passport applications to attend the WIDF meetings in Europe[5] (Johnson-Odim & Mba 1997, 145–146). Finally, only after Nigerian independence in 1961 could Ransome Kuti visit Moscow and Prague. However, according to the authors, in the 1960s, Ransome Kuti established contacts with many other organizations, both in Africa and internationally, and she even attempted to establish WILPF membership for Nigeria[6] (Johnson-Odim & Mba 1997, 148–149). Thus, on the basis of the study made by Johnson-Odim & Mba, it is possible to suppose that Ransome Kuti's involvement with the WIDF was not a significant part of her life, while the ideological and physical distance between her and the federation was quite large at most times.

However, as I already said, Ransome Kuti was elected one of the vice-presidents of the WIDF at the Congress in Copenhagen, and her picture in traditional Yoruba dress could be found among those of other WIDF leaders (*Za ravnopravie* 1953). Together with the representative of Communist China and the Egyptian female leader Ceza Nabarawi, the two other WIDF vice-presidents from outside of Europe, Ransome Kuti differed from the rest of the WIDF leaders by her non-whiteness and, in particular, she was the only one in the picture wearing non-European dress. It is possible to imagine that Ransome Kuti's difference was very important from the perspective of the WIDF's representational logic; she encompassed "the whole world" of women from the Global South having "non-European" appearance and clothes. Nevertheless, the archival materials from GARF partly confirm the conclusions made by Johnson-Odim & Mba, Ransome Kuti's functions in the WIDF before Nigerian independence seem to be mainly representational. In fact, the Women's Union of Nigeria was not able to send a delegation to the 1953 congress in Copenhagen (GARF 2 1350, p. 8). However, it is important to note that as early as 1953, the possibility of becoming part of the WIDF seems to have been important for Ransome Kuti and her organization. Indeed, the Union of Women of Nigeria expressed its pride on the occasion that its president, Ransome Kuti, had been elected one of the vice-presidents of the federation (ibid.)

Nevertheless, the contacts with the WIDF, and women from state socialist countries, seem to have continued to be important for both sides in the years to come. From time to time, Ransome Kuti informed the WIDF about the activities of Nigerian women, and the archive collection contains a postcard from 1958, in which she sends her Christmas and New Year's greetings to the Committee of Soviet Women (GARF 3 310).

The documents from the Moscow archive also suggest that Ransome Kuti's election intensified the exchange of information between her, on the one hand, and the WIDF and CSW, on the other. The CSW archival collection preserved informational material about the women's movement in Nigeria from February 1953. The file contains the "Constitution, Rules and Regulations for the Women's Union of Abeokuta" organized and led by Ransome Kuti in still-colonial Nigeria. The Constitution was published by Bosere Press in Abeokuta in two languages – English and Yoruba (GARF 2 1350, p. 4). According to the Constitution, the Union had "Unity, Truthfulness, Cleanliness, Selflessness" as its motto while the Union's main objectives included "cooperation among all the women in Egbaland", "promotion and defence of the social, economic cultural and political rights and interests of the women in Egbaland"; "encouragement of mass education for women through teaching its members to read and write"; "cooperation with other organizations seeking economic and political freedom and independence of the people" (GARF 2 1350, p. 4a). The pamphlet also stated that the membership in the Union was open "to all women in Egbaland irrespective of tribe, creed or status" (GARF 2 1350, p. 4a). Even if some of the Union's slogans could indicate the influences of Christian or charity thinking (cleanliness, selflessness), the Union's goals were very ambitious and, at the same time, contained a number of practical tasks aimed at the transformation of women's role in the society. Women's organization with such goals and open membership could well fit into the activities propagated by the WIDF, which seemed to indicate the promise of a successful cooperation.

The archive also preserved a translated article from the Finnish women's magazine (published by the Democratic League of Finnish Women, member of the WIDF) *Uusi Nainen* from 8 August 1952 containing an interview with Ransome Kuti (GARF 2 1350, p. 5, in Russian translation). This publication presented Ransome Kuti as a Black teacher, the wife of a Black priest, and a leader of a Nigerian women's organization with 8,000 members. The interview gives an impressive picture of the Union's demands and activities; free school education and free medical care shared programme space with defence of equal political participation of women in local-level elective institutions. The organizational efforts were also big; the article claimed that in order to guarantee the financial independence of the organization, women opened a small textile cooperative and were planning to open a small printing house to spread the messages of the Union (GARF 2 1350, p. 5). The interview also presented Ransome Kuti in a more feminist look, when compared to the Constitution of the Women's Union I discussed above. Indeed, according to the publication, she noted that in Nigeria "women have to work a lot because men are like lords and most women after getting married are converted almost into slaves... Women are responsible for food and clothes for children. But sometimes, women also have to take care of their husbands" (GARF 2 1350, p. 5). She also described the multiple responsibilities of women in the context of a cross-sectional system of oppression; the lack of social security and welfare (it is possible to suppose that this is an accusation against the colonial regime as well) and gender inequality. According to Ransome Kuti in this publication, because of the absence of free schooling and women's responsibility for childrearing, it is women who have to collect money for the education of their children and, thus, work particularly hard (GARF 2 1350, p. 5). Even if as a result of double translation some of the ideas of Ransome Kuti experienced some modifications, it is possible to say that Ransome Kuti was a political leader who was able to earn sympathy and establish contacts with women's organizations in different countries.

As opposed to the Constitution of the Women's Union and the article in the periodical publication of the WIDF member from Finland, another document from the same period, preserved in the Moscow archive, suggests rather that the organization of the Nigerian women was quite different from the WIDF's early members, whether in Europe or in Latin America. The report on the congress of the Union of Nigerian Women that took place from 31 July to 1 August 1953 (about one month after the WIDF congress in Copenhagen) stated, for example, that the congress in Abeokuta commenced with a prayer that was read by Ms. I.I. Okala, described as the first lady adviser of Onitsha (GARF 2 1350, pp. 9–10, in Russian translation). The protocol not only mentioned prayers, but also stated that a particular prayer was offered for Ransome Kuti's long life as a leader of the women's organization. The Congress also took place in a colonial setting, and Kuti read greetings from the governor of Nigeria, Mr. John MacPherson, who regretted that he could not attend the congress due to his trip to London. It is also remarkable that women's organizations from Germany and the USA sent their greetings to the congress. While the congress discussed several issues that corresponded to the WIDF's vision of women's rights, including the universal franchise, a demand that women would constitute not less than 30% of the local legislative bodies, and the importance of school education for children – the congress also discussed other issues, including Nigerian territorial unity (GARF 2 1350, pp. 11–12). While such a short report in translation cannot explain how the Nigerian women's organization functioned, it is possible to say that this organization was a grassroots organization that, having its own tasks, forms, and rules of operation, was open to cooperation with different organizations, including the WIDF, on the basis of common interests. Ransome Kuti seems to have had very broad autonomy for her organization within the WIDF.

On the other hand, the high status of Ransome Kuti in the WIDF – she continued to keep her post of vice-president for a rather long time, from 1953 to 1975 (WWW 1975 1:3) – along with her receiving the Lenin Prize in 1970, indicate that she was very important for the WIDF's international image and, in particular, for its image in the African countries. Indeed, using Ransome Kuti's own words from the quotation at the beginning of this section, it was a time when "many international and other organizations want to get African women under their influence"; it made the presence of a well-known Black African women's rights activist among the WIDF leaders of crucial importance for the federation.

At the same time, due to the rather free character of membership of the Nigerian organization in the WIDF, the federation publicly presented a rather selective picture of its leader. For example, an article on Ransome Kuti by Barbara Kaufman published by the WIDF journal in 1960 – "In her country she is loved and respected by women" – focused mainly on the union's activism against the colonial administration in 1947. The article also recalled some important moments from Ransome Kuti's life (ZM 1960, 10, pp. 17–19). Noting that Ransome Kuti was one of the first female students in the same middle school that was attended by her future husband, the article, however, did not mention that she became the wife of a priest. Nor was there any mention of her interests in British social policy, her organization for middle-class Black women in Abeokuta, or her attempts to cooperate with women's organizations other than the WIDF. Vice versa, the main aim of the article seems to be to present Ransome Kuti as a supporter of the WIDF ideology and practice; this message was also conveyed through the visual images accompanying the text. One of them, for example, presented Ransome Kuti as a vice-president of WIDF in one of the council meetings together with Cotton, and Tsan Chai from China, and another photo showed her with the WIDF representative from Norway. The text and images, thus, suggested Ransome Kuti was fully involved in the WIDF's everyday life.

Hence, while Ransome Kuti continued to occupy the position of WIDF vice-president for more than 20 years, her influence on the federation's programme documents and practical activity seems to have been limited, with the most important period corresponding to the height of the anti-colonial struggle in Africa and the 1963 Moscow congress. During other periods of the WIDF's work, Ransome Kuti seems taking a less active part in the federation's decision-making, and in its transnational work. Ransome Kuti's long history of cooperation with the WIDF could be explained thus, through both not very intensive interactions with the WIDF, and a rather selective picture of her presentation as a WIDF leader by the federation's official media.

Organizing women in Northern Africa and the Middle East

I will start by quoting the protocol of a 1954 meeting at the WIDF Secretariat in Berlin, when Fatima Ahmet Ibrahim, the leader and one of the organizers of the Sudanese Women's Union, visited the WIDF for the first time. Describing the tasks of the Sudanese Women's Union to the members of the WIDF Secretariat, Ahmed Ibrahim stated:

> The Sudanese women started to understand that their liberation is connected to the liberation of their country. They are starting to participate more and more actively in the defence of the democratic rights of the people, for freedom and peace.
>
> (GARF 2 1482, p. 9)

When addressing the WIDF Secretariat, Ahmed Ibrahim was 21 years old, and a member of Sudan's communist party. Coming from a country with a history of complicated relationships between different groups of the population as a result of the imperial divisions of the African territories and the imperial management of the population[7] (see, e.g., Reina 2010; Mahjoub 2018), Ahmed Ibrahim was the representative of the Muslim North. Thus, a focus on her biography can help us understand how WIDF activities developed in the Middle Eastern and North African countries.

This section is dedicated to several female activists from the region. Ahmed Ibrahim's biography, in the context of the WIDF, is particularly interesting due to her WIDF career after the end of the Cold War. In 1991, she was elected the WIDF's president, the first one who was non-White and represented the Global South (de Haan 2012, p. 18). Salwa Zayadeen from Jordan was another remarkable person who worked at the WIDF's Secretariat in the 1960s. Both of them belonged to a younger generation of WIDF activists, but their role in the federation was quite different. Before discussing their biographies, I want to say a few words about one more activist from the Middle East, one of the first from this region who became a part of the WIDF leadership, in the 1950s, Ceza Nabarawi.

Nabarawi (also spelled as Nabaraoui, 1897–1985), a well-known Egyptian feminist, was elected WIDF vice-president along with Ransome Kuti at the 1953 WIDF congress in Copenhagen. While the biography of Nabarawi is well researched (especially the early period of her life), the available literature in combination with the WIDF archival material and journal publications about her indicate that the example of Nabarawi offers a quite unique case of participation of women from the Global South in the WIDF leadership. Nabarawi belonged to the generation of Egyptian feminists who became active after Egypt became independent in 1923 (Badran 1995; Bier 2010). She and her relative and feminist colleague, Huda Shaarawi, were co-founders of the Egyptian Feminist Union in 1923. They advocated changes in laws regulating marriage age, access of women to university education, and their political participation during the interwar period. Both of them also became involved in transnational women's activism by participating in the International Alliance of Women (IAW). However, Nabarawi decided to leave the IAW and join the WIDF after the Second World War. This decision was most probably influenced by the IAW's patronizing attitudes towards women in dependent countries and former colonies (see, e.g., Bier 2010, pp. 160–161) as well as by the WIDF's firm position on the Palestinian question. According to Sara Salem, the Palestinian question had a special importance for the women's movement in all Arab countries[8] (see below on Jordan's women's movement). In particular, in an extensive interview with Nabarawi published by the WIDF journal in 1959 – "The first to discard the veil" – she spoke directly on her growing conflicts with the IAW's leadership after the division of Palestine in 1948, and the founding of the state of Israel, as an important reason for changing her affiliation. Her disillusion with the IAW, according to the WIDF journal, became greater after the beginning of the Korean War in 1950 (*WWW* 1959 2: 18–21). Thus, the interview suggests that, in the case of Nabarawi, joining the WIDF, the Cold War political adversary of the IAW, was a conscious choice conditioned by a changed political situation, and a preference for a transnational political ally whose position better corresponded with the regional expectations of women.

The Moscow archive materials show that the during the 1950s–early 1960s, Nabarawi played an important role in the work of the WIDF, particularly by managing the WIDF's contacts in the Middle East and Northern Africa. Nabarawi was a valuable source of information regarding the women's movement in Arab countries, as well as on the internal situation in Egypt; the WIDF leadership highly valued her reports and inside information. For example, in 1957, Nabarawi warned the WIDF general secretary, Angiola Minella about the "not fully democratic" attitude of Nasser's government towards women's organizations (GARF 4 115, pp. 93–94). In her interview with the WIDF journal discussed above, Nabarawi herself proudly informed the readers about her representing the federation in different conferences of Asian and African solidarity (including the African and Asian Women's Conference in Cairo in 1957 and the All African People's Conference in Accra in 1958[9]). Nabarawi's role was especially important in the 1960s, as the Cold War adversaries competed hard for influence over African women (see Ransome Kuti's quote in the previous section). At the same time, other archival materials suggest that, similarly to Ransome Kuti, Nabarawi missed several WIDF leadership meetings due to the political situation in her home country, and financial problems (see GARF 3 790, p. 56; GARF 3 803, p. 106).

While both vice-presidents from the Global South elected in 1953 had their formative years in the colonial period, and both partly received their education in the West, in the rest of this section, I will look closely at two activists who began to be politically active mainly in the 1950s.

Due to a long period of political repression in Sudan after 1971, Fatima Ahmed Ibrahim (1933–2017) was arrested several times,[10] and after the Al-Bashir coup in 1989 and the growing Islamization of Sudan, she spent many years in exile (mainly in the UK). After her death in 2017, the *Guardian* published an obituary that characterized her as a "feminist political activist" and a "pioneer in the field of women's rights".[11] While the WIDF was not mentioned in this article, Ahmed Ibrahim was described as a co-founder of "the Sudanese Women's Union, which went on to campaign for and secure the right of women to vote, receive maternity pay and a pension". According to the *Guardian*, Ahmed Ibrahim joined the Sudanese Communist Party at the age of 19 because at that time it was the only party that allowed female membership. The obituary also stated that in 1993 Ibrahim "received a UN award for outstanding achievements in the field of human rights, and the Ibn Rushd prize for freedom of thought in 2006".

While, in the 1960s, Sudan was seen as a progressive country in terms of respect for women's rights (Mahjoub 2018, 221), and Ahmed Ibrahim was one of the first elected female MPs in Sudan, internationally, she seems to have become better known rather late in her life, after the end of the Cold War. By then, Ahmed Ibrahim was considered a female politician with a post-colonial and Muslim feminist stance. Her article published in the international anthology *Frontline feminisms* in 2000, for example, discussed the history of the women's movement in Sudan, and criticized both fundamentalist and Western interpretations of Islam. In this article, Ahmed Ibrahim indicated her sympathies with Islamic feminism: "By studying Islam from its source, the Quran, we could prove that Islam neither prohibits women's involvement in politics, nor their equality" (Ahmed Ibrahim 2000, 134). According to another Sudanese women's rights activist, Rogaia Mustafa Abusharaf, Ahmed Ibrahim criticized the Western preoccupation with female circumcision, seeing it as the biggest problem for Sudanese women. Ahmed Ibrahim saw the "circumcision" as "a symptom of woman's troubles in the society" and of her discrimination (Mustafa Abusharaf 2000, 156), thus she considered it important to change woman's status in society in order to fight the "circumcision".

However, none of the named publications mention the WIDF's activities during the Cold War, nor do they feature Ahmed Ibrahim's role in the federation.[12] Thus, it is particularly interesting to look at the WIDF archives and publications concerning her activity.

Sudan was a country where the WIDF did not seem to have any contacts prior to 1953 and, thus, the visit by young Fatima Ahmed Ibrahim (1933–2017) in 1954 that I described at the beginning of this section was an important event, and she was invited to present her organization before the members of the Secretariat. According to the brief report sent to Moscow by the Soviet representative after this meeting, Ahmed Ibrahim enthusiastically reacted to the WIDF's proposal to visit Sudan and her organization (GARF 2 1482, p. 2, from 26 July 1954). The Soviet representative also stressed that this meeting in Berlin showed that the Sudanese organization expected several kinds of aid from the WIDF, including helping with developing a solidarity campaign in the countries of the Global South.

In presenting her organization, Ahmed Ibrahim started by stating that women in Sudan are not allowed to go out alone, do not have rights with regard to their children, and that possibilities for getting an education in Sudan are quite limited for both men and women (GARF 2 1482, pp. 5–6). However, she stressed important changes that happened there, including the creation of women's organizations:

> At the beginning, it was the union of literate women, but now it has opened its doors to working and peasant women; it defends their demands and makes its influence grow.
> (GARF 2 1482, p. 8)

Due to these changes and, in particular, to the participation of women from poor families, paying special attention to the problem of membership fees was important: "the fees should not hinder women from becoming members of the organization" and "other possibilities of financing should be taken into account". Ahmed Ibrahim also named several demands that were made by her organization. They included opening maternity hospitals, kindergartens, and preparing a growing number of midwives, the expansion of educational institutions for girls, the creation of centres teaching housekeeping, higher (than present) salaries and equal pay with men for working women, and more opportunities for women to get jobs (GARF 2 1482, pp. 8–9).

This programme, along with Ahmed Ibrahim's expressed interest in participating in the WIDF's meetings (two representatives from Sudan promised to attend the next council meeting), got a very positive reaction from the WIDF's headquarters in Berlin. However, even though contacts between the WIDF and the Sudanese Women's Union (SWU) were established in 1954, the active participation of the Sudanese women in the WIDF seems to have begun much later. The first time an activist from Sudan took part in a WIDF bureau meeting was when Batun Babiker Dzarrug attended the event in Berlin in December 1962. The WIDF president, Eugenie Cotton, expressed particular happiness on this occasion (GARF 3 794, p. 2). Picture of Ahmet Ibrahim also appeared on the cover of the WIDF journal in 1963 (ZM 1963, 2).

The early 1970s was probably the period of the most active and successful cooperation between the WIDF and the SWU, and this was connected with the organization of a big international seminar in Khartoum on the liquidation of illiteracy among African women. The importance of this conference for the country organizer was demonstrated by the presence of Sudan's president, Jaafar Nimeiry, who made a speech at the opening of the conference (WWW 1970, 3: 6–10). In his speech, Nimeiry indicated the importance of the liquidation of illiteracy among women for the government and, thus, contributed to the visibility of the women's movement in Sudan.

The presentations made at the conference by the participants from Sudan and other African countries focused on the African experience with women's education. For example, the representative of Sudan, Abdel Aal, stressed in her talk that in order to popularize the literacy courses and to attract more women, the SWU was working broadly with the population. The organization was also trying to establish contacts with the husbands of women attending the courses. Due to the important role that the husband used to play in African and Arab families, according to Aal, the husband's approval of his wife's activity was important "not only from the practical, but also from the moral point of view" (GARF 3 2421, p. 47). In her turn, Ahmed Ibrahim, in her speech "Urgent measures to meet women's demands in the field of education", advocated women's education as benefitting the family; according to Ahmed Ibrahim, the differences in the level of education between a husband and a wife is often is a cause of many other problems, including divorce and (male) polygamy (GARF 3 2421, p. 132). Furthermore, Ahmed Ibrahim pronounced herself against those activists and politicians in Sudan who considered starting cultural change in society by first changing how women looked, i.e. by attacking the traditional clothes women wore ("the national dress", in Ahmed Ibrahim's words). In general, explaining her vision of emancipation, Ahmed Ibrahim showed herself as a rather postcolonial feminist in Mohanty's terms, her position differed not only from the "Western", but also from the "Soviet one":

> emancipation of women was not just the discarding of the robe, this is a formal liberation, no more nor less. True emancipation is freedom from ignorance, superstition, lies and bigotedness, emancipation from poverty, disease and thirst.
>
> (GARF 3 2421, p. 135)

Thus, it is possible to say that the SWU presented its strategy as an attempt to combine the liquidation of illiteracy with solving social problems and the defence of the nation, and it welcomed solving the problems of illiteracy without making loud declarations on women's discrimination by men or religion.

At the same time, the archival documents show that the conference was expected to have an ideological programme as well, and had to showcase the achievements of women's education in the state socialist countries. Ahmed Ibrahim seemed to have supported the idea of organizing a special event dedicated to the 100th anniversary of Lenin's birth. However, due to the unstable situation in the country after the coup d'état and persecution of the communists, those plans were difficult to realize. The representative of the WIDF from Jordan, Leyla Zayadeen, who made two trips to Khartoum in the process of preparing the conference, reported to the Secretariat in November 1969 that Ahmed Ibrahim considered it difficult to organize such a celebration; it could be used by the reactionary forces to present the seminar as a "communist event" (GARF 3 2122, p. 163). Still, as the report on the conference published by the WIDF journal shows, some kind of celebration of Lenin's anniversary took place during the conference (WWW 1970, 3) and, thus, had to be supported and realized by the local organizers.

Hence, Ahmed Ibrahim demonstrated her capacity to organize a conference for women's rights and, in spite of the adverse political atmosphere, to cooperate with male politicians. The conference materials also show Ahmed Ibrahim as a person who could oppose the Westernized vision of modernity; she defended women's right to education without attacking "traditional dress" or Islam. After that conference, and in spite of the changed political situation in Sudan in 1971 after the coup d'état, Ahmed Ibrahim seems to have kept contacts with the WIDF, which allowed her to become the first president of the WIDF from the Global South after she was released from prison and left Sudan for the UK in 1990.

The second female activist from the same region who belonged, as Ahmed Ibrahim, to a younger generation of WIDF collaborators, was Salwa Zayadeen from Jordan, a figure who continues to be rather unknown outside her country. Zayadeen lived in exile in Berlin between approximately 1958 and 1970 and worked in the Secretariat as a "political collaborator" (*politicheskii sorrudnik*), i.e. she had not been officially dispatched to the Secretariat by a national women's organization. During these years, Zayadeen worked as a clandestine activist, and in some of the documents available to me, she is referred to only as "Leyla" from Jordan.

The documents note that Jordanian women took part in many meetings and congresses and, it seems, that Leyla was already participating in the WIDF council meeting in Prague in 1959. There, she was one of those proclaiming the importance of anti-colonial goals being more visible in the WIDF's programme and stressed, in particular, that "although our century is a century of peaceful co-existence, it cannot be co-existence between the colonizers and the colonized" (GARF 3 221, p. 18, in Russian). In 1963, "Leyla" attended the WIDF congress in Moscow (GARF 3 967, pp. 35–37). The protocol of the commission on national independence stated that in her intervention, "Leyla" approached the difficulties of the post-colonial situation through sharing her personal story; while her country was independent and had its own representation in the UN, the expectations of people in her country that standards of living would raise and more schools for children would be built were not fulfilled. On the contrary, the current political situation was that that many people were imprisoned, her husband had already been in prison for six years (GARF 3 967, p. 35). Reflecting on this story, with the aid of several other WIDF documents and some information that I found on the Internet,[13] it is possible to claim that Leyla (or Leyla

Zayadeen, as she is referred to in some of the WIDF documents) is a well-known figure in the Jordanian and Palestinian women's movements, Salwa Zayadeen. After the coup d'état of 1957 and the arrest of her husband, Salwa and two her small children escaped Jordan and arrived in the GDR. Zayadeen might have changed her name in order to conceal her identity.

The history of the women's movement in Jordan, and its complex connections with the communist party and the Palestinian movement, was explored in a dissertation by Jordanian researcher Abeer Dababneh (2005). Dababneh interviewed Salwa Zayadeen in the early 2000s, and described her as one of the important figures of the women's movement in the country (Dababneh 2005, 91). According to Dababneh, the Jordanian Women's Union (JWU) was created in 1954, and was connected with the communist party. The JWU was guided by the ideas of socialist feminism, but also defended the national agenda (Dababneh 2005, 98–100). In the mid-1950s, women in Jordan not only demanded the right to vote, but also the opportunity to receive military training (in particular, after the Suez crisis of 1956); in the 1950s, the JWU included many prominent Palestinian women (Dababneh 2005, 98).[14] The Union was banned by the government in 1957, but in her interview with Dababneh, Salwa Zayadeen insisted on the existence of a clandestine women's organization between 1957 and 1974 (Dababneh 2005, 102–103).

The Moscow archive documents show that after the outlawing of the JWU in 1957, Jordanian women wrote to the WIDF expecting its support for Jordanian political prisoners and exiled people. In a letter from 13 March 1962, for example, arrests and torture in prisons was mentioned, and the letter stated that women decided to send this information to the WIDF because they thought that the federation was also preoccupied with the situation in Jordan (GARF 3 803, p. 6). In this context, the work of Zayadeen in the WIDF Secretariat was very important; similarly to Seza Nabarawi, Zayadeen had a lot of knowledge on the context of women's activism in the region, and had many contacts there. Zayadeen's knowledge of Arabic was also of great importance for the WIDF's work in the region. The WIDF's contacts with women's organizations in Jordan were practically lost in 1964 (GARF 3 1220, pp. 12–13), but Zayadeen travelled a lot through the Middle East and other parts of the world collecting information for the WIDF and maintaining contacts between women's organizations in Arab countries. In particular, Zayadeen had a crucial role in the preparation of the seminar on women's education in Khartoum in 1970, and visited Sudan two times. Also, on her way back, Zayadeen visited several other countries – Syria, Iraq, and the United Arab Republic (Egypt) – where she had meetings with the representatives of women's organizations in the name of the WIDF (GARF 3 2122, p. 163).

Unlike several other representatives of African and Asian countries Zayadeen fully supported the WIDF's position (coinciding with the official Soviet one) concerning the Soviet-China split in the early 1960s and condemned the developments in China. According to the letters of the Soviet representative in Berlin, Zinaida Lebedeva, to the SWC, after the publication of an important ideological article on Soviet disagreements with China in *Pravda* on 7 January 1963, the opinions of those women who worked in the WIDF's Secretariat in Berlin differed a lot. Leyla Zayadeen supported the Soviet position, however, and said that the article gives "substantial arguments for discussing all the important questions with the Chinese representatives" (GARF 4 169, p. 4). Using information received from Zayadeen, Lebedeva informed Moscow that the government of Jordan demanded that its political prisoners sign papers where they would promise to refuse to support the Soviet line. According to Zayadeen, the prisoners were shown Chinese material criticizing developments in the USSR and, according to Lebedeva, in personal conversation, Leyla expressed her preoccupation with the possible reaction of her imprisoned husband. According to Leyla, her husband, who was "arrested before all the conflicts and divisions among Soviet, Chinese and Albanian communists", might sign such a paper criticizing Soviet policies (GARF 4 169, p. 16).

Some other letters to Moscow from the Soviet representative in the Secretariat during the same period demonstrate that after her arrival in Berlin, Leyla's personal situation was very difficult. In a letter from 1963, Zinaida Lebedeva characterized Zayadeen as a very active and hard-working person who needed help; Leyla's children were seriously ill with rheumatism and were treated in hospital in Berlin. With reference to the doctor, Lebedeva suggested that Zayadeen's children probably needed a change of climate and professional care at a sanatorium, and asked her employers in Moscow to offer Zayadeen's children a course of medical treatment at some specialized sanatorium near Moscow (GARF 4 169, p. 16).

While it is not possible to discover how this situation with the children was solved, the documents show that in later years, Salwa Zayadeen continued actively working in the Secretariat until her return to Jordan in 1970 (I discussed her letter written upon her return in Chapter 5). However, in spite of her happiness at returning to her home country and meeting her husband again, the archival materials show that Zayadeen's status as a well-known women's rights activist in Jordan was mainly lost during the 12 years of her work in Berlin, and she was seen by the new women's organization, the Arab Women's Organization in Jordan, led by Emily Naffa, as a person who spent too much time abroad. This new Jordanian women's organization, at that moment, had the support of the WIDF. For example, in her letter to the WIDF (to Hugel) from 14 December 1970, Naffa made a clear distinction between her organization that "has been legally recognized by the government" and Salwa Zayadeen, who "has never been a member of the executive committee" and who spent too much time abroad (GARF 3 2772, p. 51). Thus, it seems that the contacts and experience that Zayadeen acquired during her 12 years of work in Berlin could not be transferred into political capital for the women's movement at home. On the other hand, it seems that Salwa Zayadeen continued her cooperation with the WIDF, and that in May 1974, she attended the WIDF Bureau meeting in Warsaw (GARF 3 3410, p. 1).

Thus, using the examples of Ahmed Ibrahim and Zayadeen's biographies, it is possible to say that these women were inspired by leftist and socialist theories of women's rights, supported the anti-colonial and national struggles in their countries, and were interested in learning more about the achievements of the state socialist countries with regard to women's rights and social reforms in general. It was these broader interests that made them look for connections, and ask for support from the WIDF. Their choice to join communist parties, probably, was not defined by purely ideological considerations, but rather followed a practical choice; they were looking for a political organization that could give them a place and provide support for their broader aspirations of social change.

However, during the years of their participation in the WIDF, both women suffered a lot as both defenders of women's rights and leftist/communist activists. Both of them were involved in political confrontations at different levels, including those inside the communist movement, and both became victims of repression. Still, it seems that both women saw their cooperation with the WIDF as important. Also, both women received ideological and financial support from the WIDF during their activist careers.

Conclusion

Employing a biographical perspective for several women from the Global South who took part in the work for the WIDF at different periods of its history shows the complex reasons and forms of participation of the female activists in the federation's work. Some of these women seem to have combined their work for and with the WIDF with other ideas, beliefs, political agendas, and organizational memberships that sometimes contradicted the official ideology of the WIDF. The limited material available to me does not allow me to fully explore the (positive and negative) impact of the cooperation of female leaders from different countries with the WIDF on the work of their national organizations. However, it is quite clear that all of them acquired new international experiences and received international acknowledgement for their struggle for women's rights through participation in some of the WDIF's sponsored events, or as members of its governing bodies. If nothing else, the election of one of these women, Fatima Ahmed Ibrahim, to the presidency of the WIDF in the year the Soviet Bloc collapsed shows the importance of her previous participation in the federation.

At the same time, the biographies of several prominent WIDF activists explored in this chapter confirm findings made in previous chapters regarding the serious limitations of the influence of female leaders from the Global South had on the WIDF's ideology and decision-making. Yet attention to individual biographies allows us to see that the role of these women in the organization, and their possibility to influence its programmes, events, and practical work differed a lot, depending on the home region and political affiliation of the leaders. In particular, an Argentinian communist, Fanny Edelman, seemed to be at the centre of discussions on the federation's most important decisions. Also, it was she who travelled throughout the world representing the federation and bringing its message. Most of the other women I discussed in this chapter did not attain such an influence in the federation, for different reasons. It is particularly remarkable that Funmilayo Ransome Kuti, who for many years was the WIDF's vice-president and practically the only one representing women from Sub-Saharan Africa in the WIDF's leadership in the 1950s–1960s, did not seem to play a prominent role in the WIDF's decision-making and management. For some other women, like Fatima Ahmed Ibrahim or Salwa Zayadeen, support from the WIDF seemed to be very important; however, their biographical stories indicate that this support was not enough in order for them to become recognized as important political figures in their home countries, or internationally, during the Cold War.

Notes

1 For more on the Club of International Friendship (*KID*), see in Gradskova 2014.
2 Edelman noted that they two cooperated as representatives of their respective organizations – the WIDF and the PAWO (1996, 180).
3 See, for example, http://www.derechos.org/nizkor/arg/apdh/20.html.
4 Ghana's president, Kwame Nkrumah, was a person with whom Ransome Kuti kept a good relationship all her life (Johnson-Odim & Mba 1997, 51); most probably they first met as members of the West-African Students' Union in London in 1946 (Johnson-Odim & Mba 1997, 126–127).
5 She was also denied her passport when she wanted to visit a women's conference in San Francisco in 1958 (Johnson-Odim 2009, 57).
6 According to Johnson-Odim and Mba, the cooperation with the WILPF was only partly successful, not least due to the organization's patronizing attitude, and attempts at "leading" and "teaching" African women (1997, 149).
7 South Sudan became an independent state in 2011.
8 According to Salem, "The question of Palestine was one of the key issues of the Nasser period. It was understood that the British occupation of Egypt, the formation of the state of Israel, and the emergence of American imperialism were key components of women's activism" (Salem 2017, 598).
9 The All African People's Conference in Accra, Ghana was organized by the president of Ghana, Kwame Nkrumah. The CIA reports show that the participants of this and the next one – in 1960 in Tunis – were observed closely. In particular, the report described the leadership of the organization in the 1960s as controlled by a "gamut of Communist thought (i.e. militant Chinese, Orthodox Soviet and Yugoslav nationalists)" (1961, 2). The WIDF, having the role of observer at the conference in Accra, was characterized as "the international Communist Women's front". (1961, 5).
10 Jaafar (Gaafar) Nimeiry, who became Sudan's president in 1969 through a military coup, in the beginning supported socialist ideas, however, in 1971–1972, he changed his political orientation and started a repression against the Communist Party of Sudan. Ahmed Ibrahim's husband was executed in 1971 (Ahmed Ibrahim 2000, 136; see also Detailed Vita of Fatima Ahmed Ibrahim).
11 https://www.theguardian.com/world/2017/aug/21/fatima-ahmed-ibrahim-obituary.
12 WIDF is not mentioned in the publications.

13 A Jordanian blog wrote about Yacoub Zayatddin, a medical doctor and communist who was elected member of parliament from Jerusalem in 1956, but was arrested in 1957 when the Jordanian government decided to ally with the "West". His wife Salwa and two children were sent to a remote village from where they later escaped to the GDR (https://www.alaraby.co.uk/english/blog/2015/4/7/my-communist-hero). Thus, this blog suggests that "Leyla" and Salwa Zayadeen are the same person – the episode of escaping Jordan with two children and moving to the GDR is a rather remarkable one.

14 In the 1950s, Jordan included the West Bank territories.

8 The WIDF on the eve of the IWY and during the UN decade for women

As I showed in the previous chapters, the federation experienced substantial changes during the mid-1960s, one of them being a growing number of members from the Global South. The inclusion of new women's organizations not only led to the federation's numerical growth, but also contributed to raising its international visibility and prestige. This could be seen as one of the factors that contributed to the federation's prestige regaining its official status in transnational governing bodies. While the WIDF continued to participate in some UN meetings and activities after losing its official status in the ECOSOC in 1954, it finally regained its status in 1967, after several unsuccessful applications. This status of transnational NGO further reinforced the WIDF's cooperation with the UN, and its participation in UN-related events.

Accordingly, this chapter explores continuities and changes in the WIDF's ideology, and its campaigning work with regard to the countries of Africa, Asia, and Latin America during the 1970s–1980s – the period of "normalization" of the WIDF's international status. In particular, I analyse how the WIDF's new place in global governance, and the changed composition of its members, influenced the federation's vision of the problems faced by women in Africa, Latin America, and Asia. I also explore changes in their place in the federation, and how this impacted on their influence over its activities. The first section of this chapter concerns aspects of the WIDF's internal situation during, and in connection with, the UN Decade for Women. I then go on to explore how the WIDF addressed the problems of women from the Global South, and how the federation worked with them within that new context. The final section of this chapter looks closely at certain events, solidarity campaigns, and the WIDF's new regional initiatives, in order to explore how cooperation with women's organizations from the Global South was developing, what problems and conflicts became visible, and how much power was exercised by organizations from the Global South.

The WIDF and the UN agenda on equality and non-discrimination

The WIDF's role with regard to the adoption of CEDAW, and in UN conferences during the UN Decade for Women, has already served as an object of scholarly interest. De Haan showed convincingly that it were the representatives of several countries of the Eastern Bloc connected with the WIDF who insisted on the UN's adoption of the *Declaration on the Elimination of Discrimination Against Women* (DEDAW) in 1967,[1] and in 1972 they proposed the UN-supported International Women's Year (Pieper Mooney 2013b, 224; de Haan, 2018, 234–236). The IWY, and the UN conference in Mexico City, has been of particular interest for researchers (Antrobus 2004; Ghodsee 2010; Bonfiglioli 2016; Olcott 2017). They showed that, along with the celebration of equality and solidarity, the UN conference in Mexico City demonstrated deep divisions between women – these divisions were particularly strong between women from the Global North and those from the Global South (Ghodsee 2010; Bonfiglioli 2016; Olcott 2017).

Ghodsee's recently published book, *Second World's Second Sex* (2018), further problematized how the events of the UN Decade for Women were presented in women's history. In particular, she focused on the contribution of state socialist ("Second World") women. According to Ghodsee, women from the Global South, with the support of the WIDF and women's organizations from the state socialist countries, constituted a strong force at all of the UN women's conferences (Mexico 1975; Copenhagen 1980; Nairobi 1985) and were able to make their claims heard. In particular, the *Forward-Looking Strategies for Advancement of Women*, which was adopted by the last UN conference of the decade (in Nairobi), named "imperialism, colonialism, neo-colonialism, expansionism, apartheid and all other forms of manifestation of foreign occupation, domination and hegemony, and the growing gap between the levels of economic development between developed and developing countries" as the main obstacles to the advancement of women (Ghodsee 2018, 2009-210). At the same time, using as examples the Bulgarian WIDF representatives Elena Lagadinova and Ana Durcheva,[2] Ghodsee showed that the cooperation between women's organizations in Africa and the WIDF also led to certain problems, and that the conflicts became particularly visible during the preparations for the conference in Nairobi (Ghodsee 2018, 199–200).

While the WIDF's participation in the UN-sponsored events of 1975–1985 is not yet fully studied, and probably deserves a book of its own, in this section I limit myself mainly to exploring further some implications of the Cold War confrontation on the WIDF's transnational activities during these years. In particular, the archival documents from Moscow allow me to question some of the descriptions of the WIDF's intentions, and the self-positioning of its leadership with regard to the different events of the decade. I also want to contextualize the WIDF's attitudes towards UN activities with the help of some documents describing internal discussions in the organization. Thus, this brief review of the WIDF's internal developments will help me with my analysis of the federation's work in the Global South presented in the next two sections.

WIDF as a global women's rights actor during the IWY

The important context of the IWY was the development of the mass, grassroots radical feminist movement in Western Europe and the USA, often referred to as "second wave feminism". This feminist movement was interwoven with other radical movements of the 1960s, including the student movement, the gay and lesbian movement, solidarity with anti-colonial and anti-racist movements worldwide, as well as the spread of leftist and socialist ideas of different kinds (see Gildea et al. 2013). All of this contributed not only to a higher visibility of ideas regarding the equality of women with men, but also to an intensification of the transnational discussion on different kinds of injustices. These grassroots movements influenced changes in how gender differences were seen by society; in many countries, these movements led to changes of legislation with regard to marriage, divorce, work, abortion, as well as on taxation, towards the achievement of greater gender equality (see Florin & Nilsson 1999; Allen 2008; Elgán 2015). Due to these changes in legislation and practices, as well as in grassroots mobilization, the language of the discussions around gender inequalities and discrimination in many countries of Western Europe and North America became both more radical and more specific than what the WIDF could offer.

However, the WIDF's leadership continued making efforts to promote the WIDF as the world's leading women's transnational organization. Thus, the WIDF was eager to firm up its international image by demonstrating its participation in the prestigious institutions of global governance. For example, according to the WIDF journal, in 1975, the WIDF included 117 organizations from 101 countries[3] (*ZM* 1975, 1); the first page also stated that the WIDF had the status of category "I" in the UN (ECOSOC), the consultative status of category "B" in UNESCO, and that the federation was also on the special list of the ILO (*ZM* 1975 1: 1). After naming all these important transnational memberships, the journal also proudly added that it was the only journal in the world that is written for "all the women".

This improved international status was used by the WIDF to gain influence. This is particularly apparent in documents and publications about two World Congresses organized by the WIDF during the UN Decade for Women – in Berlin in 1975 and in Prague in 1981. Of these, it was the first one that has received the most attention from researchers. Celia Donert showed that the summer 1975 congress in East Berlin was a rather representative event in the sphere of women's rights. At the same time, however, it demonstrated serious limitations of the state socialist approach to women. Furthermore, according to Donert, the congress was widely used by the GDR for propaganda purposes and to showcase its superiority over "the West" (Donert 2014, 76–77).

The documents from the Moscow archives confirm these findings, suggesting that the ambitions of the organizers of the WIDF World Congress in Berlin with regard to showing the strength of the "Eastern Bloc" were quite large. In 1973, Edelman, the WIDF general secretary, expressed her hopes that

> 1975 will be a big event for the democratic women's movement and all the progressive forces of the world, it will make visible the importance of the WIDF's and other organizations' contributions to the advancement of women.
> (GARF 3 3162, p. 15)

The planned congress had to commemorate the 30th anniversary of the federation, and at first, the WIDF's leadership had some hopes it could organize it in Paris, where the WIDF had been founded (GARF 3 3162, p. 20). However, due to political difficulties in the context of the Cold War, these expectations could not be realized. Yet the WIDF leadership made many efforts to make its congress internationally visible.

The archive documents show that the WIDF delegation promoted the WIDF congress at a July 1974 consultative meeting of representatives of 36 NGOs having official status at the ECOSOC[4] in Geneva. Among other things, the WIDF relied on the support of Helvi Sipilä, the special adviser to the UN secretary-general on social development and humanitarian issues, and an important official involved in organizing the IWY (report to Moscow by Titova, GARF 3 3414, p. 59). According to Titova, Sipilä, in her speech in Geneva, honoured Hertta Kuusinen and noted how important she was, as the former WIDF president, for the IWY (GARF 3 3414, p. 54). Sipilä also had a private meeting with the delegation of the WIDF on its request (GARF 3 3414, p. 59). According to Titova, after listening the WIDF delegation's plans for organizing the World Congress in Berlin, Sipilä was interested in the financial aspects of the organization of this event and suggested "that the financial factor could be used to explain the choice of place" for holding the congress by the WIDF leaders (GARF 3 3414, p. 60). Thus, explaining the choice of East Berlin as being for economic reasons, according to Sipilä, "could calm down those who are worried about the idea of the organization of the World Women's Congress". Finally, Sipilä also promised to come to the preparatory meeting for the congress, and to give a speech there (GARF 3 3414, pp. 60–61). The WIDF journal published a long article by Sipilä, accompanied by a large photo of her, in the beginning of the second issue from 1975 (ZM 1975 2: 4–5), and during the whole year, the WIDF congress continued to be presented as an obvious part of International Women's Year, and a continuation of the UN conference in Mexico. In addition to the important UN representative, the WIDF also managed to attract several important transnational and regional organizations, some of them from the Global South. The Communique from the International Preparatory Committee for the World Congress for International Women's Year from 6 February 1975 reported proudly that many international organizations took part in the preparatory meeting for the congress; they included, among others, the WILPF, the Pan-African Women's Organization, AAPSO, and the All-Arab Women's Federation (Bulletin 1975, p. 2, collection of the WIDF documents in IISH).

Preparation for the WIDF congress in Berlin was the main focus of several WIDF bureau meetings: in Tihany, Hungary, in the autumn of 1974; in Berlin (February 1975), where the special preparatory committee was created; and in Bucharest (April 1975). Even though the WIDF world congress was initially supposed to be similar to the previous WIDF World Women's Congresses (in Copenhagen in 1953 and in Moscow in 1963), the new challenges of feminist activism in the USA and Western Europe made the organizers change this tradition. Instead, Moscow suggested that the congress should be open to men. A letter by Xenia Proskurnikova, vice-president of the CSW, to Titova from 2 September 1974 stated that it is important "to formulate the Congress theme in such a way that it would be written there what it is dedicated to, but it would not be stated whose congress it is" (GARF 3 3414, pp. 86–87). This letter likely explains why the word "women" disappeared from the final variant of the official title of the congress: "World Congress for International Women's Year".

In spite of such an intense focus on its own congress, the WIDF also began its preparations for the UN's sponsored programme for IWY well in advance, as it was crucial to have a high degree of visibility at such an important international event. Thus, the symbol of the IWY was displayed in the WIDF journal, and the journal also published a lot of material dedicated to the IWY. In her speech at the April 1975 bureau meeting in Bucharest dealing with preparations for the IWY, Freda Brown stated the importance of the UN conference in Mexico, and of the IWY (GARF 3 3691, p. 55). In particular, Brown thanked the French delegation for proposing the IWY idea to the WIDF leadership many years earlier, and welcomed making compromises while cooperating with women's organizations in the framework of the IWY: "In the process of this work, I would like to underline that we must be ready to make concessions, we must be ready to negotiate". However, the invitation to negotiate made by Brown was immediately followed by statement on the non-negotiable "basic principles" that made the notion of negotiation quite weak:

> I am not suggesting that we are compromising on our basic principles, on these we will stand very, very firm. Let me just give you an example. There are some radical women's organizations that want in this year just to discuss the status of women. They do not want to discuss peace, they do not want to discuss national independence. For us, it is absolutely vital that the question of peace and the question of national independence be integrated with all our discussions. For we recognize that women's equality means nothing unless we have lasting peace, unless we have won national liberation.
>
> (GARF 3 3691, p. 69, in English)

The official WIDF documents and publications attempted to bring the events in Mexico and in Berlin together, as if they would have the same international status and support from women's organizations in different countries. For example, a report written by Freda Brown for the WIDF bulletin after Mexico and before Berlin stated that:

> We should appreciate that the Congress will bring together organizations that in fact have never sat down before together to discuss questions; we can say we will have an historical event. At Mexico in the speeches, reports and documents, the importance of NGO participation was stressed over and over again. At our Congress we will have a widely representative gathering of people's organizations. The delegates will represent thousands of others, and when they speak, their speeches will be based on the opinion of many other people.
> (WIDF Bulletin 1975, n 4, pp. 2–3, IISH)

Further, Brown also suggested that that "these Mexican documents should be studied in preparation for the Congress" (WIDF Bulletin 1975, n 4, pp. 2–3, IISH), meaning the WIDF congress in Berlin.

While the participation of the WIDF in the IWY, and its congress in Berlin, could be seen as successes – the WIDF drew a lot of international attention to its activities – further developments during the UN Decade for Women indicated growing problems in the federation's internal situation, and for its international position.

Growing uncertainties during the UN Decade for Women

The international prestige and the optimism that the WIDF had at the beginning of the UN Decade for Women gradually disappeared over the course of the decade. By the time of the UN's second conference in Copenhagen, the international context of the WIDF's activities was less favourable for the federation than before. This was connected to the Cold War confrontations, but also to developments in the Global South. Despite the initially positive reaction of the Soviet Union and the WIDF to the "throwing down of the criminal shah's regime",[5] the Islamic revolution in Iran (1979) not only destroyed the UN's initial plans to organize the second UN conference in Tehran, but also interrupted the WIDF's cooperation with Iranian women, and weakened its position in Asia. Furthermore, Soviet political and military interventions in the "Third World" such as the intervention in Afghanistan in 1979, its support of the Sandinista government in Nicaragua (after 1979), and of the Salvadoran guerrillas, made the WIDF's situation even more difficult. In particular, the Soviet intervention in Afghanistan contributed to worsening the WIDF's relationships with most Islamic countries, and, as Ghodsee has shown, resulted in new accusations of the WIDF being dependent on the Soviet Union (2010). Finally, the Eastern Bloc experienced growing pressure for political changes and economic reforms from inside; this pressure contributed to the crisis of the system in 1989. The most visible symptoms of this crisis were the Solidarity movement in Poland (1980), and growing dissident activism in many other state socialist countries. It is important to note that, ironically, the UN Decade for Women was also the last decade of state socialism before the start of Gorbachev's Perestroika.

During the UN decade, the WIDF became increasingly involved in the UN-led transnational space of the politics of women's rights and gender equality. Nevertheless, the federation continued with its own agenda of peace, anti-imperialism, anti-colonialism, and children's rights that were often framed as being in opposition to (Western) feminism. For example, in the context of the mass protests in Europe against the Reagan Administration's decision to creation new European military bases in the early 1980s, the WIDF's anti-war campaign could be seen as twofold. On the one hand, it was a response to the new situation in Western Europe where thousands of women took part in the anti-war movement, but, on the other hand, using the image of the well-identified enemy, American militarism, could help the federation divert attention away from the Soviet intervention in Afghanistan.

The tone of anti-war publications by the WIDF from the 1980s was quite dramatic, and reminded one of the famous WIDF pamphlet against the war in Korea from 1951. For example, the WIDF's appeal to women in connection with the UN-designated Day of Peace (25 October) in 1981 informed its readers: "The danger of nuclear war is threatening humankind as never before. It threatens each woman, each man, each child – your child – as never before" (ZM 1981, 4: 3).

The UN declaration announcing 1979 as the International Year of the Child provided a good opportunity for the WIDF to return to its activities for the rights of children. While this UN-sponsored year never enjoyed the same global prominence as the IWY, it became central for the WIDF's work in 1979; its principal journal had the International Year of the Child as its main theme (ZM 1979). The WIDF's central event to celebrate that year was a conference on children's rights in Moscow and, according to the WIDF journal, the preparations for the conference started at the 1975 Congress in Berlin. Indeed, one of four working groups created by the Berlin Congress in 1975 was responsible for preparations for the International Year of the Child (ZM, 1979 4: 4–5). It seems that the attention to the rights of children contributed to the possibility of escaping the conflictual moments of the transnational discussion on women's rights.

In spite of this focus on the International Year of the Child, the events of the UN Decade for Women continued to occupy important places in the WIDF's work plans and publications during 1975–1985. The propaganda and monitoring of the adoption of CEDAW was one of the important directions of this work. For example, Freda Brown, in her article "1975. The end of the Year. The Beginning of a Decade 1976–1985" (WWW 1977, 1: 7–9), mentioned that the participants of the WIDF Congress in Berlin supported the idea of the adoption of the Convention, and she wanted to "assure the commission that the 121 national organizations of the WIDF would publicize and popularize the convention once it was formulated" (*WWW* 1977 1: 7–9). At the same time, the WIDF continued to insist that the state socialist countries had already solved the problem of women's rights. Thus, an article by Titova in the same issue stressed the differences between the state socialist countries and all others:

> the representatives of the socialist countries where all the rights for women are embodied in laws [...] pointed out that women in the majority of countries suffered from discrimination because motherhood is not recognized as a social function, and that many states do not want to take over the responsibility of creating the prerequisites that are necessary to enable women to combine their duties as mothers, working women and citizen and to become equal members of society.
> (*WWW* 1977 1: 13–15)

Plans for the WIDF's participation in the Copenhagen UN conference of July 1980 were discussed in the context of the growing Cold War confrontation at the WIDF bureau meeting in Berlin on 30 April 1980. As in the case of 1975, the bureau, however, also discussed plans for organizing the next WIDF congress – the World Congress in Prague in 1981 (GARF 3 5076). The report to the bureau meeting prepared by the WIDF general secretary, Vire-Tuominen, proudly stated that the WIDF was active in many UN committees, including those on the situation of women, human rights, and against racism and race discrimination (GARF 3 5076, p. 62). At the same time, in her speech on the WIDF's preparations for the UN conference in Copenhagen, the WIDF's president, Brown, stated that the "progress achieved in the first half of the UN decade is often slow, while changes are not all the same everywhere" (GARF 3 5076, p. 130). As for the practical aspects of preparation for the conference in Copenhagen, Brown particularly stressed that the UN conference should correspond to the interests of women from the Global South, and that they should be adequately represented at the conference. In particular, she expressed doubts that the interests of women "from the Third World" could be represented by those participants who would come to Copenhagen with economic support offered by the USA through its conference organizational committee. According to Brown, "in reality it would be women who usually are living in western countries and are under the influence of the west" (GARF 3 5076, p. 141). That is why, according to Brown, it was particularly important that every member organization of WIDF send its own delegation to the forum "in order to give to the public opinion the real picture of the situation in their countries and tell about successes and problems" (GARF 3 5076, p. 141).

The WIDF protocols discussing the UN conference in Copenhagen suggest that after the excitement and uncertainty regarding the first UN conference in Mexico, and the parallel organization of the WIDF's own long-planned congress in 1975, the WIDF saw the second UN conference as an event that was important for the WIDF's visibility, but was still a part of the usual business. In her report for the WIDF council in 1980, the WIDF eneral secretary, Vire-Tuominen, proudly stated that the WIDF accomplished a lot during the NGO forum in Copenhagen:

> WIDF organized 17 seminars, 2 film projections, and wide distribution of our printed materials including a special issue of our journal prepared during the forum. Our president Freda Brown chaired two panels, and our experts participated in several panels.
> (GARF 3 5077, p. 90)

As for the UN conference in Nairobi, it was presented by the WIDF's journal as a discussion on the ratification of CEDAW, along with the conference's general atmosphere and guests, as well as by focusing on the NGO forum (ZM 1985, 3). At the same time, even the WIDF's official publication presented the conference participants as clearly divided. Indeed, "Women from the developing countries dealt with such problems affecting them as lack of drinking water, food, medicaments, and educational opportunities"; women from Latin America "accused the United States monopolies of using a high interest policy on credits". At the same time, women from Western Europe, United States, and Canada spoke about the connection between unemployment and cuts to social services. Finally, "Soviet women spoke about their activities for peace". These divisions, however, did not prevent Freda Brown from concluding that this forum was "a great success" (*WWW*, 1985 3: 4).

At the same time, as I said, the WIDF also continued with its own agenda, and in 1981 arranged its next World Congress in Prague, which was held on 14–15 October. Its preparations were discussed at the WIDF bureau meeting in Berlin in 1980 (GARF 3 5077, pp. 86–87). The Congress was attended by 1000 participants from 133 countries (ZM 1981 4). A documentary about this congress produced by Soviet filmmakers – *Women's Word about Peace* – continued mainly with the WIDF's established narrative (part of the leading narrative of the documentary seems to be also used for the article published in the journal, ZM 1981). The film starts by showing happy mothers with children on the streets of Prague, while the main part of the film discussed the difficult situation for women and children in countries such as Northern Ireland, Kampuchea, and El Salvador.

Like Berlin, the Prague Congress also made connections to the UN Decade for Women, and paid attention to the importance of the UN conferences. Vire-Tuominen began her speech in Prague by acknowledging the importance of the UN Decade for Women (GARF 3 5311, p. 7); she also stressed the importance of the meeting in Copenhagen. At the same time, she reaffirmed that the WIDF had taken part in the preparations for the conference through its activities in the UN preparatory committee, and in the meetings of the regional commissions that analysed the realization of the Plan of Action adopted in Mexico. Vire-Tuominen also proudly stated that "women representing different social groups and having different political opinion in the developed capitalist countries are cooperating with us more and more" (GARF 3 5311, p. 15). On the other hand, Vire-Tuominen definitely valued the unity of women's actions, and noted that in some countries, national member organizations of the WIDF cooperate with "some feminist organizations in fighting the arms race, and in the work of liquidating discrimination against women" (GARF 3 5311, p. 66).

Still, in spite of the WIDF's active participation in all three UN conferences (Mexico, Copenhagen, and Nairobi) and many other UN-organized events connected to the UN Decade for Women, it seems that the WIDF's own World Congresses in Berlin and Prague had a more central meaning in the WIDF's work. For example, in her memoirs, Fanny Edelman, an active participant in many events of the decade (first as general secretary, later as WIDF vice-president), wrote that during the Decade for Women, the WIDF organized three big events: Berlin 1975; Moscow (conference dedicated to the Year of the Child) 1979; and Prague 1981 (Edelman 1996, 226–227).

Some of the WIDF's documents from the last years of the period under review show that the WIDF's leadership saw developments in the world as problematic; it suggests that during the second part of the UN Decade for Women, the WIDF's position in the Cold War battle worsened still further. At the WIDF bureau meeting in Berlin in 1980, for example, Brown, after reminding that many of the federation's founding members fought against fascism, described the current situation as also being very dangerous:

> this meeting of the bureau takes place in a very complicated international situation. We are very worried while observing the attempts to turn back positive changes that occurred over the last 10 years. Aggressive American imperialists, their allies in NATO, and with the support of the aggressive Chinese leadership are trying to impose its political and economic domination over different peoples.
> (GARF 3 5076, p. 12, from 12 April 1980, in translation to Russian)

Thus, it is possible to see that here all of the enemies of the state socialist countries are brought together and accused of some unclear plan of world domination. This enormous threat, according to Brown, could be confronted by creating a "strong women's movement for the defence of peace, a movement that could unite broad masses of people and overcome national, social and religious barriers" (GARF 3 5076, p. 13).

In practice, the catastrophic feelings of the WIDF president were connected not only to the politics of the USA or China, or to the general world situation, but, rather, to growing internal problems in the federation and disputes among its members. For example, the archives preserved (in Russian translation) the Declaration of the National Bureau of the Union of French Women (UFF), which was addressed to the participants of the

WIDF's 1980 bureau meeting (GARF 5077, pp. 268–279). In this letter, the UFF expressed its discontent with the WIDF due to a lack of democratic decision-making, and the WIDF's unlimited support for the viewpoint of the "socialist countries" and the use of the experiences of these countries as a positive example for other countries to follow. UFF leaders also criticized the place played by peace issues in the WIDF's work; according to the UFF, it diverted attention away from other issues, including women's rights. In discussing the planned congress in Prague in 1981, the authors of the declaration stated that the upcoming congress can be dedicated to discussing the problems that are "of a particular importance for a big international organization; its role, main directions of its activity, and its functioning" (GARF 5077, p. 269). For example, the declaration stressed that

> it is important that the organization, like the Secretariat, avoid making any changes [in the discussed earlier documents aimed for the congress participants] in the months and weeks before the congress.
> (GARF 5077, p. 277, in translation to Russian)

Further, the UFF proposed using the UN CEDAW convention as a common platform for discussions in Prague. The UFF Declaration also suggested changing the logistics of the congress; a short introductory speech should be followed by small group discussions on important topics based on the text of the UN Convention. These topics, according to the members of the French organization, included:

> end of discrimination in legislation and in practice, advancement in the sphere of work and education, recognition of the economic role of woman in agriculture, maternity as a social function and responsibilities of parents and of the state, women's participation in cultural, economic and political life, solidarity of women fighting poverty, participation of women in the struggle for freedom and independence, and in anti-war activism.
> (GARF 3 5077, p. 277)

Here it is possible to see that the UFF suggested focusing increasingly on issues connected with the advancement of women, and placed the WIDF's traditional concern with peace in last place. Such a proposal of structuring the work of the congress could also potentially lead to a discussion regarding how the rights of women in the state socialist countries differ between legislation and practice. Finally, the declaration of the UFF endangered Soviet influence on the work of the WIDF by critiquing the special role of the Secretariat.

Later, the privileged place of state socialism in the WIDF's ideology was questioned by Jeannine Zaidner, the UFF representative, who voiced the UFF's concerns at the WIDF bureau meeting in December 1980. After recognizing that ratification of the CEDAW declaration met with difficulties in France, Zaidner stressed that "we cannot give privilege to one social system", clearly indicating the state socialist countries (GARF 3 5077, p. 285).

The correspondence between Berlin and Moscow suggests that the WIDF's internal and external situation became even more tense at the time of the preparations for the UN conference in Nairobi. The WIDF's general secretary, Vire-Tuominen, had a business meeting with some representatives of the CSW in Moscow on 8 June 1983 when she visited the USSR with her daughter for medical care (GARF 3 5871, p. 3). Lilia Berezhnaia, one of the leading members of the CSW, sent a report summarizing this meeting to Valeria Kalmyk, who was the Soviet representative at the Secretariat in Berlin at that time. During the conversation in the CSW, Vire-Tuominen stated that national organizations of the WIDF in some countries – the UK, Norway, Denmark, Sweden – were very weak, while the organization in the Netherlands ceased operations altogether. According to Vire-Tuominen, the last was connected with difficulties in the communist parties of the respective countries (GARF 3 5871, p. 12). During the meeting, Vire-Tuominen spoke also about growth of anti-Soviet attitudes in Finland, and suggested that, in this situation, it would be particularly important to maintain relationships with all people and organizations in the world that the WIDF used to cooperate with in the past.

Probably as a result of the falling popularity of the WIDF in Europe, its Secretariat chose to make the protection of peace even more central than it was before (and thus decided to do the opposite to what the Union of French Women suggested). For example, in the same conversation in Moscow, Vire-Tuominen supported the plans of Brown, the WIDF's president, to take part in the peace march from Dortmund to Brussels in the coming months; she also thought it important to send a delegation to the peace camp in Greenham Common (GARF 3 5871, p. 11).[6] Peace activism also seems to have taken over some of the WIDF's work with women in the Global South. Vire-Tuominen noted that:

> Brown managed to convince Elena Lagadinova that a school of peace for Europe, USA, and probably, some representatives of the socialist countries should be organized in 1984 in Sofia in place of courses for cadres of African women.
>
> (GARF 3 5871, p. 11)[7]

Paradoxically, the last period of the WIDF's activities was when the federation received its highest evaluations from the UN. One of the last issues of the WIDF journal published in 1991 contains an article by Javier Perez de Cuellar, secretary general of the UN, who noted that "during all these years, the federation has played an important role in promoting equality of women's rights" and wished "all the success in your work" to the WIDF on the occasion of its 45th anniversary (ZM 1991, 1).

From anti-colonialism to development? speaking the language of transnational women's rights in the Global South

In the late 1960s, organizations from the countries of the Global South constituted more than half of the WIDF's members, which meant that the federation continued to pay a lot of attention to the problems and concerns of women from Africa, Asia, and Latin America. However, due to several factors, the WIDF's evaluation of these countries, and its character of work with women's organizations there, experienced changes in the late 1960s–1970s. On the one hand, cooperation with global governance bodies led to the WIDF participating in multiple discussions about poverty, development and sustainability, i.e. dealing with, in part, the language of post-colonial and transnational humanitarian organizations (developmentalism was already central at Bandung; Eslava et al. 2017, 22). On the other hand, changing discourses were a result of assumptions made by the Soviet political leadership, and by international communist party leaders and experts, on the lack of perspectives for revolution and socialism in most of the newly independent countries of Africa and Asia. By the mid-1960s, hopes for socialist scenario for Africa, for example, had declined significantly,[8] while Soviet policies in Africa generally became more pragmatic (Mazov 2008; see also Matusevich 2003). Growing competition with China in Asia and in the Global South diminished hopes for the development of the Soviet variety of state socialism there (MacFarlane 1985).

As a result of these changes, the WIDF seemed to have adopted to the new realities, not least through changing its language when addressing the problems of the Global South. According to the new geopolitical denominations, women's organizations started to be seen as belonging to different geopolitical and economic entities: developed countries – more industrialized and with higher standards of living; developing countries – those who still were not industrialized enough and whose level of life was much lower; and, finally, countries that were considered to be following the socialist path of development. The last group included first of all North Vietnam, Cuba, and North Korea, but later also some other countries, including some in Africa. While Western Europe, North America, Australia, Japan and most of the state socialist countries in Europe were assumed to belong to the first category, most of the countries of Asia, Africa, and Latin America belonged to the second one. Thus, even if the issues of anti-colonial and anti-Apartheid struggle and solidarity continued to be important for the WIDF, the federation started to see the problems of development/underdevelopment as central for women from Latin America, Africa, and Asia.

This is particularly visible when analysing the WIDF periodical publications. An article by Nicole Martin about a UNESCO-supported seminar on education of woman in postcolonial Africa that was held in Dakar, Senegal in 1963 stated that the legacy of colonialism is "extreme poverty and ignorance" and that, among other factors, "the strict customs and religion" were hindering women's education (*WWW* 1963, 3: 23–25). Along with stating that reducing arms spending around the world by only one percent could guarantee the literacy of the African women, the article also implied that there were many local obstacles on the way to full literacy, and also to the broad public participation of the African women. Thus, these obstacles on the way to development should also be dealt with in order to guarantee women's rights.

Later, in 1966, most probably as a part of the preparing to regain its official status in the UN,[9] the WIDF announced a new programme for its journal; the editors planned to produce more a "serious" publication for "women from the whole world", starting from that year. Indeed, the journal promised to provide its readers with expert analysis of the situation of women's rights, and not just offer information about different events and national organizations (ZM 1966, 1: 3). Alongside political documents, such as parts of the official speech made by the leader of the Sudanese women's organization, Fatima Ahmed Ibrahim, at the WIDF council meeting in Salzburg, the first issue of the journal in 1966 published three articles signed by PhD degree holders in different disciplines.[10] One of those was an article by Raisa Smirnova, a researcher from the Africa institute in Moscow,[11] on the cooperative movement in Africa (WWW 1966, 1: 19–22); another one, titled "Family planning and the demographic problem", was authored by Nora Federici, a professor of geography from the University of Rome. This latter article defended woman's individual choice concerning the number of children (and thus – abortion on demand), but also addressed fears of "overpopulation" due to rapid population growth "in some economically underdeveloped (*slaborazvitye*) countries" (ZM 1966, 1: 44–45). Federici claimed, however, that attempts at controlling the birth-rate in countries with low economic development and cultural backwardness could not be successful without an improvement in the population's economic and cultural living standards. That is why, according to the author, the governments of some countries of the Global South (e.g., India) were not particularly successful in distributing contraceptives. Thus, it is possible to say that the new scientific approach of the WIDF to the problems of countries of the Global South included evaluating the ideas of its Cold War political adversaries, and use of a less political and more scientific language for criticizing their ideas. The article showed that the countries of the Global South had a high fertility rate, which could probably be a problem for development. However, the problem of development according to the WIDF could not be solved only with the help of birth control, but needed broader social reforms, or, in other words, the reforms that were named in the earlier WIDF programmes.

In the 1970s, the term "developing" countries was widely used by the WIDF journal to denote the countries of Asia, Africa, and Latin America (see, e.g., WWW 1977, 1: 5). This concept was seen as rather neutral and academic – it differed from labelling the countries of the Global South as poor or "underdeveloped". For example, in presenting its report at the international conference "Population and Development", organized by UN in Bucharest in 1974, the WIDF delegation rejected the division of countries into "rich and poor", and insisted that the socialist countries were the real friends of the "developing" ones (WWW 1975 1: 53). The WIDF journal continued to demand rights for women in the countries of the Global South, and to accuse colonialism and imperialism. The WIDF stated that the improvement of the situation of women in developing countries needed broader reforms and programmes. At the same time, the WIDF continued to criticize developmental organizations from the West, and also some of the governments of the newly independent states, for their focus on fertility regulation programmes. For example, the above-quoted report on the UN conference "Population and Development" in Bucharest denounced fears of "excess population" (WWW 1975, 1: 53–55). The report claimed that human intelligence and productive capacity can produce more than is needed for survival, but that, due to the lack of inclusion of women into the workforce, "the capacity and the labor of the majority of women in the world are not utilized for the socially useful production" (WWW 1975 1: 54–55). This report also supported "the right of conscious maternity" for women, but focused mainly on economic factors, including women's participation in the labour force and the redistribution of wealth (WWW 1975, 1: 54–55).

This vision of the problem of development was reflected in the WIDF's attempts to further support regional and national initiatives and events aimed at improving women's access to education, including vocational training, and women's rights in the family. For example, one of the important and widely commented events that the WIDF co-organized was the seminar on the liquidation of illiteracy in African countries in Khartoum in 1970 that I have already discussed. It was there that the doctor of historical sciences Rahimbabaeva, representing the WIDF and the CSW, discussed the Soviet experience of emancipation and education of women in Soviet Uzbekistan in detail, and stated the importance of development of culture and education:

> a new modern economy can only be built on the basis of well-developed technology, enriched with the latest scientific discoveries, and this requires a high standard of culture for all the people.
> (GARF 3 2421, pp. 29–44)

The report on a seminar regarding women's education in Latin America that was organized with the support of the WIDF in Lima in 1974, and published by the WIDF journal in 1975 (WWW 1975 2: 9–23), also stressed the importance of access to education for all. In order to improve the situation of education, the article suggested that women should be included in social security provisions, while governments should solve the housing problem and fight discrimination at the work place (WWW 1975 2: 23). Thus, the solution of the problem of education again was presented as a part of broader social reforms that the WIDF documents defended from the early days of the federation. Another article in the WIDF journal from the same year was a report by the WIDF representative, Hanaa Bousha, on an international seminar in Lebanon that brought together representatives from the UN, ILO, AAPSO, and some other international organizations. The seminar was dedicated to reforms of women's rights under "Arab legislation" (*WWW* 1975 1: 46–47). According to this article, women's position in society would be improved if states adopted new laws regarding divorce and child custody. However, Bousha especially stressed the problem with "insufficiencies in implementation of certain principles that acknowledge the rights of women, such as equal pay for equal work, for instance" (*WWW* 1975 1: 46–47).

The archival documents show that in later years the WIDF continued to support local and regional events in different countries of the Global South that were connecting women's rights with a more fundamental transformation of society and the world, including the New International Economic Order (NIEO). The ideas of NIEO were developed by the Non-Aligned countries, and aimed to transform trade regulations in order to eliminate global inequalities and the poverty of the Global South. These ideas received UN support in the mid-1970s, and the representatives of the WIDF not only took part in discussions, but also supported seminars on this topic with women's organizations in the Global South. Thus, in 1980, the WIDF, in cooperation with the government of Madagascar, organized the seminar on the "Situation of woman and family in connection with the New International Economic Order". Representatives of 11 national women's organizations from East and South African countries, and 200 participants from Madagascar, attended the seminar (GARF 3 5077, p. 94).

Thus, it is possible to say that in the 1970s, obstacles on the way to the advancement of women in the Global South were seen by the WIDF from a new perspective. The WIDF publications and documents suggested that the "developing" countries require more investment to improve the cultural and educational level of women, and that achieving equal rights for women there will take a long time. It suggested a further move from discussing the fight against imperialism (how it was discussed for example, at the WIDF congress in Moscow in 1963) to work on changing legislation, creating a system of social security, and changing women's cultural levels. Even if these changes were not addressed explicitly as "modernization", due to the word's association with Western politics, and even if religion was never openly attacked in WIDF documents, it could be said that the WIDF connected its expectations in the change of women's status in the developing countries with the modernization of societies, and it was the aspirations of modernization that sustained the cooperation with the WIDF in the Global South.

Reading the WIDF's documents and publications from the 1970s to 1980s suggests that the WIDF started making more distinctions between the countries of Latin America, Asia, and Africa. For example, a review of the situation of the women's organizations of Africa prepared by Soviet researchers from the Africa Institute in Moscow for the WIDF in 1978 indicates several problems of building relationships with different women's organizations. The possibility of the WIDF establishing relationships with these organizations depended on their level of development, the political situation in the country, their leadership's attitude to the Soviet Union, and the acceptance of socialist ideas (GARF 3 4524). The report was signed by E. Gaievskaia and E. Markosova, and stated that while the struggle for liquidation of the "colonial empires in Africa is mainly finished", the countries have chosen different developmental strategies (GARF 3 4524, p. 1). Thus, some of them, such as Algeria, Congo, Guinea, Mozambique, Angola, Tanzania and some others, could be seen as countries of "socialist orientation", while others cannot. Further, the report stated that the WIDF meets a lot of problems in its work related to both difficult internal political situations in many countries of Africa, and activities of the "bourgeois international and national women's organizations that are trying to keep the females masses of Africa under its control" (GARF 3 4524, p. 10). Finally, the report named several transnational organizations that hindered the WIDF's work with African women: ICW, IAW, the International Council of Social-Democratic Women, and the International Agricultural Association of Women. While these organizations offered a variety of activities, including charitable ones aimed at women, different courses, seminars, and courses for cadre preparation, their activity "could limit possibilities of the African women's movement" and "make it strictly feminist" (the last meaning "Western-like").

As for Asia, a discussion on the distribution of the federation's journal in Arabic that took place at the WIDF bureau meeting in Cuba in 1973 also suggests that there were quite limited possibilities for the growth of the federation in the Middle East. While the journal was sold in countries like Iraq, Israel, Yemen, Jordan, Kuwait, Lebanon, Mauritania, and among the Palestinian organizations in different countries, there was no growth in distribution in other countries of the Middle East and North Africa (GARF 3 3162, pp. 42–45).

In the 1970s–1980s, the WIDF continued to financially support women activists who were taking part in the events organized by the federation, and by different solidarity campaigns. As before, such campaigns were expected to be financed through membership fees that differed from country to country (see, e.g., GARF 3 1396, p. 35). The CSW and women's organizations from other state socialist countries played a particular role in providing this support. At the same time, the CSW, as before, was quite careful when counting money and choosing the countries and persons it would support. For example, the archive materials preserved a letter containing a list of organizations that Moscow wanted to invite to the WIDF council meeting in 1972, in Varna, Bulgaria (GARF 3 2941, p. 4, letter sent to Rahimbabaeva 27 January 1972) This list included women's organizations from Burundi, Mali, Guinea, Zambia, India, Ceylon, Bangladesh, Nepal, the Democratic Republic of Vietnam, South Vietnam, Laos, and Cambodia (GARF 3 2941, p. 5).

However, Moscow wanted to share the costs of the invitation. In her letter to Rahimbabaeva, Proskurnikova stated that the CSW is:

> ready to pay for the travel of two representatives of women's organizations of Cameroon, Congo and Ceylon. If the Secretariat will decide to invite one representative of these organizations, the committee is ready to receive these delegations in the USSR before the council meeting so that one representative of these countries could return home, and one attend the council meeting in Varna.
> (GARF 3 2941, p. 21, 29 January 1972)

The documents also show that, with time, the number of women from the Global South who required support with their travel expenses was increasing. Thus, the CSW started to use the facilities of the Soviet state more broadly, first of all, Soviet state aviation – Aeroflot. For example, in a letter from the CSW to Valeria Kalmyk, Soviet representative in the Secretariat, from 1983, it is possible to read that the Committee has positively answered the request of the WIDF to support the travel of 80 representatives of Asia, Africa, and Latin America to the WIDF's council meeting in Budapest, via Moscow (GARF 3 5871, p. 24, 15 August 83). The supported participants had to travel by Aeroflot, except for those parts of their route not serviced by that airline. Those parts of the travel – that had to be paid for in hard currency – were supposed to be covered from the WIDF budget.

The WIDF also established fellowships for prominent women from countries of the Global South to study in Soviet universities (unfortunately, I could not find the year when these fellowships began to be distributed). In a letter from the CSW from 1984 (GARF 3 6164, from 1984) to the Algerian women's organization, the CSW invited the leader of the organization, Fatima Djaghroud, and two other members to visit the Soviet Union. They were also asked about contacts with a former WIDF fellowship holder from Algeria with whom the CSW wanted to keep in contact.

Successes and disappointments of the WIDF work in Africa, Asia, and Latin America

This section will look at the WIDF as a worldwide organization where women from Latin America, Asia, and Africa acquired some power and influence. During the 1970s–1980s, not only were women from countries outside Europe not well represented in the WIDF's leadership, but also, at the end of that period, they constituted a majority in the official governing bodies of the federation.

Already in the 1970s, the WIDF bureau and council included a remarkable number of women from Latin America, Asia, and Africa. In the first issue of the WIDF journal, *Women of the Whole World*, from 1977, it is possible to read that the members of the bureau included five vice-presidents from countries outside Europe: Fathila Bettahar (Algeria); Vilma Espín de Castro (Cuba); Aruna Asaf Ali (India); Ha Tsi Que (Vietnam); and Fuki Kushida (Japan) (*WWW* 1977 1: 3). It is possible to say that half or more of the vice-presidents represented countries outside of Europe, because there were only three from European countries: Valentina Tereshkova (USSR); Ilse Thiele (GDR); and Giselle There (France). However, this information could be also read differently – out of eight vice-presidents, only the representatives of India[12] and Japan[13] were not members of the communist party in their countries.

In those years, the countries of Africa, Asia, and Latin America were also well represented among the ordinary members of the bureau (not vice-presidents). In 1977, the bureau included the representatives of Angola, Argentina, Chile, Costa Rica, Guyana, North Korea, Mongolia, Mozambique, Palestine, Somalia, South Africa, Sudan and Uruguay – 13 countries altogether. Only four members of the bureau represented European and North American countries, including state socialist ones – Czechoslovakia, UK Canada, and Portugal.

In 1981, representation of women from the Global South in the WIDF governing bodies increased still further. The WIDF's vice-presidents were Fatima-Zohra Djaghroud (Algeria), Fanny Edelman (Argentina), Aruna Asaf Ali (India), Vilma Espín de Castro (Cuba), Salome Moyane (Mozambique), Isam Abdel Hadi (Palestine), Nguen Thi Dinh (Vietnam), Ilse Thiele (GDR), Fuki Kushida (Japan), Luisa Amorim (Portugal), and Valentina Tereshkova (USSR). Thus, there were seven vice-presidents from "developing countries", two from European state socialist countries and (if we include the WIDF president and general secretary) – four from the "developed" countries (Australia, Finland, Japan, and Portugal). Thus, representatives of the Global South constituted the majority, even if two of them (those of Cuba and Vietnam), most probably, would be defined as representatives of state socialist countries of the Global South (*ZM* 1981, 4: 3). At the same time, the ordinary bureau members included representatives of 11 countries from the Global South (Angola, Ethiopia, Chile, Guyana, Yemen, Costa Rica, North Korea, Mongolia, South Africa (women's section of ANC), Sudan and Uruguay) versus representatives from the UK, Canada, and Czechoslovakia. Thus, even if the representatives of North Korea, Vietnam, Mongolia, and Cuba could probably be counted as state socialist (and thus, belonging already to the "Second" and not the "Third" World) in the early 1980s, it would be still 14 representatives of the countries of the Global South in the bureau consisting of 27 members including the vice-presidents – thus, the majority.

These data suggest that the problems of low representation of women from countries outside Europe that were characteristic of the WIDF in the late 1950s–early 1960s (see Chapter 6) were successfully overcome in the later period of the Cold War. However, it is important to explore how much power with regard to the WIDF agenda and other important decisions these representatives actually had in the 1970s–early 1980s. What did participation mean for them? Even if full answers to these questions cannot be found in the sources available to me, below, I will analyse some campaigns and events from this period that could help to understand the ways in which representatives of countries of Africa, Asia, and Latin America could influence these campaigns, and what limits inside the federation they might have had.

Education, cooperation and ideology in the WIDF's work for development

As I have already shown, the WIDF saw the liquidation of illiteracy, girls' education and professional education for women as important goals in the advancement of women; it participated in several international conferences on improving women's literacy skills and education in the 1960s, and organized its own seminar in Tashkent in 1962. The seminar on the elimination of illiteracy among women in Africa that took place in Khartoum, Sudan, in 1970, unlike the 1962 seminar, not only took place in Africa, but the practical aspects of its organization became a responsibility of African women, members of the Sudanese Women's Union and its head, Fatima Ahmed Ibrahim. The seminar brought together representatives of 21 African countries (*WWW* 1970, p. 4) and not only offered its participants the opportunity to meet activists from other regions of Africa, but also to confirm and to strengthen the relationships of pan-African (and African-Asian) solidarity already established at the conferences in Cairo in 1958 (see McGregor & Hearmann 2017, 161–176). The seminar also created a space to discuss the similarities and differences of women's work with illiteracy in different countries, compared to the example of the work for the elimination of illiteracy in Sudan. Thus, it was a good opportunity for African women to learn from one another as well as from the recent Cuban campaign to liquidate illiteracy (GARF 3 2421, pp. 67–94).

The WIDF was led at the seminar in Khartoum by its president, Hertta Kuusinen, who greeted the seminar participants and gave a special interview to the WIDF journal. In her speech, Kuusinen acknowledged the negative role of the colonial legacy, and stressed the historical roots of global disparities in women's status (GARF 3 242, pp. 110–116). In particular, she said:

> In 1960, when many African countries gained independence, the situation faced by the new states in this respect was disastrous. The burdensome heritage of imperial exploitation – economic and cultural backwardness resulting from foreign domination, the theft of national wealth, various kinds of discrimination – meant a vast army of illiterates which in itself was one of the obstacles in the fight to overcome ignorance. Where racial discrimination is the rule, there are countless victims of illiteracy among the colored population.
> (GARF 3 2421, p. 111, document in English)

The archival documents show that the WIDF saw this seminar as important, and that it was ready to support its organization financially, as well as to look for other sponsors, like UNESCO. The report sent by Rahimbabaeva to Moscow in 1969 shows that the seminar in Sudan was discussed at the Secretariat meeting on 19 September 1969 and, according to the preliminary calculations, the seminar itself would cost $38,000; the WIDF was also planning to pay travel costs for a number of participants (GARF 3 2122, p. 107). However, while relying on the Sudanese organizers in many cases, the WIDF also wanted to guarantee the seminar would be free of intrusion from its political and ideological adversaries, not least the "Chinese Marxists". The event was to show sympathies toward Soviet policies, not Chinese ones. Still, it seems that the WIDF and the Sudanese organizers of the seminar shared several common beliefs with respect to the importance of women's education and ways of improving it. It also seems that both parties were dependent on mutual support from one another; not only did the Sudanese organizers, and other African women, need the expertise and financial support of the WIDF, but the support of the African women's organizations continued to be important for the WIDF's international image in the 1970s, not less than in the 1960s.

Later on, the WIDF continued to organize educational events for cadres, and also continued with its attempts to organize the WIDF bureau in countries outside Europe. In March 1974, the WIDF was one of the co-organizers (with UNESCO) of a regional seminar on the elimination of illiteracy and improving education for women in Algiers, the Algerian capital (GARF 3 3414, p. 75). The importance of this seminar for the African continent was stressed, in particular, through its venue – the congress palace, where the conference of the Non-Aligned countries had taken place. Three representatives from each African country, and from movements fighting for the independence of their countries, were invited to the conference, and delegations from the Soviet Union and Cuba also participated (GARF 3 3414, p. 3). The description of this seminar was accompanied by an unusually informative financial report. Titova noted that after long conversations, UNESCO agreed to contribute only $2,500 – "we hoped for $5–10,000 but..." (GARF 3 3414, p. 76); the WIDF itself financed the travel expenses of the participants ($35,000),[14] while the Algerian organizers were responsible for the guests' accommodations, as well as for synchronous translation of the conference into three languages – French, English, and Arabic (GARF 3 3414, p. 75). Thus, it is possible to say that, at least in some cases, the WIDF acted as the main sponsor of events organized in the Global South.

The seminar on ending discrimination against women in the sphere of education in Lima in 1974 that I already mentioned was aimed at women from Latin America, and enjoyed financial and organizational support from the Federation of Cuban Women (FMC) (GARF 3 3414, p24; pp. 69–71). In February 1977, an international seminar "Overcoming the colonial heritage", was organized by the WIDF in cooperation with the Revolutionary Women's Union of Guinea in Conakry. The WIDF's journal stated that this seminar was "attended by delegations from women's organizations of 27 African countries, delegations of women's organizations from 24 countries of the Middle East, delegations of the socialist countries, of Asia and Latin America, as well as by representatives of international organizations and specialized agencies of the UN and the Organization of African Unity" (*WWW* 1977, 2: 48–49). However, these seminars, and others organized in Latin America in later years, were never described in the WIDF journal in as detailed a manner as the first big event organized in Africa – the 1970 seminar in Khartoum.

After about 10 years since a WIDF meeting occurred outside of Europe, in 1973, WIDF's bureau meeting was held in Havana, Cuba. According to the protocols, this bureau meeting enjoyed particular attention from the Cuban government, including a personal greeting from the country's leader, Fidel Castro (GARF 3 3162, pp. 53–58, from 30 April to 5 May 1973). The meeting was opened by Vilma Espín,[15] president of the FMC. In her speech, Espín stressed that this event was a recognition of the special importance of the Cuban women's organization in the women's struggle on the Latin American continent (GARF 3 3162, pp. 9–12). It seems that this bureau meeting was the last that the WIDF held outside of Europe; the meeting undoubtedly indicated the growing role of Cuba and Cuban women in the WIDF, and the growing role of women's organizations in Latin America as a whole for the WIDF. In 1974, for example, FMC came up with an initiative to support several events aimed at Latin American women – together with the seminar on education in Lima that I mentioned earlier, Cuba was also ready to support the WIDF seminar for women of the Caribbean (GARF 3 3414, pp. 24–25). At the same time, it is important to note that at that time, approximately, the FMC followed the line of the Cuban Communist Party much more closely than it had done earlier (see Espín 1985, pp. 48–49) and, most probably, became more trusted by the Soviet Union.

In concluding this part, it is possible to say that many women's organizations in the Global South saw cooperation with the WIDF as an opportunity to develop and organize different regional and international events that would have been difficult to realize without external financial and logistical support.

After this review of WIDF's co-organization of different events with women's organizations in different countries of the Global South during the 1970s, in the next part of this chapter, I am going to look closer at the WIDF's work to support women's organizations that were involved in armed struggle or were taking part in anti-dictatorial protests and could not work legally.

Showing solidarity, making friends

The WIDF was founded as an anti-fascist and democratic organization, thus clearly placing itself in the left political sector. Along with supporting rights for women, the WIDF's pro-Soviet position in the Cold War confrontation, in particular in the case of the wars in Korea and Vietnam during the 1950s, contributed to the image of this organization as one promoting anti-colonial ideas and supporting the anti-colonial struggle (see Armstrong 2016). On the other hand, due to changes in the women's movement in Western Europe and North America in the 1970s, as I have already noted, the WIDF could not expect a significant growth of its popularity among the feminist left there, and its international prestige and membership increasingly depended on women and women's organizations from the Global South. All of this contributed to a further expansion of the WIDF's solidarity work in the 1970s–1980s.

Although the majority of countries in Africa and Asia were already independent by the end of the 1960s, anti-colonial wars and military confrontation continued in several places, including Vietnam (till 1974), Angola (1961–1974 war for independence, 1975–2002 civil war) and Mozambique (1964–1975 war for independence, 1975–1992 civil war). Following the agenda of anti-racism, the WIDF became more and more involved in support of the fight against Apartheid (see Sandwell 2018), while continuing to pay attention to the anti-racist movement in the USA – in particular, organizing a solidarity campaign after the arrest of Angela Davis in 1970. While the WIDF's initial agenda on anti-fascism included supporting women in Spain, Portugal, and Greece, the non-democratic regimes of Europe in the 1950s, the hard situation of women under the new dictatorships on the Latin American continent, first of all, under the Pinochet military junta that came to power in Chile in 1973, made anti-fascist solidarity relevant for the WIDF agenda again. Finally, the WIDF expressed its support for several other countries, people, and regions that were considered victims of war or imperialist attack. While one of the central objects for such solidarity were the Palestinian people, victims of Israeli occupation, other objects of solidarity related to military conflicts were multiple. Of course, all these campaigns require a separate investigation, but here I want to write briefly on just three of them: solidarity with Vietnam, Chile; and the anti-Apartheid campaign in South Africa. In particular, I pay attention to what WIDF solidarity work consisted of, how the political and humanitarian aspects of solidarity were connected, and what these campaigns meant for women's organizations from the Global South in the WIDF.

As McGregor has shown, the distribution of information through different WIDF-associated media was one of the most important ways of organizing solidarity (2016). Along with media campaigns, the WIDF continued its practice of sending commissions to investigate the situation of the rights of women, organizing special conferences, collecting signatures, and offering keynote roles in its meetings to important female leaders from countries torn apart by war, or under dictatorships. As I showed at the beginning of the chapter, representatives of most of the countries that were in the centre of solidarity work, such as Chile, Angola, Mozambique, Palestine, Vietnam, and the ANC (South Africa) were members of the WIDF bureau in the 1970s–1980s. Participation of the representatives of these countries in the

WIDF leadership contributed to their closer contacts with the WIDF Secretariat, and offered them many opportunities to transfer information about the situation in their countries to other organizations and global governance bodies. Indeed, the theme of the violations of rights in Chile under the dictatorship, and the rights of the Black population in South Africa, were constant topics in the WIDF journal during these years.

The WIDF campaign of solidarity with Vietnam was the longest one; it continued from the earlier years of the federation (the period of anti-colonial war against France) through solidarity with the pro-Soviet Democratic Republic of Vietnam (DRV), and through the Vietnam War, which ended in 1973 with the peace agreement between the representatives of Northern Vietnam and the USA. As previous research has already shown (Armstrong 2016; McGregor 2016), the WIDF's solidarity with Vietnam was realized through many different channels, and widely used anti-war rhetoric. The important aspect of this campaign was the WIDF's coordination of the activities of its member organizations from different countries (including those in other French colonies like Algeria[16]; see Drew 2014). The repertoire of solidarity actions could be evaluated, for example, on the basis of a report by Jasovich, the WIDF general secretary, at the 1965 WIDF council meeting in Salzburg. Describing WIDF solidarity with Vietnam, Jasovich spoke about declarations denouncing aggressive American politics, letters to President Johnson and, after that, about sending reports on these actions to the UN general secretary. Jasovich also noted that the Secretariat planned sending a WIDF delegation to the DRV (but had to postpone it on the advice of the Vietnamese organization) and, in contact with the national organizations from Finland, Sweden, Netherlands, Belgium, Norway, Italy, France, and Austria, the WIDF decided to organize visits of delegations of women from South Vietnam to these countries. In the last case, the national organizations were to make arrangements for visas, and to cover the cost of the Vietnamese women's stay in their countries (GARF 3 1396, pp. 33–34). Thus, as it is possible to see, the solidarity actions were quite ambitious, and presupposed a good coordination of efforts with the national member organizations of the WIDF in Europe.

During the years of the American war in Vietnam (1965–1973), solidarity with Vietnamese women was at the heart of all WIDF events and this campaign is well documented in the WIDF official journal. For example, in 1965, almost every issue had articles discussing the difficult situation of women in Vietnam (ZM 1965 2: 14; ZM 1965 4: 8; 1965 5: 26). In particular, issue 9–10 from 1965 published a biographical article dedicated to one of the most famous military leaders of South Vietnam, Nguen Thi Dinh (ZM 1965 9–10: 14–16). While expressing solidarity with the guerrilla struggle in the South, the WIDF journal drew attention to reforms in women's status in the northern part of Vietnam that followed the socialist path of development. As I already said, the issue 1 from 1966, dedicated to women's rights, published colourful figures showing how women were represented among government officials, university students, and workers, and how many North Vietnamese children attended nurseries and kindergartens (ZM 1966, 1: 29–31).

During the later period, one of the WIDF's widely celebrated projects was the construction of a maternity hospital and medical research centre in Hanoi. The preparations started already in 1969 (GARF 3 2122, pp. 72–73), while the bureau meeting in Budapest in October 1970 discussed the architectural project and term of construction. In order to get the best results, an international team of architects, gynaecologists, and paediatricians was sent by the WIDF to Vietnam that same year; the group included experts from France, the GDR, and the Soviet Union, and had to evaluate the situation at the place (GARF 3 2430, p. 10). The group travelled through Soviet territory and, according to the archival documents, this travel was paid for by the Soviet member of the federation; the CSW informed the WIDF general secretary that it paid $4000 for the travel of the WIDF delegation on the route Moscow–Hanoi–Moscow (GARF 3 2240, p. 18, from 9 August 1970). The centre was built in 1975, and was considered an important achievement by the WIDF (WWW 1975, 1: 43; Gryzunova 1975, 55).

Due to the worldwide recognition of the heroism of Vietnamese people, and protest against the American aggression (see, e.g., Wu 2017), the WIDF's many-years-long solidarity campaign led to the federation being rewarded in terms of its international popularity and prestige. Unlike the 1950s, when the WIDF president, Cotton, underwent trial for organizing solidarity with Vietnam in France, in the mid-1970s, the WIDF could enjoy its popularity and, sometimes, even benefit from it. For example, a 1974 letter from Titova, the Soviet representative at the Secretariat, informed Moscow about the WIDF delegation sent to the congress in Hanoi dedicated to the celebration of the end of the war. In this letter, Titova suggests that while the "voice" from Vietnam in that historical moment had great authority internationally, the congress should adopt a document in support of the WIDF's congress in Berlin as a part of the UN's IWY (GARF 3 3414, p. 76, 1974). Thus, by using the "voice" from Vietnam, the WIDF hoped to resolve tensions around other activities ("*golos*" *iz Vietnama imel by bolshuyu silu*). On the other hand, the same letter suggests that the women's organization from Vietnam could get more influence inside the WIDF and, in particular, contribute to the development of other solidarity campaigns. Titova wrote that the WIDF delegation to the celebration ceremony, along with Vaillant-Couturier and Wanda Tycner (Poland), included Elena Pedraza, the Chilean representative; Titova stated that the last was included on request of the Vietnamese side. Considering that the ceremony took place in 1974, about a year after the military coup in Chile, the event in Vietnam clearly could have contributed to claiming more solidarity for Chilean women.

The WIDF's reaction to the military coup in Chile was swift (Pieper-Mooney 2013a); as early as September 1973, the WIDF had a special meeting in Berlin in memory of Chilean president Salvador Allende (Gryzunava 1975, 67). The federation started its solidarity work by sending a special international delegation to Chile consisting of representatives from several women's organizations (GARF 3 3414, p. 76). According to a letter from Titova, the women's delegation to Chile would consist of the representatives of five countries (France, the USA, Argentina, Germany (West Berlin), and Belgium), and the WIDF was represented by Margot Mrochinski from West Berlin. The delegation had to assess the situation of violations of the rights of women in Chile, and should avoid being labelled as "communist". The last consideration influenced the choice of delegation's members.

Akin to the situation in Vietnam, but probably to an even bigger extent, in the case of Chile, the WIDF applied for support to the international organizations. In this case, the WIDF could use its improved international status and prestige, as well as repaired relationships with other transnational organizations to make the solidarity campaign with Chile broader. On the other hand, it seems that several transnational organizations were interested in involving the WIDF – a well-known transnational organization – in their solidarity activities. For example, in 1976, UNESCO sent a letter to the WIDF headquarters informing them that the violations of human rights in Chile will play a more important role in its work, and that they wanted to invite the WIDF representative to the 99th session of UNESCO's executive committee to discuss these issues (GARF 3 3962 from 13 January 1976). Such invitations, in their turn, contributed to spreading information about the situation in Chile, and corresponded to the interests of Chilean women in the WIDF. A report of the WIDF bureau meeting in Berlin in 1980 shows that representatives of several countries, including Chile and the South African ANC, with support of the WIDF, took part in many international events, including those organized by the UN (GARF 5075, p. 66). Their participation opened an opportunity to raise issues of the violation of the rights of women in these countries at the international level. As well as supporting the intervention of Chilean women in international events, the Secretariat collected information about violations of rights in Chile, and published reports about the situation of women and children in Chile in the WIDF journal (see, e.g., ZM 1977, 2: 34–37; 1977 3: 22–26; 1985, 2: 40–41).

At the same time, these actions were realized not without conflict, and, in some cases, were affected by ideological considerations and Soviet geopolitical interests. Thus, one of the letters of the Soviet representative to the Secretariat suggested that the WIDF's campaign of solidarity with Chile had to consider the plans of the Chilean Communist Party (in particular, Volodia T., most probably Tetelboim,[17] was mentioned). In this letter, Titova informed her addressee in the CSW that while Fanny Edelman was ready to answer he Chilean friends' request for supplies of food for women and children, and started looking at the possibility of opening a bank account with this aim in Western Europe, the Chilean communists needed money (for their clandestine activities, most probably), and not food. Thus, according to her letter, Titova succeeded in postponing, for some period, negotiations between the WIDF and the Red Cross regarding food supplies (GARF 3 3414, pp. 76–77).

The anti-Apartheid struggle also received the support of the WIDF during almost the entire period of the Cold War. Anna Davud from South Africa spoke against Apartheid in the WIDF Congress in Copenhagen (Za ravnopravie 1953, 191–192). As was said earlier, as early as 1958, the federation's journal published a long article explaining the discriminatory system of Apartheid (ZM 1958 7–8: 17–19). After that, the journal periodically published information about women's life under Apartheid, some of the materials being very emotionally loaded. For example, in 1960 the journal published the article "The Wonderful women of South Africa" by Elsie Beeching. The text was accompanied by pictures of some African women, one of them with her husband and 10 children; the woman was described as the head of the trade union of the can manufacturing industry who had to leave her country due to discrimination (WWW 1960 2: 21). The journal also published information about developments in the anti-Apartheid struggle. The collected information was also sent to other members of the federation, together with information about solidarity actions taking place in different countries.

For example, the archives of the CSW preserved information about a solidarity event that took place in Moscow in 1970. A letter by Balakhovskaia from the CSW in August 1970 informed Hugel, the WIDF general secretary, about a meeting organized in Moscow on 6 August, the day of solidarity with the struggle of South African women (GARF 3 2440, p. 63). The meeting was held in a medical research institute named after Gamalei, in Moscow,[18] and was led by one of the secretaries of the CSW, Zinaida Fedorova. Along with researchers from the Institute of Africa and Soviet women activists, the meeting also included a presentation from the representative of South Africa, student Nomawa Shongazi, who expressed her gratitude for support and solidarity, as well as a greeting from the representative of Zambia.

In the 1970s, human rights violations in South Africa, in no small measure because of the activities of women's organizations including the WIDF, won greater international visibility. Thus, in 1973 and 1976, the WIDF sent a delegation to South Africa in order to collect material about situation of women and children under Apartheid (WIDF 40 1985, 28–29). As in the case with Vietnam and Chile, the WIDF took part in many international events connected to the anti-Apartheid struggle. For example, the WIDF bureau in Berlin on 9–11 December 1980 discussed the report on the WIDF's participation in the international seminar "Situation of woman under Apartheid", which took place in Helsinki in May 1980 (GARF 3 5077, p. 95). The seminar was organized with the support of the UN commission on racism, racial discrimination, Apartheid, and decolonization and had support from UNESCO. The WIDF report stated that the federation led the working group and "did a lot of work preparing the seminar" (GARF 3 5077, p. 95).

Solidarity with the anti-racist struggle of South African women allowed the WIDF to draw attention to other systems and cases of racial discrimination. For example, in her speech at the WIDF bureau in Havana in 1973,

Hertta Kuusinen stated the WIDF's support for struggle against racial discrimination, and then moved to the "situation of women and people that were suffering under Portuguese colonialism – in Angola, Mozambique, Guinea-Bissau, and the Cabo Verde". She then discussed the heroic fight of the people of South Africa and Namibia against Apartheid, and also noted the "long lasting struggle of people of Zimbabwe against the regime of Ian Smith" (GARF 3 3162, p. 37).

Furthermore, as soon as the news of the arrest of Angela Davis became public in 1970, the WIDF took an active part in the campaign to support Davis (GARF 3 2440, p. 110). She maintained ties with the WIDF and the CSW after her liberation in 1973. For example, in 1981, the federation journal published a two-page interview with her, under the title "Racism is a danger to the world". In her interview, Davis discussed the work of the "National Union against racist and political persecution" against the Ku Klux Klan, stated that the women's movement in the USA is changing from being mostly feminist and middle-class to include working women, and becoming more oriented towards peace. She also stated that her organization supports solidarity campaigns for the liberation of the ANC leader, Nelson Mandela (*WWW* 1981, 4: 22–23).

Aside from these central solidarity campaigns, during its meetings, the WIDF continued to express its solidarity with women of many different countries and organizations. For example, in the protocols of the WIDF bureau meeting in Berlin 14–24 July 1980, the WIDF preserved a long solidarity declaration adopted by the bureau (GARF 3 5076, pp. 166–175). The declaration reported greetings to women of Vietnam, Laos, and Kampuchea, demanded the USA remove its military bases from South Korea, expressed support for women in India and Japan fighting against nuclear arms, as well as "the actions of women in Australia, New Zealand, and other countries of the region for democratic rights, peace, and progress". The long list also included "tribute to the women of Africa, who, in a historically short period, have made an important contribution to the profound changes which have transformed this large continent, formerly oppressed by 5 colonial powers, into a continent of dozens of states" (GARF 3 5076, p. 168); a salute to "the victory of the women of Zimbabwe" and condemnation of the "criminal Apartheid regime". The declaration stated that "The WIDF bureau calls for intensification of solidarity with the women and children of South Africa and Namibia, who are subjected to continual threats, assault, torture, and assassination by the Apartheid regime". The declaration also greeted "the women of Angola, Mozambique, and Ethiopia who are participating with great courage in the reconstruction of their countries" and reiterated "its firm solidarity with the Palestinian women and people" (GARF 3 5076, p. 170). While condemning the Israeli settlement policy, the federation greeted the "democratic women of Israel who oppose the imperialist policy" and demanded peace in the Middle East (GARF 3 5076, p. 171). The declaration also saluted "the great victory of the people of Nicaragua", expressed solidarity with women in Grenada, and condemned "genocidal repressions and fascist terror" in El Salvador (GARF 3 5076, p. 173). The WIDF also declared "its solidarity with the indigenous peoples of many countries who are struggling against racial discrimination, impoverishment, involuntary sterilization, and the destruction of their country". The countries of North America and Europe appeared only at the end of the declaration – the bureau expressed its support for "women of United States and Canada who are confronting economic crises" and the "women of the Western European countries who are defending their social, economic, and political rights" (GARF 3 5076, p. 175).

Female cadres and regionalization

During the 1970s–1980s, many women's organizations in Latin America, Asia, and Africa continued to experience frequent changes both inside and around the organizations; these changes were connected with the instability of newly independent countries, as well as changes of political regimes and conflicts inside the women's movement. Obviously, the changes happening in the women's organizations did not always happen in the direction that the WIDF leadership would have wanted to see. This soon made the WIDF's work with women's organizations from the Global South become not less (and often more) difficult than its work with women's organizations from Western Europe (such as the Italian or French organizations, conflicts with whom I discussed before).

For example, in 1980 the Iraqi Women's League[19] sent the WIDF a letter describing the current situation of the organization, and demanding it be re-admitted to the WIDF. The League reminded the WIDF that, during its many years of existence, their organization, "based on democratic grounds", had established good contacts with women in both cities and the countryside. However, after the establishment of the Baathist regime, the members of the League were persecuted, and in 1979 they re-established their organization clandestinely (GARF 3 5077, p. 283). The authors of the letter also informed the WIDF that, despite "the repression and persecution of the democratic forces in the country", the organization could make stronger contacts with their sisters in other Arab countries, and with the democratic movement. During the UN conference in Copenhagen in 1980 the League collected the signatures of 1040 women from 75 countries demanding the liberation of women and children prisoners in Iraq. Further, the authors of the letter stated that the official organization of Iraqi women, the General Federation of Iraqi Women, "stopped being a women's organization and became an instrument in the hands of the Baath party regime" (GRAF 3 5077, p. 283). Thus, the authors of this letter demanded that the WIDF's bureau should decide about the League's membership status in the WIDF, and invite Dr. Dulami (the head of the League), then traveling through Berlin, to discuss issues related to the membership (GARF 3 5077, p. 284). Later that same year, the League of Iraqi Women sent the bureau another letter condemning Iraq's attack on Iran on 22 September 1980, and described the Baath regime as "dictatorial" (GARF 3 5077, p. 286). While the archive files do not contain the reactions or answers of the WIDF leadership to these letters, it is easy to suppose that the leaders were not particularly happy to receive them – the Baath party and Saddam Hussein were close allies of the Soviet Bloc. Thus, the WIDF hardly took any action to welcome the readmission of this organization to the WIDF.

Due to the growing diversity of women's member organizations of the WIDF, with respect to their status, problems, and ideologies, the WIDF leadership experienced difficulties following them and, even more importantly, in making efforts to control them. The enormous size of the transnational organization contributed to its prestige, but did not make internal communication easier. All of this required more attention to the professional skills of female leaders, as well as the establishment of smaller units that allowed for discussing similar problems. The Cold War pressure with regard to competition over women in the countries of the Global South also continued to be important; the IWY showed a growth of women's organizations striving for international cooperation. In the late 1970s, many organizations from non-European countries had much more choices when making possible alliances, and sources of financing, compared to the early 1960s. It was probably this growing globalization of the women's movement, together with the internal difficulties of the federation in supervising its members, that contributed to the WIDF's decision to strengthen its work with women's organizations on the regional level and thus transfer more power to the regions.

In 1976, the federation decided to establish regional centres for preparing female cadres that would work with the problems of women's rights in their countries (GARF 3 5799, p. 1). One such centre had to be created in Latin America, and the USSR's closest ally there, Cuba, was made responsible for its organization. Another centre, for women of Asia, was to be created in state socialist Mongolia. According to Ghodsee, Bulgarian women took the initiative to organize a similar centre for cadres from Africa to take summer courses in Bulgaria (Ghodsee 2018).

The centre created in Havana, Cuba, in 1978, seems to be the first and the most stable and successful one. The WIDF journal wrote about this centre on two occasions – in 1983 and in 1985. The article published in 1983 was written by Fanny Edelman and Nancy Ruiz (the head of the centre) and celebrated the centre's 5th anniversary. They emphasized the importance of the centre through mentioning the solidarity efforts of different people and organizations that made its creation possible. At the same time, the authors stressed that the space where the courses in Cuba were taught belonged to the whole federation – "our house":

> We entered the house which since that day has been ours. The Cuban government had presented it to us. Workers and craftsmen had renovated and embellished it. Solidarity goods from across the oceans sent

> by our friends from national organizations and from the socialist countries, enriched our house and further beatified it.
>
> (WWW 1983, 1: 34)

They also stressed the importance of the centre in the context of the UN Decade for Women; the centre discussed and disseminated the programme for the decade. Finally, the article also stressed the high level of qualifications of its personal:

> The pedagogical work and the methods of instruction are reconciled with the extent of knowledge and peculiarities of every student in order to bridge over any arising differences.
>
> (WWW 1983 1: 34)

According to Ruiz, all students of the centre were activists and "came in order to improve their knowledge, to collect valuable experience" (WWW 1983 1: 35).

The second article, titled "The good work done by the WIDF regional centre in Havana", was written by Nancy Ruiz and published in 1985 (WWW 1985 3: 7–8). As its title shows, the article was very positive about the work of the centre, and described its curriculum as very informative:

> The curriculum covers the points contained in the WIDF Programme – winning and defending the rights of women and children, peace and disarmament, national independence and democratic freedoms – as well as the history of the women's movement, the history of America, the mass media and women, and the United Nations system.
>
> (WWW 1985 3: 7)

Both of the authors writing about the centre were activists in the Latin American women's movement, and presented this centre as having large regional importance. At the same time, both stressed the leading role of the FMC in designing its programmes and in selecting the participants. Thus, it is possible to suppose that the creation of such a centre in Havana in practice also meant lesser control and influence of the WIDF's central leadership, and Moscow, over the WIDF's cadre politics on the regional level.

These ideas could be further supported by the archival materials available in Moscow. A report on the work of the Havana centre from 28 April 1980, created by P. Yulchinskaya for the CSW, was mainly based on the official publications of the Cuban press (like the journal *Mujeres*) and the data provided by the Soviet Embassy in Cuba (GARF 3 5799, pp. 1–3). The report confirms, thus, that Moscow and the CSW did not have first-hand information about the centre (and, most probably, were not at all involved in planning its work). The report stated that the decision to create this centre was made at the WIDF bureau meeting on 23–26 November 1976. The centre opened on 16 January 1978, with the participation of members of the Cuban government, WIDF representatives, and representatives of the FMC and other Cuban organizations. According to this report, the Havana centre was not only a place for teaching Latin American female cadres, but contained an archive, and functioned as a research centre dedicated to the women's movements on the Latin American continent. This implied that the centre took it upon itself to collect material on the regional level (GARF 3 5799, pp. 4–8), something that the CSW did with the archive I used for writing this book. Unlike the archive in Moscow, the documents preserved in Havana seem to be mainly in Spanish, which made them only partially accessible to the WIDF's controls. This contributed to a certain independence of the centre; the possibility of establishing and maintaining own contacts with organizations and individual activists in the region, as well as it being able to establish priority when selecting candidates and teaching programmes locally (even though the report stated that the programmes are elaborated together by the FMC and WIDF).

According to the Soviet report, the centre was supported by the Cuban government, and also received support from women's organizations of some socialist countries. The Havana centre's programme included disciplines such as: history of the women's movement in Latin America; forms of cooperation of women's organizations on the international, national and regional level; importance to women of the IWY and the UN Decade for Women; the NIEO; Latin American economic systems; the Andean Community[20]; struggle for independence and its defence; struggle for democratic freedoms against Apartheid, race discrimination, and fascism (GARF 3 5799, p. 2). The students of the courses (two representatives of every country of the region and some African participants) were expected to spend three months in Havana and guaranteed free medical treatment in Cuba. Thus, similarly to the Soviet case, the courses also showcased the benefits of the socialist system, in this case, mainly, the Cuban one.

The archive documents from the same period show, however, that the attempt to open a similar centre in Mongolia was much less successful (GARF 3 4949, p. 1). A report to the CSW's leadership from 5 February 1979 stated that Comrade Udval, the head of the Committee of Women of Mongolia, on the occasion of her transit travel via Moscow on 16 October 1978, visited the CSW and informed its members about the situation regarding the opening of the centre in Ulan-Bator, Mongolia. Unlike the reports and publications on the centre in Havana, this short report suggested that both sides assumed that Moscow would play an important role in financial and logistical aspects of the centre's work. Udval stated that the financial means that the Committee of Mongolian Women had could only cover a one-and-a-half-month-long course for 30 women. This course could be organized only once a year, during the summer, when it was possible to accommodate the female students from Asia at the university dorm. Furthermore, language differences seem to play a more important role here; the Committee of Mongolian Women could guarantee translation into English and French; however, it would not be able to pay for the participants' travel to Ulan-Bator and back. Thus, the Mongolian women's organization hoped for help from other socialist countries in covering the participants' travel expenses. The committee also planned to ask the WIDF, or socialist countries, for help with buying a bus, two typing machines in English and French, and a rotator. Finally, Udval also informed members of the CSW that teachers at the school should come from the Mongolian Communist party's school.

On the basis of this report, it is possible to say that Udval did not show any particular enthusiasm concerning plans for opening the centre for female cadres, and was rather following pressure from Moscow. While I did not find any other documents or publications about this centre in the WIDF journal, it is possible to suppose that the centre never started to function or, even if did, it was very poor in the quality of its teaching resources, taking into account the diversity of the participants and problems connected to women's status in Asia.

The Havana centre, however, seemed to have corresponded to the WIDF's expectations. In her 1980 report for the WIDF's bureau in Berlin, the WIDF general secretary, Vire-Tuominen, not only noted the good work of the centre, but also suggested that its experience was used for the courses for African and Asian women that were opened in Bulgaria "thanks to the generous support of Bulgarian women" (GARF 3 5077, p. 97).

Conclusion

On the basis of the studied material, it is possible to say that during the 1970s–1980s, the WIDF was fully immersed in the field of transnational women's rights and was seen by many international governance bodies and women's organizations as an important and respected organization for promoting women's rights globally. In particular, the WIDF mastered a less ideological and more juridical language when addressing different aspects of women's rights, including those for women in the countries of the Global South.

At the same time, due to the rise of grassroots women's organizations and the radical feminist movement in Western Europe and North America, the WIDF lost much of its attractiveness to women's organizations in the "West". This made it continue to expand its activities in the Global South, and organizations from Latin America, Asia, and Africa came to constitute the majority of the WIDF's active members. The WIDF offered an opportunity for establishing contacts and cooperation between women's organizations from different countries in the Global South, and expanded its solidarity work. Women's organizations from these countries also received support in the form of expert advice, seminars, and training as well as financial aid for financing some events, training female activist cadres, and for the education of some female students in the state socialist countries.

The WIDF on the eve of the IWY 191

While actively participating in all of the UN-sponsored events of the IWY and the UN Decade for Women, the federation was quite successful in competing for influence over women from the Global South against other transnational organizations defending women's rights, such as the IAW or the ICW. However, growing conflicts inside the organization, together with less a favourable context of the main Cold War confrontation at the end of the period under research led to a partial loss of the WIDF's strength, and contributed to its further regionalization.

Notes

1 This declaration later became the basis for the CEDAW, adopted in 1979.
2 Both were members of the Union of Bulgarian Women.
3 The number of countries and organizations seem to have grown even during the same year – issue 4 names 121 organizations from 106 countries.
4 ECOSOC consists of representatives elected by the UN and holds its sessions for one month once a year. The session is also attended by the organizations having the special status of NGO.
5 From the speech by Mirjam Vire-Tuominen at the WIDF bureau meeting in Berlin in 1980 (GARF 3 5076, p. 16).
6 Greenham Common women's peace camp (UK) was started by women protesting against the plans of the British government to allow cruise missiles to be stored there.
7 This was the school that Ghodsee wrote about (2018).
8 The Nkrumah government in Ghana lost power in 1966, while developments in Algeria did not follow revolutionary expectations in the second half of the 1960s.
9 As I wrote earlier, the WIDF never stopped its cooperation with the Commission on the Status of Women. For example, Issue 6 from 1965 published a report on the 18th session of the UN CSW in Teheran (WIDF was represented by Betty Harrison). The article reflected the discussions during that session, including those on political rights for women de jure and in practice, and family legislation in many countries that preserved the inequality of the statuses of husband and wife (ZM 1965, 6: 17–18).
10 Issue 2 from 1968 contained four articles whose authors had title Dr., the articles were dedicated to different aspects of family legislation and women's rights.
11 The institute was created in 1959.
12 Aruna Asaf Ali (1908–1996) left the Communist party in the 1950s. She participated in the struggle for independence, was one of the founders of the Federation of Indian women in 1954, and rejoined the Congress Party of India in the 1960s. https://www.theguardian.com/world/1996/jul/30/india.guardianobituaries
13 Fuki Kushida (1899–2001) was a feminist and peace activist, https://www.latimes.com/archives/la-xpm-2001-feb-08-me-22689-story.html
14 Titova noticed that only $2,500 would be left in the WIDF's account after that, until the next deadline for membership fees (GARF 3 3414, 75).
15 Vilma Espín was the leader of the FMC that subsumed the Democratic Federation of Cuban Women, a member of the WIDF before 1960 (see Chase 2015). It was also widely known that Espín, participant in the Cuban guerrilla movement, was a partner of the brother of the leader of Cuban revolution, Raul Castro.
16 Abassia Fodil, participant at the 1953 WIDF congress in Copenhagen, stated that women and dock-workers organized protests in Algerian ports (*Za ravnopravie* 1953).

17 Volodia Tetelboim, leader of the Chilean Communist Party in the 1990s.
18 Institute of Epidemiology and Microbiology.
19 The Iraqi Women's League started its cooperation with the WIDF in the late 1950s (see ZM 1958 11:28) and included members of the Communist Party. However, the Baathist regime later established its own women's organization, General Federation of Iraqi Women.
20 The Andean Community is a free trade zone created by Colombia, Chile, Ecuador, Peru, and Bolivia in 1969.

9 The WIDF and the end of the three worlds
Concluding remarks

After the researchers of the women's movement "rediscovered" the WIDF during the 2010s, and a new interest on the positive side of state feminism in the "Communist countries" developed inside the field of gender history (see Zheng 2017), research on different aspects of the work of this organization in different countries attracted attention. Both the forgetting and the rediscovery of this organization raises many questions about its role in disseminating an awareness of women's rights' history globally, as well as questions about the organization's embeddedness within the Cold War. This "rediscovery" adds new questions to the already started discussion on meaning of postsocialism for feminist knowledge production (see e.g., Suchland 2011; Asztalos Morell & Gradskova 2018, 1–18; Kulawik 2020). In particular, they concern experiences from the Communist "East"; how do these experiences influence the established narrative on the progress of women's rights in the post-Second World War period as a result of pressure from the independent women's movement (from the "West"). This also makes it important to re-evaluate the place of an organization that was dependent on the "Eastern Bloc" in theorizing a place for state socialist histories of activism with respect to "feminism" and agency (see de Haan 2016).

This analysis of the WIDF's archive in Moscow through post-colonial lenses showed that the vision of women from outside Europe and North America as "uniform and dominated" described by Mohanty, in a modified version, was present in the WIDF. This vision was grounded on the unconditional belief in the superiority of modernity and modernization (similar to the role that modernity and development was seen to play in the "West"). However, in this particular case, it was the Soviet and the state socialist modernity that was considered superior. Furthermore, multiple silences and problems in following particular stories that were discussed by Stoler (2009) in the case of the colonial archive of the Dutch East Indies were characteristic for the logic of documents that were created and preserved in files dealing with the WIDF in the Moscow archive. The classified letters between the CSW and the Soviet representatives at the WIDF Secretariat, in particular, show how, and from where, the systems of knowledge and classification of the "women of the whole world" was constructed.

The analysed materials allow me to make three conclusions regarding the WIDF's activities for the rights of women of the "whole world":

The Cold War competition was very important in determining how women's rights were recognized globally. At the same time, the idea of rights for women in its different interpretations must be seen as an idea that transcended the "East/West" dividing line. The documents analysed in this book suggest that the WIDF was very active in promoting the idea of the importance of women's rights to work, equal pay, education, and social security, everywhere in the world. The WIDF started doing this transnationally before the mass feminist mobilization in the "West", known as "second wave" feminism, began in the 1960s. However, it seems that the Cold War competition was an important factor for both facilitating the recognition of the rights for women globally, and for the radicalization of the WIDF's own demands and statements.

Indeed, the analysed documents indicate that the global promotion of women's rights was, to a large extent, the outcome of the specific context of the Cold War confrontation. In particular, the "rights for women" was a strategy used by the Soviet Union and the "Eastern Bloc" to find more friends and sympathizers in the "West"; the changing goals of Soviet foreign policies played an important role for the choice of, and changes in, the WIDF's rhetoric, partners, and financial priorities. However, in time, the Cold War logic made women's rights and their global implementation an important battlefield of the cultural struggle between the USA and the Soviet Union; this field included a number of actors and positions that could not be foreseen in 1945 when the federation was founded.

Many of the WIDF demands concerning women's rights were modelled on the Soviet practices with rights for "women workers". These demands were perceived by the world to be quite radical in the late 1940s, but became normalized through the women's movement of the 1960s, and the UN documents of the 1970s. At the same time, these demands gained strength and acceptance only because of their broader popularity, and support from women's organizations and individual female leaders in different countries and continents.

The "Soviet front" theory is not a good explanation for most of the WIDF's work for women's rights. The studied archival documents show that changes in the WIDF's policies that occurred from 1955 to 1985 cannot be explained as Soviet "decisions"; they were a result of internal discussions, lobbying, and conflicts. The Soviet women's organization, the ACSW/CSW, was one of the founding members of the WIDF and did everything possible to maintain its influence on the WIDF's cadre politics, and its ideology, up to the end of the Cold War. The main instrument of Soviet influence was the Secretariat, as well as the coordination of WIDF activities and cadre politics through communist parties' female representatives in the federation from different countries. This instrument, however, was too complex, and its effectiveness was quite low. In practice, many female leaders-Communist party members had independent opinions on the global work for women's rights, and defended their positions at the Secretariat, as well as at the WIDF bureau meetings and congresses. The agency of these communist (and even more in the case of leftist independent) women in the WIDF led to multiple conflicts and developments that did not correspond to the Soviet or "communist" interests or expectations. Hence, the studied materials show that, in spite of the existence of Soviet projects with respect to the WIDF's activities, and attempts at realizing them, the WIDF was a much more complex organization than just a "sympathizing organization" (Petersson 2013) or a public diplomacy entity.

Women from the Global South became one of the most important factors influencing the Cold War cultural confrontation and the transformation of the WIDF itself. One of the most important and unexpected outcomes of the WIDF's activities was the strong presence of representatives of the Global South in the federation and its leadership in the 1970s. At the same time it is important to have in mind that, the Cold War logic sometimes led the WIDF to defend the rights of women from the Global South more radically than it would have in the absence of such a pressure.

After the beginning of the mass decolonization process in the late 1950s, many representatives from Asia, Africa, and Latin America joined the federation. The new participants were influenced by different ideas, connected with the struggle for independence and anti-imperialism, but most of them aspired to rapid modernization and the development of their countries. Thus, the change of women's status in society was broadly seen as an important condition of modernization and cultural transformation. The participation of these women changed the character of the federation and made it, by the 1970s, a broader alliance of left-oriented Global South women in cooperation with the Eastern Bloc. After many European communist women stopped being so active in the WIDF (particularly after the radical new wave of feminism arose in 1968), members from countries outside Europe constituted the majority of WIDF members and influenced all the decisions of the federation.

The WIDF especially attracted women from the Global South because it emphasized its differences from the "Western" global feminist efforts that were criticized by Black and "Third World" feminists (see bell hooks 1989; Mohanty 2003). Women from Africa, Asia, and Latin America were attracted by the WIDF's declared readiness to accept the representatives of the Global South as independent subjects of politics (thus, making a contrast to the "Western" perception of "Third World" women as those in need of help and guidance, see Mohanty 2003). Many of the new WIDF participants from the Global South were also happy to join an organization that saw the struggle for social rights and anti-racism as an important one.

In its turn, the mass participation of the new women's organizations in the WIDF resulted in the heterogeneity of the federation and growing tendencies towards regionalization.

Due to its visibility in the field of international politics, and its permanent defence of human rights, gender equality, anti-racism, and anti-colonialism, the WIDF acquired a lot of influence in the countries outside Europe. The achievements of the state socialist modernity that multiple guests could see while visiting not only Moscow, the GDR, or Czechoslovakia, but, in particular, Central Asia and the Caucasus, were quite convincing for many female leaders from the developing countries. The achievements of the previously "backward" and "underdeveloped" colonial borderlands (of the Russian Empire) confirmed the possibility that other developing countries could find ways to solve the problems of development and change women's status without the aid programmes designed by the First World countries (frequently, former colonizers). In particular, the documents show the significant role played by Soviet women of colour (like Rahimbabaeva) – those incorporating Soviet and post-colonial identities, who became a presentation of a different Sovietness for the outside world, especially for women from the Third World.

The analysis of the biographies of some of the representatives of Asia, Africa, and Latin America in the WIDF shows that their identities were very complex and multilayered, while their interest and degree of involvement with the WIDF's work varied considerably. Many of the female leaders from the Global South who cooperated with the WIDF belonged to the middle class and educated elite of the late colonial/early post-colonial society. At the same time, they often had experiences of multiple and cross-sectional injustices. The regional and ethnic identities of these leaders were no less important in their interactions with the WIDF than their political, educational, or religious ones. Thus, they had a combination of views that were connected to their multiple intersectional belongings and experiences of discrimination, and only some of their views and demands found support in the WIDF. This meant that the alliances women from the Global South made with the federation were more strategic than ideological (including the cases of those women who were members of a communist party, such as Ahmed Ibrahim). Further, it allowed them to build alliances more freely with women's organizations on the other side of the Iron Curtain, in the "West". The constant suspicion of the WIDF's ideological leadership towards the behaviour of these activists from the Global South is probably why women from Asia, Africa, and Latin America could only attain the top positions in the organization after the end of the communist system. On the other hand, the lack of strong centralism in the WIDF as well as the lack of subordination between the leaders of the Global South and the Secretariat in Berlin in some cases allowed to first to have a broader repertoire of actions while working at both the national and local levels. The African, Asian, and Latin American female leaders could not be compelled to only use those forms of actions and ideas promoted by the WIDF.

Thus, the example of the WIDF shows that women's rights was an important ideological weapon of the "Eastern Bloc". The bloc was always ready to show that it performed better in realizing such an important aspect of human rights. This provided the means of attracting new supporters from other geopolitical entities (and thus more allies in the cultural Cold War), but, probably even more importantly, it enabled the bloc to win some battles at the UN, UNESCO, and other global governance bodies. The end of the Cold War, and the elimination of the division between the three "Worlds", seems to have eliminated the pressure to introduce more rights for women that was connected to the competition.

Appendix

WIDF congresses
1945 – Paris
1948 – Budapest
1953 – Copenhagen
1958 – Vienna
1963 – Moscow
1969 – Helsinki
1975 – Berlin
1981 – Prague

WIDF bureau meetings outside of Europe
1960 – Jakarta (Indonesia)
1962 – Bamako (Mali)
1973 – Havana (Cuba)

WIDF presidents
1945–1968 – Eugénie Cotton (France)
1969–1974 – Hertta Kuusinen (Finland)
1975–1991 – Freda Brown (Australia)

WIDF general secretaries
1946–1955 – Mari-Claude Vaillant-Cotourier (France)
1956–1957 – Angiola Minella (Italy)
1957–1963 – Carmen Zanti (Italy)
1963–1967 – Rosa Jasovich-Pantaleon (Argentina)
1967–1972 – Cecile Hugel (France)
1972–1978 – Fanny Edelman (Argentina)
1978–1985 – Mirjam Vire-Tuominen (Finland)

Heads of the Committee of Soviet Women
1941–1968 – Nina Popova
1969–1991 – Valentina Tereshkova

Soviet representatives in the WIDF's Secretariat
    1946–1949 – Tatiana Kosheleva
    1950–1951 – Zinaida Gurina
    1951–1955 – Galina Goroshkova
    1956–1957 – Zoya Ivanova
    1958–1959 – Maria Skotnikova
    1960–1963 – Zinaida Lebedeva
    1964–1967 – (?) probably Xenia Proskurnikova
    1969–1972 – Zukhra Rahimbabaeva
    1973–1977 – Valentina Titova
    1978–1986 – Valeria Kalmyk

List of Literature

Archive materials

Arbetarrörelsens Arkiv och bibliotek (ARAB, Flemingsberg) – Fond 3340, Svenska Kvinnornas Vänsterförbund – foreign correspondence.
CIA. (1956). *Women's International Democratic Federation. A Compilation of Available Basic Reference Data.* https://www.cia.gov/library/readingroom/document/cia-rdp78-00915r000600140010-9, Accessed August 20, 2020.
CIA. (1961). The All African People Conference. https://www.cia.gov/library/readingroom/docs/CIA-RDP78-00915R001300320009-3.pdf, Accessed August 20, 2020.
CIA. (1963). *The Third Afro-Asian People Solidarity Conference.* https://www.cia.gov/library/readingroom/docs/CIA-RDP78-00915R001400380004-1.pdf, Accessed August 20, 2020.
Institute of International Social History – archival collection of WIDF documents (IISH, Amsterdam).
Russian State Archive of Social and Political History (RGASPI). Fond 17 (Central Committee of the Communist Party of the Soviet Union), opis 137, Vneshnepoliticheskaia Kommissia (1949–1952).
State Archive of the Russian Federation (GARF), fond 7928, Antifascist Committee of the Soviet Woman.

Periodicals

Women of the Whole World – 1969, 1970, 1975–1985 (some years incomplete).
Zhenshchiny mira – 1953, 1958–1984 (some years incomplete).

Other publications

Ahmed Ibrahim, F. (2000). Sudanese Women under repression, and the shortest way to equality. In: M. Waller & J. Rycenga eds., *Frontline Feminisms: Women, War and Resistance.* New York: Garland, pp. 129–139.
Allen, A.T. (2008). *Women in Twenties Century Europe.* Basingstoke: Palgrave McMillan.
Alvarez, S. (1994). La (trans)formación de (los) feminism(s) y la politica de genero en la democratización de Brasil. In: M. Leon ed., *Mujeres y Participación Política: Avances y Desafíos en América Latina.* Santa Fe de Bogota: TM, pp. 231–282.

Andreen, A. (1974). *Svenska Kvinnors Vänsterförbund: En Femtioårs Berättelse av Andrea Andreen*. Stockholm AB: Esselte (first published in 1964).
Antrobus, P. (2004). *The Global Women's Movement*. London: Zed Books.
Anzaldúa, G. (1991). *Borderland: The New Mezstiza la Frontera*. San Francisco: Aunt Lute Books.
Armstrong, E. (2016). Before Bandung: The anti-imperialist women's movement in Asia and the Women's International Democratic Federation. *Signs*, 41(2), pp. 305331.
Asztalos Morell, I. & Gradskova, Y. (2018). The gendered subject of postsocialism: State-socialist legacies, global challenges and (re)building of tradition. In: Y. Gradskova & Asztalos Morell, I. eds., *Gendering Postsocialism: Old Legacies and New Hierarchies*. New York: Routledge, pp. 1–8.
Autio-Sarasmo, S. & Miklossy, K. (eds.). (2011). *Reassessing Cold War Europe*. London: Routledge.
Badran, M. (1995). *Feminists, Islam, and Nation: Gender and the Making of Modern Egypt*. Princeton, NJ: Princeton University Press.
Bechmann Pedersen, S. & Noack, Ch. (2020). *Tourism and Travel During the Cold War*. London: Routledge.
Berger, M. & Weber, H. (2014). *Rethinking the Third World: International Development and World Politics*. Houndmills: Palgrave Macmillan.
Bier, L. (2010). Feminism, solidarity, and identity in the age of Bandung: Third world women in the Egyptian women's press. In: Ch. Lee ed., *Making a World After Empire: The Bandung Moment and Its Political Afterlives*. Athens: Ohio University Press, pp. 143–172.
Bier, L. (2011). *Revolutionary Womanhood: Feminisms, Modernity and the State in Nasser's Egypt*. California: University of California Press.
Bonfiglioli, Ch. (2012). *Revolutionary Networks: Women's Political and Social Activism in Cold War Italy and Yugoslavia (1945–1957)*, PhD Dissertation, Utrecht University. https://dspace.library.uu.nl/bitstream/handle/1874/254104/Bonfiglioli.pdf?sequence, Accessed August 20, 2020
Bonfiglioli, Ch. (2016). The first UN world conference on women (1975) as a Cold War encounter: Recovering anti-imperialist, non-aligned and socialist genealogies. *Filozofija I Drustvo*, xxvii(3), pp. 521–531.
Bonfiglioli, Ch. (2016a). On Vida Tomšic, marxist feminism, and agency. *Aspasia*, 10, pp. 145–151.
Bracke, M. & Mark, J. (2015). Between decolonization and the Cold War: Transnational activism and its limits in Europe, 1950s–90s. *Journal of Contemporary History*, 50(3), pp. 403–417.
Byrne, J. J. (2016). *Mecca of Revolution: Algeria, Decolonization, and the Third World Order*. New York, NY: Oxford University Press.
Casola N. (2015). *El PC Argentino y la Dictadura Militar*. Buenos Aires: Imago Mundi.
Chaperon, S. (2000). Feminism is dead: Long live Feminism: Women's movement in France at the liberation. In: C. Duchen & I. Bandhauer-Schöffmann eds., *When the War was Over: Women, War and Peace in Europe, 1940–1956*. London: Leicester University Press, pp. 146–161.
Chase, M. (2015). *Revolution Within the Revolution: Women and Gender Politics in Cuba, 1952–1962*. Chapel Hill: The University of North Carolina Press.
Christiaens, K., Goddeeris, I. & M. Rodriguez eds. (2014). *European Solidarity with Chile, 1970–1980*. Frankfurt am Main: Peter Lang.

Cissé, J. M. (2009). *La Fille du Miló*. Paris: Presence Africaine.

Dababneh, A. (2005). *The Jordanian Women's Movement: A Historical Analysis Focusing on Legislative Change*. PhD Dissertation. University of Leicester.

David-Fox, M. (2012). *Showcasing the Great Experiment: Cultural Diplomacy and Western Visitors to Soviet Union, 1921–1941*. New York: Oxford University Press.

de Haan, F. (2010). Continuing Cold War paradigms in Western historiography of transnational women's organizations: The case of the Women's International Democratic Federation (WIDF). *Women's History Review*, 19(4), pp. 547–573.

de Haan, F. (2012). The Women's International Democratic Federation (WIDF): History, main agenda and contributions (1945–1991). In: Th. Dublin & K. Kish Sklar eds., *Women and Social Movements (WASI) Online Archive*. http://alexanderstreet.com/products/women-and-social-movements-international

de Haan, F. (2013). Eugénie Cotton, Pak Chong-ae, and Claudia Jones: Rethinking Transnational Feminism and International Politics. *Journal of Women's History*, 25(4), pp. 174–189.

de Haan, F. (2016). Introduction. Forum: 10 years After. Communism and feminism revisited. *Aspasia*, 10, pp. 102–110.

de Haan, F. (2017). La Federación Democratica Internacional de Mujeres (FDIM) y America Latina, de 1945 a los años setenta. In: A. Valobra & M. Yusta eds., *Queridas Camaradas. Historias Iberoamericanas de Mujeres Comunistas*. Buenos Aires: Miño y Davila, pp. 17–44.

de Haan, F. (2018). The Global Left-Feminist 1960s: From Copenhagen to Moscow and New York. In: Ch. Jian, M. Klimke, M. Kirasirova et al. eds., *The Routledge Handbook of the Global Sixties: Between Protest and Nation-Building*. London: Routledge, pp. 230–242.

Desfosses, H. (1980). Population in Soviet perspective. In: R. Duncan ed., *Soviet Policy in the Third World*. New York: Pergamon Press.

Devinatz, V. G. (2013). A Cold War Thaw in the International Working Class Movement? The world federation of trade unions and the international confederation of free trade unions, 1967–1977. *Science & Society*, 77(3), pp. 342–371.

Djagalov, R. & Salazkina, M. (2016). Tashkent '68: A cinematic contact zone. *Russian Review*, 75(2), pp. 279–298.

Donert, C. (2013). Women's rights in Cold War Europe. *Past and Present* 218(8), pp. 180–202.

Donert, C. (2014). Whose Utopia? Gender, ideology and human rights at the 1975 world congress in East Berlin. In: J. Eckel & S. Moyne eds., *The Breakthrough: Human Rights in the 1970s*. Philadelphia: University of Pennsylvania Press, pp. 68–87.

Donert, C. (2016). From communist internationalism to human rights: Gender, violence and international law in the Women's International Democratic Federation mission to North Korea, 1951. *Contemporary European History*, 25(2), pp. 313–333.

Drew, A. (2014). *We Are no Longer in France: Communists in Colonial Algeria*. Manchester: Manchester University Press.

Eckel, J. & S. Moyn eds. (2014). *The Breakthrough: Human Rights in the 1970s*. Philadelphia: University of Pennsylvania Press.

Edelman, F. (1996). *Banderas, Pasiones, Camaradas*. Buenos Aires: Dirple.

Edelman, F. (2001). *Feminismo y Marxismo. Conversaciones con Claudia Korol*. Buenos Aires: Cuadernos Marxistas.

Egefur, F. (2020). *Gränslösa rörelser för fred 1889–1914*. Lund: Lund University.
Elgán, E. (2015). *Att ge sig själv makt: Grupp 8 och 1970-talets Feminism*. Göteborg: Makadam.
Embong, A. R. & Abdulla, Z. (2019). The Japanese Invasion of Malaysia in WWII. In: J. Suchoples, S. James & B. Törquist-Pliewa eds., *World War II Re-explored*. Berlin: Peter Lang, pp. 135–148.
Engel, B. (2004). *Women in Russia*. Cambridge: Cambridge University Press.
Eslava, L., Fakhri, M. & Nesiah, V. eds. (2017). *Bandung, Global History, and International Law: Critical Pasts and Pending Futures*. Cambridge: Cambridge University Press.
Espín, V. (1985). Entrevista concedida a Mirta Rodriguez Calderón, el periodico Granma. *Mujer de Cuba. Vilma Espín*. La Habana: Federacion de Mujeres Cubanas, pp. 37–50.
Fainberg, M. (2016). Introduction to: Radio free Europe information item #687/54 (29 January 1954) "The Decline of Family Life". *Aspasia*, 10, pp. 89–93.
Faraldo, J. M. (2016). An antifascist political identity? On the cult of antifascism in the Soviet Union and post-socialist Russia, In: H. García, M. Yusta, X. Tabet & C. Climaco eds., *Rethinking Antifascism. History, Memory and Politics 1922 to the Present*. New York: Berghahn, pp. 202–228.
Fitzpatrick, Sh. (1996). Supplicants and citizens: Public letter-writing in Soviet Russia in the 1930s. *Slavic Review*, 55(1), pp. 78–105.
Fitzpatrick, Sh. (2015). Impact of the opening of Soviet archives on Western scholarship on Soviet social history. *The Russian Review*, 3, pp. 377–400.
Florin, Ch. (2006). *Kvinnor Får Röst*. Stockholm: Atlas.
Florin, Ch. & Nilsson B. (1999). Something in the nature of a bloodless revolution. In: R. Torstendahl ed., *State Policy and Gender System in the Two German States and Sweden 1945–1989*. Uppsala: Uppsala University, pp. 1–77.
Frazier, J. (2017). *Women's Anti-war Diplomacy During the Vietnam War*. Chapel Hill: University of North Carolina Press.
Friedman, J. (2015). *Shadow Cold War: The Sino-Soviet Competition for the Third World*. Chapel Hill: University of North Carolina Press.
Funk, N. (2014). A very tangled knot: Official state socialist women's organizations, women's agency and feminism in Eastern European state socialism. *European Journal of Women's Studies*, 21(4), pp. 344–360.
Gaer, F. (2009). Women, international law and international institutions: The case of the United Nations. *Women's Studies International Forum* 32, pp. 60–66.
García, H., Yusta, M., Tabet, X. & Climaco, C. eds. (2016). *Rethinking Antifascism. History, Memory and Politics 1922 to the Present*. New York: Berghahn.
Gerdov, Ch. (2019). Hanna Rydh och den onämnbare andre. *Tidskrift för genusvetenskap*, 40 (1), pp. 75–95.
Ghodsee, K. (2010). Revisiting the United Nations decade for women: Brief reflections on feminism, capitalism and Cold War politics in the early years of the international women's movement. *Women's Studies International Forum*, 33, pp. 3–12.
Ghodsee, K. (2018). *Second World, Second Sex*. Durham: Duke University Press.
Gildea, R., Mark, J. & Warring, A. (2013). *Europe's 1968. Voices of Revolt*. Oxford: Oxford University Press.
Giorgi, A. L. (2017). Entre la lucha contra la carestía y por los derechos de la mujer. Las comunistas uruguayas durante la segunda mitad del siglo 20. In: A. Valobra & M. Yusta eds., *Queridas Camaradas. Historias Iberoamericanas de Mujeres Comunistas*. Buenos Aires: Miño y Davila, pp. 215–234.

Gordon-Nesbitt, R. (2015). *To Defend the Revolution is to Defend Culture. The Cultural Policy of the Cuban Revolution*. Oakland, CA: PM Press.

Gradskova, Y. (2007). *Soviet People with Female Bodies: Performing Beauty and Maternity in Soviet Russia, in the Early 1930s-1960s*. PhD Dissertation. Stockholm: Stockholm University.

Gradskova, Y. (2014). The Soviet Union: "Chile is in our hearts." Practices of solidarity between propaganda, curiosity and subversion. In: K. Christiaens, I. Goddeeris, & M. Rodriguez eds., *European Solidarity with Chile, 1970–1980*. Frankfurt am Main: Peter Lang, pp. 329–346.

Gradskova, Y (2018). *Soviet Emancipation of Ethnic Minority Women. Natsionalka*. Cham: Springer.

Gradskova, Y. (2019). Women's International Democratic Federation, the "Third World" and the global Cold War from the late-1950s to the mid-1960s. *Women's History Review*, https://tandfonline.com/doi/full/10.1080/09612025.2019.1652440

Grigorieva, R. (2010). *Golub mira Niny Popovoi. K 65-litiyu pobedy v Velikoi Otechestvennoi voine, sozdaniia MDFZh I 45-litiyu prisvoeniia Moskve zvaniia goroda-geroia*. Moskva: Tonchu.

Gryzunova, M.G. (1975). *MDFZh 1945-1975*. Moskva: Znanie.

Hajimu, M. (2015). *Cold War Crucible. The Korean Conflict and the Post-War World*. Cambridge, MA: Harvard University Press.

Hanson, P. & Johnson, S. (2014). *Eurafrica. The Untold Story of European Integration and Colonialism*. London: Bloomsbury.

Hasegawa, T. ed. (2011). *The Cold War in East Asia. 1945–1991*. Stanford: Stanford University Press.

hooks, b. (1989). *Talking Black. Thinking Feminist, Thinking Black*. Boston, MA: South End Press.

Hong, Y.S. (2015). *Cold War Germany, the Third World, and the Global Humanitarian Regime*. Cambridge: Cambridge University Press.

Hugh Lee, S. (2011). Military occupation and Empire building in Cold War Asia: The United States and Korea, 1945–1955. In: T. Hasegawa ed., *The Cold War in East Asia. 1945–1991*. Stanford: Stanford University Press, pp. 98–121.

Ilic, M. (2011). Soviet women, cultural exchange and the Women's International Democratic Federation. In: S. Autio-Sarasmo & K. Miklossy eds., *Reassessing Cold War Europe*. London: Routledge, pp. 157–174.

Iriye, A. (2013). *Global and Transnational History*. Basingstoke: Palgrave Macmillan.

Jian, Ch. (2011). Reorienting the Cold War: The implications of China's early Cold War experience: Taking Korea as a central case. In: T. Hasegawa ed., *The Cold War in East Asia. 1945–1991*. Stanford: Stanford University Press, pp. 81–97.

Jo Plant, R., Sanders, N., Weintrob, L. & van der Klein, M. (2012). *Maternalism Reconsidered: Motherhood, Welfare and Social Policy in the Twentieth Century*. New York: Berghahn Books.

Johnson-Odim, Ch. (2009). "For their freedoms": The anti-imperialist and international feminist activity of Funmilayo Ransome-Kuti of Nigeria. *Women's Studies International Forum*, 32, pp. 51–59.

Johnson-Odim, Ch. & Mba, N. (1997). *For Women and the Nation. Funmilayo Ransome Kuti of Nigeria*. Chicago: University of Illinois Press.

Kalinovsky, A. (2018). *Laboratory of Socialist Development: Cold War Politics and Decolonization in Soviet Tajikistan*. Ithaca: Cornell University Press.

Kamp, M. (2006). *New Woman in Uzbekistan, Islam, Modernity and Unveiling under Communism*. Seattle: University of Washington Press.

Kanet, R. (1988). Soviet propaganda and the process of national liberation. In: R. Kanet ed., *Soviet Union, Eastern Europe and the Third World*. Cambridge: Cambridge University Press, pp. 84–114.

Katsakioris, C. (2019). The Lumumba University in Moscow: Higher education for a Soviet–Third world alliance, 1960–1991. *Journal of Global History*, 14(2), pp. 281–300.

Katsakioris, C. (2020). Students from Portuguese Africa in the Soviet Union, 1960–1974: Anti-colonialism, Education, and the Socialist Alliance. *Journal of Contemporary History*. doi: 10.1177/0022009419893739.

Kirasirova, M. (2018). Building anti-colonial Utopia: The politics of space in Soviet Tashkent in the long 1960s. In: Ch. Jian, M. Klimke, & M. Kirasirova et al. eds., *The Routledge Handbook of the Global Sixties. Between Protest and Nation-Building*. London: Routledge, pp. 53–66.

Koivunen, P. (2011). Overcoming Cold War Boundaries at the World Youth Festivals. In: S. Autio-Sarasmo & K. Miklossy eds., *Reassessing Cold War Europe*. London: Routledge, pp. 175–192.

Kotila, P. (2006). The "Red Lady of Finland". *Science & Society*, 70(1), pp. 46–73.

Kozlova, N. (2005). *Sovetskie liudi. Stseny iz istorii*. Moskva: Evropa.

Kozlova, N. &Sandomirskaja, I. (1996). *"Ya tak khochu nazvat kino"*. *'Naivnoe pismo' – Opyt sotsio-lingvisticheskogo chteniia*. Moskva: Gnosis.

Kryshtanovskaia, O. (1995). Transformatsiia staroi nomenklatury v novuyu rossiiskuyu elitu. *Obshchestvennye nauki I sovremennost*, 1, pp. 51–65.

Kulawik, T. (2020). Introduction. European borderlands and topographies of transnational feminism. In: T. Kulawik & Zh. Kravchenko eds., *Borderlands in European Gender Studies: Beyond the East-West Frontier*. London: Routledge, pp. 1–38.

Larberg, E. & Andreen Sachs, M. (2015). *Andrea Andreen: För Livets Skull*. Stockholm: Publit.

Lebon, N. & Maier, E. (2010). *Women's Activism in Latin America and the Caribbean: Engendering Social Justice, Democratizing Citizenship*. New Brunswick, NJ: Rutgers University Press.

Lee, Ch. ed. (2010a). *Making a World After Empire. The Bandung Moment and its Political Afterlives*. Athens: Ohio University Press.

Lee, Ch. (2010b). Tricontinentalism in question. In: Ch. Lee ed., *Making a World After Empire: The Bandung Moment and its Political Afterlives*. Athens: Ohio University Press, pp. 266–286.

Leon, M. ed. (1994). *Mujeres y Participación Política: Avances y Desafíos en América Latina*. Santa Fe de Bogota: TM.

Livshin A., Khlevnyuk, O., & Orlov I. (2002). *Pisma vo Vlast*. Moskva: ROSSPEN.

Lorde, A. (1984). Notes from a trip to Russia. In: A. Lorde eds., *Sister Outsider*. Trumansburg, NY: Crossing Press, pp. 13–35.

Loomba, A. (2018). *Revolutionary Desires: Women, Communism, and Feminism in India*. London: Routledge.

Lundin, E. (2019). "Now is the time:" The importance of international Spaces for Women's Activism within the ANC, 1960–1976. *Journal of South African Studies*, 45(2), pp. 323–340.

MacFarlane, N. (1985). *Superpower Rivalry and 3rd World Radicalism: The Idea of National Liberation*. London & Sydney: Croom Helm.

McGregor, K. (2013). The Cold War, Indonesian women and the global anti-imperialist movement, 1946–1965. In: J. Pieper-Mooney & F. Lanza eds., *De-Centering Cold War History: Local and Global Change*. London & New York: Routledge, pp. 31–51.

McGregor, K. (2016). Opposing colonialism: The Women's International Democratic Federation and decolonization struggles in Vietnam and Algeria 1945–1965. *Women's History Review*, 25(6), pp. 925–944.

McGregor, K. & Hearmann, V. (2017). Challenging the lifeline of imperialism. In: L. Eslava, M. Fakhri, & V. Nesiah eds., *Bandung, Global History, and International Law: Critical Pasts and Pending Futures*. Cambridge: Cambridge University Press, pp. 161–176.

Mahjoub, J. (2018). *A Line in the River: Khartoum, City of Memory*. London: Bloomsbury.

Mark, J. & Apor, P. (2015). Socialism goes global: Decolonization and the making of a new culture of internationalism in socialist Hungary, 1956–1989. *The Journal of Modern History*, 87(4), pp. 852–891.

Mark, J., Kalinovsky, A., & Marung, S. (2020). *Alternative Globalizations: Eastern Europe and Postcolonial World*. Bloomington: Indiana University Press.

Matusevich M. (2003). *No Easy Row for a Russian Hoe*. Trenton, NJ: Africa World Press.

Matusevich, M. (2012). The Black Atlantic: African students as Soviet moderns. *Ab Imperio*, 2, pp. 325–350.

Mazov, S. (2008). *Politika SSSR v Zapadnoi Afrike. Neizvestnye stranitsy kholodnoi voiny*. Moskva: Nauka.

Mazower, M. (2008). *No Enchanted Palace: The End of Empire and the Ideological Origins of the United Nations*. Princeton & Oxford: Princeton University Press.

Mazower, M. (2013). *Governing the World: The History of an Idea*. London: Penguin.

Melasuo, T. (2019). The second world war and Africa: New considerations within colonial context. In: J. Suchoples, S. James & B. Törquist-Pliewa eds., *World War II Re-explored*. Berlin: Peter Lang, pp. 355–382.

Mignolo, W. & Vasquez, R. (2013). Decolonial aesthesis: Colonial wounds/decolonial healings. *Social Text*. http://socialtextjournal.org/periscope_article/decolonial-aesthesis-colonial-woundsdecolonial-healings/, Accessed September 28, 2020.

Mohanty, Ch. (2003). *Feminism Without Borders: Decolonizing Theory, Practicing Solidarity*. Durham: Duke University Press.

Molyneux, M. (2001). *Women's Movements in International Perspective: Latin America and Beyond*. Basingstoke: Palgrave.

Moyn, S. (2010). *The Last Utopia. Human Rights in History*. Cambridge, MA: Belknap Press.

Moumié, M. (2006). *Victime du Colonialism Française*. Paris: Duboiris.

Müller, T. (2014). *Legacies of Socialist Solidarity: East Germany in Mozambique*. Lanham, MD: Lexington Books.

Mustafa Abusharaf, R. (2000). Revisiting feminist discourses on infibulation: Reponses from Sudanese feminists. In: B. Shell-Duncan & Y. Hernlund eds., *Female "Circumcision" in Africa: Culture, Controversy and Change*. Boulder: Lynne Rienner, pp. 151–165.

Nari, M. (2004). *Políticas de Maternidad y Maternalismo Político. Buenos Aires, 1890–1940*. Buenos Aires: Biblos.

Northrop, D. (2004). *Veiled Empire: Gender and Power in Stalinist Central Asia*. Ithaca: Cornell University Press.

Olcott J. (2017). *International Women's Year: The Greatest Consciousness-Raising Event in History*. New York: Oxford University Press.
Oldfield, S. (2000). *Alternatives to Militarism 1900–1989*. Oxford: Blackwell.
Onajin, A. & Ofoego, A. (2014). Funmilayo Ransome-Kuti: And the Women's Union of Abeokuta. UNESCO online publication https://unesdoc.unesco.org/ark:/48223/pf0000230929, Accessed August 20, 2020
Paik, H. (2010). Superpower rivalry and the victimization of Korea: The Korean war and the North Korean nuclear crises. In: Ch. Chari ed., *Superpower Rivalry and Conflict: The Long Shadow of the Cold War on the 21st Century*. London: Routledge, pp. 34–49.
Petersson, F. (2013). Caught between nostalgia, anti-colonialism, international communism, transnational networks and radical spaces: A re-assessment on the historiography of the league against imperialism. *CoWoPa: Comintern Working Paper*, 28, pp. 1–31.
Petrova, L. (1956). *Za mir i Ravnopravie Zhenshchin i Schastie detei*. Moskva: Gospilitizdat.
Petrova, L. (1959). *Chetvertyi Congress Mezhdunarodnoi Demokraticheskoi Federatsii Zhenshchin*. Moskva: Znanie.
Pieper Mooney, J. (2013a). Fighting fascism and forging new political activism: The Women's International Democratic Federation in the Cold War. In: J. Pieper Mooney & F. Lanza eds., *De-Centering Cold War History*. London: Routledge, pp. 52–73.
Pieper Mooney, J. (2013b). El antifascismo como la fuerza movilizadora: Fanny Edelman y la Federación Democratica Internacional de las Mujeres (FDIM). *Anuario IEHS* 28, pp. 207–226.
Pojmann, W. (2013). *Italian Women and International Cold War Politics, 1944–1968*. New York: Fordham University Press.
Popa, R. M. (2009). Translating equality between women and men across Cold War divides: Women activists from Hungary and Romania and the creation of international women's year. In: Sh. Penn & J. Massino eds., *Gender Politics and Everyday Life in State Socialist Eastern and Central Europe*. Basingstoke: Palgrave, pp. 59–75.
Popa, R. M. (2016). "We opposed it": The national council of women and the ban on Abortion in Romania (1966). *Aspasia*, 10, pp. 152–160.
Rabenschlag, A.-J. (2014). *Völkerfreundschaft nach Bedarf: Ausländische Arbeitskräfte in der Wahrnehmung von Staat und Bevölkerung der DDR*. PhD dissertation. Stockholm: Stockholm University.
Rahimbabaeva, Z. (1949). *Zhenshchina Uzbekistana na puti k kommunismu*. Tashkent: Gosizdat UzSSR.
Rasulov, A. (2017). Central Asia as an object of orientalist narratives at the age of Bandung. In: L. Eslava, M. Fakhri & N. Vasuki eds., *Bandung, Global History and International Law*. Cambridge: Cambridge University Press, pp. 215–231.
Reilly, N. (2009). *Women's Human Rights. Seeking Gender Justice in a Globalized Age*. Cambridge: Polity.
Reina, S. (2010). The disasters of war in Darfur 1950–2004. *Third World Quarterly*, 31(8), pp. 1297–1320.
Roman, M. (2011). Forging freedom, speaking Soviet anti-racism: African Americans and alternate strategies of fighting American racial apartheid. *Critique*, 39, pp. 365–383.
Rupp, L. (1997). *Worlds of Women: The Making of the International Women's Movement*. Princeton: Princeton University Press.

Rydström, J., & Tjeder, D. (2009). *Kvinnor, Män och Alla Andra*. Lund: Studentlitteratur.

Salem, S. (2017). Four women of Egypt: Memory, geopolitics, and the Egyptian women's movement during the Nasser and Sadat Eras. *Hypatia*, 32(3), pp. 593–608.

Sandwell, R. (2018). The travels of Florence Mophosho: The African National Congress and left internationalism, 1948–1985. *Journal of Women's History*, 30(4), pp. 84–108.

Saunders, S. F. (2000). *The Cultural Cold War: The CIA and the World of Arts and Letters*. New York: New Press.

Scholte, J. A. (2005). *Globalization: A Critical Introduction*. New York: Palgrave Macmillan.

Scott-Smith, G. & Krabbendam, H. eds. (2003). *The Cultural Cold War in Western Europe 1945–1960*. London: Frank Cass.

Scott-Smith, G., Roulin, S. & van Dongen, L. eds. (2014). *Transnational Anti-Communism and the Cold War: Agents, Activities, and Networks*. Basingstoke: Palgrave.

Sluga, G. (2017). Women, Feminism and twentieth century internationalism. In: G. Sluga & P. Clavin eds., *Internationalisms: A Twentieth-Century History*. Cambridge: Cambridge University Press, pp. 61–84.

Sluga, G. & Clavin, P. (2017). *Internationalisms: A Twentieth-Century History*. Cambridge University Press.

Snyder, S. (2013). Bringing the transnational in: Writing human rights into the international history of the Cold War. *Diplomacy& Statecraft*, 24, pp. 100–116.

Snyder, S. (2018). *From Selma to Moscow: How Human Rights Activists Transformed US Foreign Policy*. New York: Columbia University Press.

Sovershenno sekretno. (2001–2005). *Lubianka Stalinu o Polozhenii v Strane*. Moskva: Institut Rossiiskoi istorii RAN.

Stoler, A. L. (2009). *Along the Archival Grain: Epistemic Anxieties and Colonial Common Sense*. Princeton: Princeton University Press.

Suchland, J. (2011). Is Socialism Transnational? *Signes*, 36(4), pp. 837–862.

Swain, G. (1992). The Cominform: Tito's international? *The Historical Journal*, 35(3), pp. 641–663.

Terretta, M. (2013a). *Petitioning for Our Rights, Fighting for Our Nation: The History of the Democratic Union of Cameroonian Women, 1949–1960*. Bamenda, Cameroon: Langaa.

Terretta, M. (2013b). *Nation of Outlaws, State of Violence: Grassfields Tradition and State Building in Cameroon*. Athens, OH: Ohio University Press.

Tlostanova, M. (2010). *Gender Epistemologies in Eurasian Borderlands*. Basingstoke: Palgrave.

Tokhtakhodzhaeva, M., Abdurazkova, D. & Kadyrova, A. (2002). *Sudby i vremia. Proshloe Uzbekistana v ustnykh rasskazakh zhenshhin-svidetelnits sovremennits sobytii*. Tashkent: Shark.

Tonchu, E. (2004). *Rossiia – zhenskaia sudba*. St Petersburg: Tonchu.

Valobra, A. (2012). "Una historia de vida en la lucha de clases": Trayectoria política de Irma Othar, 1943–1957. *Mundos de trabalho*, 4(7), pp. 292–313.

Valobra, A. (2017). Las comunistas argentinas durante la politica de frentes y la Guerra fría. In: A. Valobra & M. Yusta eds., *Queridas Camaradas. Historias Iberoamericanas de Mujeres Comunistas*. Buenos Aires: Miño y Davila, pp. 71–90.

Waters, E. (1989). In the shadow of the comintern: The communist women's movement, 1920–1943. In: S. Kruks, R. Rapp, & M.B. Young eds., *Promissory Notes: Women in the Transition to Socialism*. New York: Monthly Review Press.
We Accuse. (1951). Berlin: WIDF.
Weigand, K. (2001). *Red Feminism: American Communism and the Making of Women's Liberation*. Baltimore: John Hopkins University Press.
Wernicke, G. (2003). The World Peace Council and the antiwar movement in East Germany. In: A.W. Daum, L. C. Gardner & W. Mausbach eds., *America, The Vietnam War and the World*. Cambridge: Cambridge University Press, pp. 299–320.
Westad, O. (1999). *Brothers in Arms: The Rise and Fall of the Sino-Soviet Alliance, 1945–1963*. Stanford: Stanford University Press.
Westad, O. A. (2005). *The Global Cold War: Third World Interventions and the Making of our Time*. Cambridge: Cambridge University Press.
Wolvers, T. & S. Salvedra. (2015) The Concepts of the Global South. https://kups.ub.uni-koeln.de/6399/1/voices012015_concepts_of_the_global_south.pdf, Accessed August 20, 2020.
Wu, J. T.-Ch. (2013). *Radicals on the Road*. Ithaca & London: Cornell University Press.
WIDF 40 years. (1985). Berlin: WIDF.
Wood, E. (1997). *The Baba and the Comrade: Gender and Politics in Revolutionary Russia*. Bloomington, IN: Indiana University Press.
Yusta, M. (2016). The strained courtship between antifascism and feminism: From the women's World Committee (1934) to Women's International Democratic Federation (1945). In: H. Garcia, M. Yusta, X. Tabet, & C. Climaco eds., *Rethinking Antifascism*. New York: Berghahn, pp. 167–186.
Yusta, M. (2017). Las mujeres en el partido comunista de España (1921–1950): La estrategia internacional. In: A. Valobra & M. Yusta eds., *Queridas Camaradas. Historias Iberoamericanas de Mujeres Communistas*. Buenos Aires: Miño y Davila, pp. 45–71.
Yukina, I. (2007). *Russkii Feminism Kak Vyzov sovremennosti*. St. Petersburg: Aleteia.
Yuval-Davis, N. (1997). *Gender and Nation*. London: Sage.
Za Ravnopravie, schastie i mir. (1953). Berlin: WIDF.
Zheng, W. (2017). *Finding Women in the State: A Socialist Feminist Revolution in the People's Republic of China, 1949–1964*. Oakland, CA: University of California Press.
Zubkova, E. (1998). *Russia after the War: Hopes, Illusions, and Disappointments, 1945–1957*. Armonk, NY: M.E. Sharpe.
13 sessiia ispolkoma MDFZh. (1952). *Bukharest 18-22 iunia 1952*. Moskva: Prilozhenie k zhurnalu Sovietskaia Zhenschina.

Not-published works

Al Harbi, K. (2019). *Internationalizing a Socialist Vision of Women's Rights: The Rise and Fall of the Women's International Democratic Federation from 1945 to 1967 in the United Nations Economic and Social Council*. BA-thesis, University of Amsterdam.

Internet – resources

Detailed Vita of Fatima Ahmed Ibrahim. (2006). https://www.ibn-rushd.org/typo3/cms/de/awards/2006-fatima-ahmed-ibrahim/cv-fatima-ahmed-ibrahim/detailed-vita/

Film: "Slovo zhenshchin o mire". (1981). https://www.net-film.ru/film-8576/, Accessed August 20, 2020.

Index

Ahmed Ibrahim, Fatima 118, 147–156, 171, 177, 196
African National Congress (ANC) 19, 176, 180, 183, 185
Andreen, Andrea, 49–50, 62n18, 64–65, 71–72, 89
Arab Women's Organization 154
Asaf Ali, Aruna 176, 191n12

Banerjee, Gita 112
Beijing 82–83, 106, 120, 127
Bertrand, Simone 50, 80, 83
Betinelli, Adela 52–53, 119–120, 139
Brown, Freda 54, 57–59, 133, 162–167, 169

Chakravarti, Renu 130
Cissé, Jeanne Martin 22n2, 139
Congress of Mothers 49, 65, 70, 113–114
Copenhagen 16, 43, 47, 64, 71, 73, 75, 88–89, 110, 141, 143–145, 147, 159, 162–163, 165–167, 186, 191n16
Cotton, Eugénie 43, 49, 53–54, 56, 62n25, 64–65, 76, 86–87, 89, 96, 127, 146, 150, 182

Dasgupta, Bani 91, 97n6, 121
Davis, Angela 139, 180, 185–186

Edelman, Fanny, 55, 58, 59, 62n26, 65, 70, 113–114, 116, 117n9, 133, 137–140, 155, 161, 168, 176, 183, 187
Espín, Vilma 176, 179, 191n15

Farooqui, Vimla 50, 52
Federation of Cuban Women/FMC 104, 140, 178–179, 188–189, 191n15
Fiala, Branca 92

Gyanchand, Anasuya 122–123

Hanoi 85, 182
Havana 90, 179, 184, 187–190
Helsinki 11, 54, 56, 82, 84–85, 132, 184
Ho Chi Minh 85, 115

IAW 7, 16, 25, 72–73, 148, 174, 191
Ibarruri, Dolores 33–34, 50, 54, 62n18
ICW 7, 16, 25, 58, 174, 191
IWY 16, 19, 21, 137,158–163, 182, 187, 189–190

Jakarta 95, 118, 122, 125
Jasovich, Rosa 74, 133, 138–141, 181
Jordanian Women's Union (JWU) 153

Khartoum 85, 109, 152–153, 172, 177, 179
Kuusinen, Hertta 54–57, 62n23, 62n25, 133, 161, 177, 185

League of Iraqi Women 186
Lima 172, 178–179

Mandela, Nelson 185
Mexico City 16, 71, 159–161
Minella, Angiola 35, 45, 47–49, 53, 148
Moscow Congress 17, 69, 75, 127, 129, 132–134, 146
Moumié, Marthe 113–114, 121

Nabarawi, Ceza 94, 139, 143, 147–148, 153
Nasser, Gamal Abdel 94, 148, 156n8
National Federation of Indian Women 50, 62n19, 122
Nimeiry Jaafar 151, 156n10

212 Index

Nguen Thi, Dinh 139, 176, 181
Nkrumah, Kwame 156n4, 191n8

Ouandié, Marthe 111

Paris 10, 24, 26, 29–31, 38, 61, 63, 78, 81, 85–86, 90, 161
Parfenova, Nadezhda 39–40, 51, 83, 86, 112
Petrova, Lidiia 28, 31, 40, 68, 73, 97n2
Popova, Nina 25–28, 32–34, 38–41, 45, 47, 49, 55, 64, 67–69, 75, 76n3, 81, 95–96, 101, 104, 119, 121–122, 125, 130, 135n6
Prague 28, 79, 116, 120, 127, 134n3, 141, 143, 152, 160, 165–168
Proskurnikova, Xenia 55–57, 59, 162, 175

Rahimbabaeva, Zuhra 56–57, 108–109, 128, 172, 174–175, 178, 196
Ransome Kuti, Funmilayo 141–147, 156

Sportisse, Alice 79
Sudanese Women's Union 118, 147–150, 171, 177

Tashkent 91, 102, 106–107, 111–113, 116, 117n5, 177
Tereshkova, Valentina 55, 57, 60, 113–114, 176
Thiele, Ilse 58, 130, 176
Tsui, Lu 82

Udval, Sonomyn 189–190
Ulan-Bator 74, 189–190
Urriz, Eliza 44, 50–51, 62n21, 126

Vaillant-Couturier, Marie-Claude 33–34, 39, 53, 67, 86, 120, 122, 182
Vienna 27, 67, 71, 91, 101, 104, 107, 127
Villaroel, Emperatriz 114–116
Vire-Tuominen, Mirjam 60, 165–167, 169, 190, 191n5

WILPF, 16, 24, 63, 65, 143, 156n6, 162
Women's Union of Abeokuta 142, 144–145

Zayadeen, Salwa (Leyla) 115, 117, 126, 147, 152–155, 157n13
Zanti, Carmen 35–37, 51–54, 64, 67–69, 90, 92–95, 125–127, 131–133